San Francisco Year Zero

San Francisco Year Zero

Political Upheaval, Punk Rock, and
a Third-Place Baseball Team

LINCOLN A. MITCHELL

Rutgers University Press

New Brunswick, Camden, and Newark, New Jersey, and London

Library of Congress Cataloging-in-Publication Data

Names: Mitchell, Lincoln Abraham, author.
Title: San Francisco year zero : political upheaval, punk rock and a third place baseball team /
    Lincoln A. Mitchell.
Description: New Brunswick : Rutgers University Press, 2019. | Includes bibliographical
    references and index.
Identifiers: LCCN 2018058805| ISBN 9781978807341 (cloth : alk. paper) |
    ISBN 9781978807372 (web pdf)
Subjects: LCSH: San Francisco (Calif.)—History—20th century.
Classification: LCC F869.S357 M58 2019 | DDC 979.4/6104—dc23
LC record available at https://lccn.loc.gov/2018058805

A British Cataloging-in-Publication record for this book is available from the British Library.

"The American in Me" by the Avengers, 1978. Reprinted with permission of Penelope Houston.
"Berkeley Farms" by the Blowdryers, n. d. Reprinted with permission of Jennifer Waters.
"What Are We Going to Do?" by Code of Honor, 1981. Reprinted with permission of
Michael D. Fox—Code of Honor © 1981.

"An Elegy to Dispel Gloom" by Lawrence Ferlinghetti, from *Endless Life*, copyright © 1973 by
Lawrence Ferlinghetti. Reprinted by permission of New Directions Publishing Corp.

♾ The paper used in this publication meets the requirements of the American National
Standard for Information Sciences—Permanence of Paper for Printed Library Materials,
ANSI Z39.48-1992.

www.rutgersuniversitypress.org

Manufactured in the United States of America

For my mother, Susan Mitchell

Contents

Preface

On October 27, 2010, Newy Scruggs, a correspondent for the NBC affiliate in Dallas, stood in a San Francisco neighborhood that only a few decades earlier had been run down and mostly abandoned. There were no unused buildings and empty industrial spaces in the background anymore. Instead, a ten-year-old ballpark slowly filling up with fans clad mostly in the orange and black of their Giants was Scruggs's backdrop. The San Francisco Bay shimmered invitingly in the background as a few sailboats and other small crafts floated in a small body of water called McCovey Cove, named after one of the greatest left-handed sluggers in baseball history. Scruggs began his broadcast with the words "This is San Francisco, and (quickly changing his tone to one of surprise) I can tell you, right over there, there's some people smoking weed." For the next few minutes Scruggs continued to try to set the scene for game 1 of the World Series while jokingly comparing the culture and attitudes toward marijuana use in San Francisco and Dallas. Scruggs seemed not to be bothered by the San Franciscans around him, even those smoking marijuana, describing them in complimentary terms and referring to the ballpark behind him as the best that he had ever seen.

When the game started, there were more than 43,600 fans in AT&T Park. The San Francisco that the country saw that night featured a beautiful ballpark with views of the San Francisco Bay in the background, and a crowd that included tech millionaires who had paid hundreds of dollars to be there and to be seen there. The crowd had many fewer African Americans in the stands than in decades past, but that was true of almost every

Major League ballpark by 2010. However, there were a lot more Asians and Asian Americans at the game than there were, for example, at game 1 of the World Series the previous year when the Yankees had hosted the Phillies.

The most popular player on that Giants team was not an aging superstar whose best days were behind him, a big star who had just been traded to the Giants, or, as in the earlier part of the twenty-first century, a bloated slugger who hit better than almost anybody in the game's history but was dogged by rumors of steroid abuse. The star of this Giants team and its starting pitcher in the first game of that World Series had been the Giants' first-round draft pick only four years earlier and was already an ace pitcher unlike any other in the game.

Tim Lincecum, known as Timmy or The Freak to Giants fans of all ages, had won the National League Cy Young Award in 2008 and 2009, and after an off year (by his standards) had helped the Giants win their first two postseason series of 2010 with his excellent pitching. Lincecum could be a little wild at times, but he had great stuff and in 2010 led the league in strikeouts for the third consecutive season. Lincecum was among the elite pitchers in baseball, but he did not look like the rest of them. At a time when pitchers were generally well over six feet tall with stocky, muscular builds, Lincecum was only five feet, eleven inches, and only weighed 170 pounds. His delivery was unique, as he took a huge step with his front leg and seemed to propel both himself and the ball toward home plate. Lincecum had a baby face and long hair—not the long hair that suggested a good old boy from the South like many other ballplayers, but the long hair of a West Coast hippie. Lincecum came by that look honestly, as he had grown up outside of Seattle and had attended the University of Washington.

In 2009 during the off-season, Lincecum was busted for possession of marijuana. Unlike many ballplayers in similar situations, Lincecum made little effort to deny his use of the drug or to apologize, and he became recognized as a recreational user of marijuana. This made him even more popular in San Francisco, where T-shirts and posters with the slogan "Let Timmy Smoke" began to pop up at the ballpark. Lincecum's marijuana use, laid-back West Coast style, and sense of humor made him a perfect fit for San Francisco.

The Giants cleverly marketed Lincecum based on his personality, rather than seeking to mold him into a more normal ballplayer. It was also clear that because of the Giants' attitude and home city, Lincecum was more comfortable there than he would have been with most other teams, particularly those where the fan culture was very conservative, like the Texas Rangers, the Giants' opponents in the World Series that was about to begin.

Elsewhere around the city, people gathered at bars and in homes to watch the game. Charles A. Fracchia Jr., a forty-five-year-old lifelong Giants fan with deep roots in San Francisco, was one of many at Lefty O'Doul's, a downtown restaurant that had long been a place to watch big Giants games. In the Castro, numerous bars serving the city's still substantial gay population were packed with Giants fans. Asian Americans in the Sunset, wealthy families in Pacific Heights, Yuppies in the fully gentrified Marina, and more than a few people who had been in the crowds or on the stage at the Mabuhay Gardens, the On Broadway, or other punk rock clubs in the late 1970s and early 1980s nervously sat in front of their television screens and watched Lincecum get off to a rocky start in his first World Series game. The Giants' bats rescued him as the home team cruised to an 11–7 win. Less than a week later, the final game of that World Series was played in Texas. Lincecum got another crack at the Rangers. This time he pitched a great game, which the Giants won 3–1, and San Francisco had its first World Series championship. The Giants would repeat as World Series winners in 2012 and 2014.

Despite the city's enduring and deserved left-wing reputation, by 2010 San Francisco had become a major business center due to the tech boom. Real estate speculation was rampant, and rents for vacant apartments were skyrocketing. Within a few years, the housing crunch would lead to a rise in evictions as landlords, often with no real connection to the city, would seek to empty out entire buildings, expelling tenants who had been there for years, so they could make more money through Airbnb. The media would soon be telling the world that "San Francisco has more income inequality than developing nations, rivaling not the likes of Sweden and Denmark, but countries of sub-Saharan Africa."[1]

The San Francisco that the world saw in 2010 probably seemed very far removed from the 1970s, when a declining population and tax base, radical politics, racial unrest, some very bad Giants teams, the hangover from the Summer of Love, and a burgeoning but strange and, for many, frightening punk rock scene defined San Francisco. To fully understand the trajectory that got San Francisco to where it is now, in the first decades of this century, it is essential to understand one specific year. By the last weeks of 1978, many wondered how the city would survive, but the events of that year, including assassinations, mass murder, the ascendancy of San Francisco punk rock, and a revived baseball team, ultimately helped lay the foundation for the

San Francisco of today. The relationship between the city of Twitter, Salesforce, AT&T Park, tenant evictions, Google buses, gay political power, trans rights, banned plastic bags, and a surprisingly vibrant and avant-garde cultural scene, and the city of Harvey Milk, George Moscone, Dan White, Dianne Feinstein, Herb Caen, Jonestown, the Concerned Relatives, Bill Graham, Jello Biafra, East Bay Ray, Hank Rank, Penelope Houston, Jack Clark, Willie McCovey, Vida Blue, and Mike Ivie may not be linear or direct, but it is real.

San Francisco Year Zero

1

New Year's 1978

• •

On the corner of Sutter and Steiner Streets in what was then the Western Addition, or perhaps the Fillmore District, of San Francisco, a local Bay Area band interrupted their New Year's Eve show a few minutes after 1978 began while a man who as a young boy had fled the Nazis descended across the ballroom and onto the stage on a giant jerry-rigged model of a motorcycle. As Bill Graham landed on the stage at Winterland, the Grateful Dead hit the opening notes of "Sugar Magnolia," and 1978 in San Francisco was underway. It was a year that would be unlike any other the city had known.

By the end of 1977, the Grateful Dead were already an old band. They were mostly linked with the San Francisco of the 1960s and the acid tests, be-ins, Summer of Love, and hippies that were associated with that time. However, the Grateful Dead still had a loyal following in the late 1970s for whom New Year's shows in San Francisco were an annual ritual. That ritual lasted until Jerry Garcia, the band's paunchy lead guitarist, died in 1995. The Dead continue to play in various forms and under somewhat different names, so it turns out that New Year's Eve 1977 was, in Grateful Dead terms, the early years.

The Grateful Dead concert on New Year's Eve 1977 was a good one. The band played some of their most beloved and best-known songs, including "Sugar Magnolia," "Scarlet Begonias," "Friend of the Devil," and "Truckin,"

1

encored with "One More Saturday Night" (December 31, 1977, was a Saturday) and "Casey Jones." For fans of the more obscure, they even played a cover of Luigi Denza's 1880 composition "Funiculi, Funicula."

The Grateful Dead's New Year's show was just one of many ways San Franciscans welcomed in 1978. Fans of what was known as arena rock spent the evening at the Cow Palace at another Bill Graham event, this one with Santana, Journey, and Eddie Money performing. Disco was still very popular in San Francisco in 1978. The City on Montgomery Street and the Jack Tar Hotel on Van Ness Avenue held New Year's disco parties, which drew a much more diverse crowd than the mostly straight white audiences at Graham's events. Adherents of San Francisco's nascent punk rock culture went to the Mabuhay Gardens, known even then simply as the Mab, or occasionally the Fab Mab, to ring in the New Year with a roster of punk rock bands.

San Franciscans with something else on their minds on New Year's Eve were invited to "Meet Kyoto" at the O'Farrell Theatre, with the promise that she and "each one of our ultra women are specially trained to make your 'ultra visit' as erotic and pleasurable as possible."[1] The proprietors of the O'Farrell Theatre were the Mitchell Brothers. By 1978, Jim and Artie Mitchell were among the most prominent pornographers in the country and very much part of the cultural milieu of San Francisco. The two brothers operated a number of strip clubs, produced X-rated movies from the late 1960s through the 1980s, and were very well connected in San Francisco's political and social circles. In 1991, after years of feuding, Jim shot and killed Artie.

In the jungles of Guyana, about 4,500 miles southeast of San Francisco, a group of former San Franciscans met the New Year a little differently. The thousand or so members of the Peoples Temple enjoyed no major New Year's celebration and spent the last days of 1977 continuing to try to construct the utopia that their increasingly erratic and unstable leader, Jim Jones, had promised. The stifling humidity, inadequate food supplies, poor sanitary conditions, and extremely simple living quarters in Jonestown—the name Jim Jones had immodestly given to his jungle fantasy—did not lend themselves to a festive feeling, even on New Year's Day.

Jones had been an important figure in San Francisco's religious, political, and civic life in the early and mid-1970s. His Peoples Temple had begun to relocate to Guyana in 1974, but it wasn't until 1977 that a significant numbers of Peoples Temple members made the journey to Guyana. Jones himself had left San Francisco and moved there during the summer of 1977. By the end of that year, there were some concerns in San Francisco about what was happening in Guyana and what the true nature of Jim Jones's organization was. Some thought it had become a dangerous cult, while others continued to see it as an experiment in radical equality and progressive living.

Marshall Kilduff and Phil Tracy captured this dichotomy in a 1977 article in *New West,* writing that California's "Lieutenant Governor Mervyn Dymally went so far as to visit Jones's 27,000 acre agricultural station in Guyana, South America and he pronounced himself impressed." However, Kilduff and Tracy also concluded that "life inside Peoples Temple was a mixture of Spartan regimentation, fear and self-imposed humiliation," and described physical and psychological methods used to abuse members of the organization.[2]

A few hours after Bill Graham's motorcycle ride, another set of Mitchell brothers, these ones in fifth and seventh grade, boarded a plane in New York to return to their home in San Francisco for the rest of the school year. My brother and I were not related to Jim and Artie, but if you grew up in San Francisco in the 1970s and 1980s with my last name and had a brother, you heard a lot of jokes, as well as the occasional request for tickets. My brother and I were still a few years removed from punk rock or Grateful Dead shows. The only politics we knew were mostly from our radical left-wing grandparents in New York. As we got older, those views usually served us well in our hometown, but on more than a few occasions they made us stand out at our Catholic school, where we found ourselves in a sea of kids who came from very different backgrounds from ours. Most of their families did not share our grandparents' political views. This would be very apparent by the end of the year.

Although our beloved grandparents made sure that my brother and I shared their political positions, our passion was not yet politics or even music. Instead, it was that most all-American of activities—baseball. Our grandfather, a first-generation American born on the Lower East Side of Manhattan to Belarusian Jewish immigrants in 1907, had moved to the Bronx as a boy. A few years later, the Yankees followed him across the river from Manhattan and became his team. We rooted for the Yankees too because of our New York roots and because of him, but by 1976 or so had also become fans of our local team. The Giants were pretty bad back then, but you could get tickets in the upper deck for three bucks, and the Ballpark Express, run by Muni, the city's transit authority, was cheap and sometimes even convenient.

Inauguration Day

On the second Monday of 1978, after school had resumed and San Franciscans had recovered from the holiday season, the eleven-member board of supervisors, including five new members, was inaugurated. The swearing in of new members of the city's legislature was not the kind of thing that typically drew much attention in the San Francisco of that time, but this year was different. Among the five people being sworn in for the first time that day was Harvey Milk, one of the very first openly gay elected officials anywhere in the world, and a man who eventually became a major part of the history of his adopted hometown, and indeed the whole country.

In our house, this event went largely unremarked upon, save for my mother's happiness at seeing a left-of-center Jew from New York on the board of supervisors. Before Milk, the most well-known Jewish member of that body had been the daughter of a prominent Jewish doctor who, despite her Eastern European roots, had long been part of the more elite German Jewish community in San Francisco. Milk, however, was one of us. He came from Long Island—we were from Manhattan—and, like my mother, spoke English with a New York accent. Milk even spoke a little Yiddish.

Milk may have been a good progressive New York Jew, but he became an international icon and historical figure because of his outspoken and eloquent work for equality for gays and lesbians. As a single working mother in San Francisco in the 1970s, my mother had many gay friends and business acquaintances with whom she worked well and built relationships. In those days, most straight women, even progressive ones, didn't speak much about gay rights, but my mother was not a bigot and was not opposed to Milk.

The Catholic school where my brother and I went every day was a little different. These were the days when "f*g" was still a playground taunt hurled at a target of enmity countless times a day, even in San Francisco. School was not an environment where anybody spent a lot of time recognizing the historic significance of Milk's being on the board of supervisors. For many of our classmates, he was simply "that f*g."[3]

The official inauguration photo of that day shows Milk standing in the back row in, appropriately, the far left. He has the big smile of a man who has finally achieved something he has been working toward for years. The previous November he had been elected in his third bid for office. Next to him is another progressive Jew from the East Coast. Carol Ruth Silver had come to San Francisco from Massachusetts and been a Freedom Rider in the South before moving to California. A little to the right, physically, if not politically, was Ella Hill Hutch, only the second African American, and the first African American woman, ever elected to the San Francisco Board of Supervisors. Milk and Silver shared more than just progressive politics and their Judaism. They were friends and political allies. When I met with Silver in her home in 2018 to discuss this book, she pointed out that the kitchen table at which we were sitting was the same one where she and Milk had strategized about his 1976 race for the state assembly, which he ultimately lost.

Hutch, Silver, and Milk had all been elected the previous fall when the city had implemented district-based, rather than at-large, elections for its board of supervisors. This was a demand made by progressives and communities of color, who believed, accurately, that if supervisors were elected from individual districts, the board would better reflect the diversity of San Francisco. At-large elections, in which the entire city voted for the entire board, created a big advantage for those who could raise enough money to campaign citywide, and thus for those candidates who had the support of powerful real estate or other well-heeled interests. Changing the electoral system so that members of the board of supervisors were elected by smaller districts made fund-raising less important while rewarding candidates who were either well known in a specific part of the city or who were willing to work very hard to become well known in their district. Moreover, district elections gave opportunities for minorities and gays, who had limited city-wide appeal, to get elected in districts where they were the majority. The switch to district elections had been a major victory for progressives seeking to remake San Francisco. It was, therefore, no accident that the board of supervisors that was sworn into office in 1978 was the most diverse in San Francisco history.

In the inauguration photo—sandwiched not entirely comfortably, but still smiling, between Silver and Hutch—is another new supervisor whom the voters elected that fall in a district that had been drawn in one of the city's most conservative neighborhoods. We should probably be grateful that we will never know what was going through the mind of Dan White, who by the end of the year the world would know to be deeply disturbed, as he posed with a gay Jew, a radical Jewish woman, and a progressive African American woman. These three new members intended to create a very different San Francisco than the one envisioned by White, a working-class

conservative Catholic from the Excelsior district whom Charles A. Fracchia Sr., a San Francisco historian who founded the San Francisco Historical
Society in 1988 and currently serves as its president emeritus, described to
me as a "a real representative of the old San Francisco."[4]

San Francisco city legislators are known as supervisors because the city
and county lines are the same. Although they function as a city council,
members are also county supervisors. In general, county supervisors and city
council members are not well known outside of their city or county. Some
politicians start out at this most local of elected offices and become famous
for things they achieve later in higher offices, but very few are remembered
simply for being city legislators. In all of American history, the two most
famous city-level legislators who never went on to higher office are Dan
White and Harvey Milk. They were both elected in the same year in the
same city, and their stories remain linked to this day. Both of them got elected
in competitive multicandidate races that they won through hard work and
good retail politicking, and were briefly considered rising political stars in
San Francisco. The *San Francisco Bay Guardian*, a left-leaning community
newspaper, attributed Milk's having won to the fact that he "simply out-
politicked his opposition," while using similar language to explain White's
victory: "Dan White simply out-campaigned his 12 opponents in what was
a vigorous person-to person effort."[5] Fitzgerald's analysis of Milk's political
style and themes provides a sense of the kind of politician that Milk was:

> As an outsider running against liberals, he became at once a fiscal conservative
> and a populist: he was for "the little people" in the neighborhoods against the
> downtown interests and the landlords; he was for mass transit, better schools,
> better city services for the elderly; to pay for that he would end waste in
> government and tax the corporations and the commuters from Marin County.
> Along the way, his support came from the Teamsters, the Firefighters' Union,
> the Building and Construction Trades Council, and small businessmen; but in
> the end his main supporters were the thousands upon thousands of young gay
> men settling in the Castro.[6]

In January 1978, nobody knew how the relationship between White and
Milk would develop over the next eleven months. However, it was apparent that the two new members of the board represented very different directions for the future of San Francisco and that both were emerging as visible
representatives of those different directions.

On the day Milk, White, and the other supervisors were sworn in, the board of supervisors also had to determine who would be their leader. In a close race, the moderate supervisor Dianne Feinstein, who represented some of San Francisco's most affluent neighborhoods in the northern part of the city, defeated Gordon Lau by a 6–5 vote. Milk supported Lau, the more progressive candidate. Dan White sided with the more centrist Feinstein. That narrow vote would become very important by the end of the year. Feinstein's victory in that election showed that while the board of supervisors may have been the most progressive in the history of San Francisco, progressives still did not have the majority they needed. Getting that sixth vote would be a challenge throughout Milk's tenure on the board and would ultimately play an enormous role in the events of 1978.

The video of Milk being sworn in shows the new supervisor jubilantly repeating the oath of office. When he is finished, Milk and the man who swore him in, Mayor George Moscone, warmly shake hands and smile broadly for the cameras. It was the smile of political allies. One, by dint of the office he held, was more powerful, but both were looking forward to working together to remake their city in a more progressive direction. Milk was a gay Jew who had moved to San Francisco when he was already in middle age and began running for office only a few short years after arriving in town. Moscone was a straight Italian American Catholic whose San Francisco bona fides were second to nobody's. They made a strange pair, but long before Dan White made sure that their memories could never be separated, they had a lot in common politically. As time passed it was the supervisor, not the mayor, who would emerge as the more significant historical figure. Nonetheless, Moscone was a progressive ally of Milk's and a hugely important figure of the changing politics in the San Francisco of the 1970s.

Moscone and Milk both campaigned for office on platforms that were very different from those of typical winning candidates at the time. By the middle of the 1970s, radicalism had certainly come to most American cities, but it was still usually at the periphery of electoral politics. The exceptions were in cities such as Newark or Detroit that had African American majorities. Those cities and others elected progressive, occasionally even radical, African American mayors, but their politics were focused more on the racial and economic issues that undergirded the drive for African American political power and owed their victories to demographic changes rather than to broad progressive coalitions. In other cities, mayors such as Abe Beame and Ed Koch in New York, Richard J. Daley in Chicago, and even Tom Bradley in Los Angeles still governed with a progrowth and pro-business emphasis that pushed neighborhood interests to the side.

Moscone's statement in the 1975 San Francisco voter guide demonstrated that his priorities and allegiances were different from those of the aforementioned mayors or their equivalents in San Francisco: "I am committed to a new direction for San Francisco and will replace all members of every Board and Commission—appoint new people from neighborhoods and not from contributor's [*sic*] lists to direct our City's future—open the doors to City Hall so for once your voice can be heard. I can listen."[7] Most of Moscone's opponents used the brief space allotted in the voter guide primarily to boast about their managerial experience. Campaign promises should always be seen for what they are, but Moscone managed to persuade a very slim majority of San Franciscans that he meant those promises. When he got elected, he kept them for the most part.

One of those neighborhood people Moscone appointed was Harvey Milk, to the Board of Permit Appeals. Milk shared Moscone's commitment to neighborhoods but could be even more radical because, unlike Moscone, he was not seeking to be the city's chief executive. In a speech to members of the International Longshoremen and Warehousemen Associations at a campaign event in 1973 when he unsuccessfully sought a seat on the board of supervisors, Milk outlined a vision for the city very much in line with what Moscone would campaign on two years later: "The route of making a city an exciting place for all to live: not just an exciting place for a few to live! A place for the individual and individual rights. There is no political gain in this non-moneyed route, and thus you do not find people with high political ambitions leading this way. There are no statistics to quote . . . no miles of highway built to brag about, no statistics of giant buildings built under your administration."[8]

Milk's use of the word "exciting" is striking, as it suggests a vision of the city grounded in joy and as a place for ordinary people to live more easily and hassle free. In a flyer from that campaign, Milk fleshed out this vision: "MUNI & TRAFFIC: Free Service . . . More and better MUNI . . . Banning all autos in downtown area . . . create rapid shuttle system in the downtown area . . . CITY EMPLOYEES: ALL without exception must live in the city! PERFORMING ARTS CENTER: Neighborhood arts centers must be first!"[9] Milk was working toward a genuinely radical view not just of urban politics, but of what cities like San Francisco were for. Even as the economy was declining through the 1970s, either despite or because of his own background in finance, Milk advocated for a San Francisco where the needs of the business community took a distant back seat to the rights of all San Fran- ciscans to enjoy and share their city.

By the mid-1970s, and certainly by the time he successfully ran for the board of supervisors in 1977, Milk was a neighborhood-oriented progres- sive, but his political evolution to get there was not straightforward. In 1976, after two unsuccessful bids for the board of supervisors, Milk lost an assem- bly race to Art Agnos. Agnos was a straight white man, so it is tempting to view his victory as a defeat for progressive forces, but Agnos beat Milk from the left in that 1976 Democratic primary. Agnos had a labor background and a commitment to racial equality, was an early supporter of gay rights, and a strong progressive. More than forty years after that primary campaign, Agnos recalled Milk's 1976 platform: "His speech centered around 'We gotta get rid of these social welfare programs, we gotta make government run like a business. . . . I told him you're not gonna get anywhere in politics in this city with that rap. . . . You gotta give people hope.'"[10] Eleven years after defeat- ing Milk, Agnos expanded his progressive coalition to the whole city and became mayor of San Francisco.

Milk, who was about half a generation older than many of the young people coming to San Francisco in the late 1960s and early 1970s, probably began moving to the left around when he gave up his career in the finance sector in New York to move to San Francisco. Milk was born in 1929, so he had had adult life experience in New York. Part of that experience was being a Goldwater Republican in 1964. Supporting Barry Goldwater in 1964 was not the same as supporting moderate New York Republicans like Governor Nelson Rockefeller (who challenged Goldwater for the presidential nomi- nation that year), Senator Jacob Javits, or others. Goldwater was, in the con- text of the time, on the far right, and he lost badly to Lyndon Johnson in that 1964 election.

Milk was not the only former Goldwater supporter who became an influ- ential Democratic politician. Hillary Clinton was famously a "Goldwater girl" in 1964, but Clinton had just turned seventeen when that election hap- pened; just a senior in high school, she was not even old enough to vote. Milk, by contrast, was thirty-five when he supported Goldwater over Presi- dent Johnson. Additionally, as a Protestant growing up in the Midwest, in 1964, Clinton was in an environment where support for Goldwater was rea- sonably widespread. Milk was a Jewish New Yorker and so was likely sur- rounded by Johnson supporters. Johnson carried 90 percent of the Jewish vote in 1964,[11] so Milk was a real outlier, supporting the most right-wing major presidential candidate in a generation rather than the incumbent Democrat who, at that time, was better known for his aggressive action on behalf of civil rights than for his missteps in Vietnam.

George Moscone was a gifted politician who, unlike Milk, had deep roots in old San Francisco, but he easily made the transition to being a symbol of the new, emerging progressive San Francisco. Moscone was an Italian American who had grown up in the Cow Hollow district. Today, Cow Hollow is a second-generation Yuppie neighborhood. For the last few decades, Cow Hollow and its neighbor, the Marina District, have been the punch line of jokes and disdainful comments by hipper and more bohemian San Franciscans. Both are now neighborhoods of expensive rental flats, singles bars, pricey boutiques, and overpriced restaurants that are good but not the best in the city.

Much of the Marina is built on landfill and so was badly damaged in the 1989 earthquake, but the earthquake only briefly slowed the gentrification that was already well underway there. However, for much of the twentieth century—indeed from the 1930s when Moscone was growing up there through the 1970s and early 1980s when I lived there—Cow Hollow and the Marina were heavily Italian middle- and working-class neighborhoods. They were the kinds of places where Italian matrons in local bakeries gave free cookies to neighborhood kids sent by their mother to pick up a loaf of San Francisco sourdough. (My brother and I never tried to dissuade these kind women of their assumption that we were Italian.) Cow Hollow was also a neighborhood that was supportive of single mothers who worked hard and sent their kids to Catholic school, even if they happened to be Jewish.

To the north of Cow Hollow and the Marina district is a strip of grass called the Marina Green and then the San Francisco Bay. In the middle of the Marina was Funston Park, a good public facility with ball fields and basketball courts. By the time I was old enough to play high school baseball, the park had been renamed after George Moscone. Moscone came from a modest family but was a bright student who was able to attend St. Ignatius (SI), San Francisco's elite Jesuit high school, where he was also a basketball star. Generations of San Francisco's most influential Catholics have attended SI. During the time Moscone was mayor, the governor of California, Jerry Brown, and the Speaker of the California State Assembly, Leo McCarthy, were both also SI graduates. It was a longtime San Francisco aphorism that if you got pulled over for a speeding ticket, the police officer probably went to Riordan or Sacred Heart, two Catholic schools that were not as academically rigorous as SI. However, if you challenged the ticket in court, the judge was likely to be an SI graduate.

After college and law school, Moscone, like Milk, served in the U.S. Navy. He then practiced law for a few years before being elected to the board of supervisors in 1963 and the state senate in 1966. Moscone quickly became the majority leader of that body, making him one of the most powerful Democrats in California. However, he was willing to give that power up to be mayor of San Francisco. This may have seemed like a puzzling move to some, but for a son of Cow Hollow and an SI alum who loved his hometown, it made perfect sense.

The inauguration of the new board of supervisors, primarily because of Milk, was minor national news. The *New York Times* coverage noted that "one of the new members is Harvey Milk, an avowed homosexual who walked to City Hall with hundreds of supporters and told the city establishment, 'I want to introduce my lover' after other supervisors had introduced wives, husbands and blood relatives." In the next paragraph, Les Ledbetter, the *Times* reporter writing about the event, made sure to mention that Milk was a "former New Yorker." The article included a photo of the board of supervisors with a caption that by the end of the year would prove to be a bit of an understatement: "The 11-member San Francisco Board of Supervisors is a diverse and unpredictable group."[12]

A few weeks after the inauguration, both White and Milk found themselves mentioned in Herb Caen's column on the same day. For most of the period from the 1940s to the 1990s, a mention in Herb Caen's column was a sign that a politician, cultural figure, or society person had made it in San Francisco. Caen—who by 1978 was an influential, widely read, often funny, and sometimes progressive San Francisco institution—pointed out that Milk and antigay state senator John Briggs were both supporting Proposition 13, an initiative that would cut both taxes and services. For Milk, it was a nice mention in its suggestion that he was not an orthodox liberal, but within a few months he would change his position on Proposition 13.

White got a longer write-up, as Caen observed that "at Warren Simmons' Pier 39 project . . . new Sup. Dan White . . . is dickering for space to open a shop called the Potato Patch, aimed at spudnuts—baked, fried and browned."[13] This was vintage Herb Caen, complete with the coining of a new term—but for the man who gave us the word "beatnik," "spudnut" was a pretty modest accomplishment. However, behind the light tone, Caen was suggesting that less than a month into office, White may have been exploring ways to sell his new influence. This story finding its way into Caen's column was not good for the new supervisor.

Changing Music Scenes

One of the enduring and central paradoxes of San Francisco is that it has long been an important city culturally, economically, politically, and otherwise but has never been a very big one. This dynamic has been at the center of San Francisco's appeal for decades. At its best, San Francisco offers diversity and cultural resources approaching those of New York, while having a much smaller population. Even today, visitors to the city, particularly if they spend time in many of its diverse neighborhoods—from the techie/yuppie quarters such as the Marina District and the new hip areas of South Beach to the still fogbound and heavily Asian American Outer Sunset and the enormous expanse that is the Outer Mission—are often surprised that the city's population is well under one million.

This dynamic was acute in 1978. For example, the youth culture that had been at the center of the city's vibe beginning with the Summer of Love eleven years earlier, was still a significant part of San Francisco's cultural milieu. While the 1960s may have ended with Altamont or Woodstock in 1969, the shootings at Kent State in 1971, or at other points during the late 1960s or early 1970s elsewhere in the country, in San Francisco the 1960s lasted at least into the late 1970s. Bands such as the Grateful Dead were still strongly identified with San Francisco, and despite the influx of harder and more dangerous drugs in the early 1970s, Haight Street was still a prominent part of the global hippie scene. The left-wing politics of the era were slowly making inroads into the power politics of San Francisco, particularly since Moscone's victory in 1975 and the election of Hutch, Milk, and Silver to the board of supervisors two years later.

A young adult could have lived in San Francisco in the late 1970s much as they had in the late 1960s—and many did. They were part of the background of San Francisco of the era. Many men working in the service sector, waiting tables, driving taxis, and the like had long hair, wore tie-dye, smoked grass, and believed in the principles of peace and equality that had seemed so urgent in the 1960s. Others of that demographic became hippie business people who started small companies, joined law firms, or in some cases, moved a few dozen miles down the peninsula to dabble in computers in San Mateo and Santa Clara Counties.

These hippies, almost always described as "aging" in the media vernacular of the time, were only one piece of the complex cultural mosaic of San Francisco in 1978. There were parts of San Francisco such as the Outer Sunset where conservative and conventional values and lifestyles were still the norm. The city's substantial Latino and African American populations were immersed in cultural and political lives of their own. San Francisco had always had a large Asian American population that had its own political fights, community leaders, and cultural touch points. The Castro was beginning to become a global center of another movement. There was always some overlap between all of these San Franciscos, but the differences were at least as significant. Even within the relatively narrow demographic of white people under forty or so, the hippies were no longer the only game in town, because there was something new happening in the culture and music scene in San Francisco as 1978 began.

On January 14, only two weeks after the archetypical Bay Area hippie band, the Grateful Dead, rang in the New Year at Bill Graham's Winterland, that famous arena hosted a different show. Three local bands—Negative Trend, the Avengers, and the Nuns—representing the still young San Francisco punk rock scene, appeared on the bill with the Sex Pistols, who at that time were the most famous punk band in the world. Bill Graham had made his name, and a great deal of money, as the best and most famous promoter of the music of the late 1960s, but he had been slow to embrace punk. Most punks in turn were not fond of Bill Graham, but Graham nonetheless had finally put together a punk show at Winterland.

Speaking about that concert, Jenny Miro, the Nuns' lead singer, said, "We almost didn't get it. Bill Graham just hated us."[14] Miro's assessment of Graham may have been accurate, but more introspection on her part might have led Miro to understand why a promoter who had spent his childhood trying to stay one step ahead of Hitler's genocide might not be too excited about a band whose repertoire included a song called "Decadent Jew," which included these lyrics:

The Nazis gassed me
Burnt me too
Sterilized me
Beat me black and blue

'Cause I'm a—
Decadent Jew! Decadent Jew![15]

When I met with Henry S. Rosenthal, the drummer for Crime, who was known as Hank Rank back then and had been raised in a secular Jewish family in Cincinnati, he seemed to have a better understanding of the source of the tension with Graham: "Bill Graham represented that [music] establishment in San Francisco, and he controlled all the major venues, and he very quickly took a stance in no small part because of the liberal use of Nazi imagery [in the punk scene]. It was turned on its head, but he didn't see that."[16]

The Sex Pistols concert, or more accurately the scene surrounding the concert, was covered extensively in the local media. A full-page story on page 2 of the *San Francisco Chronicle* was provocatively titled "How I Got Punked On by the Sex Pistols." Columnist John Wasserman described the event as a human interest story:

> "Oh, how disappointing" my escort wailed as we cruised past the bedraggled line on the rain-soaked sidewalk outside the Winterland Arena, "Nobody's punked out." Her eyes, barely visible through a cloud of glitter and mascara misted over woefully as she peered in vain for like-minded souls waiting for the West Coast debut of England's notorious Sex Pistols. The bone in her nose—a chicken femur, she had pointed out earlier—trembled slightly as she fretfully ran her ring-laden hands through her orange and green crew cut.[17]

The review of the actual music appeared thirty-eight pages later. Joel Selvin's generally positive review noted that "the Pistols accounted for themselves admirably, turning out a tight tidy hour-long blitz of hard, driving rock." Selvin also added, "It was bassist Sid Vicious who served as the band's chief provocateur, standing menacingly at the edge of the stage, taunting the front rows and exchanging insults with the audience. In return, the audience showered the Pistols with an unremitting barrage of all manner of debris—coins, items of apparel, joints—which band members blithely ignored."[18]

Ten days after the concert, Joseph Torchia wrote that it had been "punk rock's greatest moment in San Francisco—promising to be the most degenerate, disgusting, delinquent night this city had ever seen—and everyone who was no one turned out to prove it."[19] Torchia's tone was much less charitable than Selvin's. His piece, which appeared in the People section, not the Music section of the paper, captured much of what many San Franciscans felt about punk rock in the movement's embryonic period. It is also safe to say that if Torchia thought January 14, 1978, was the most "degenerate, disgusting, delinquent" night in San Francisco's history, he was in for a tough few years.

In January 1978, the Sex Pistols' San Francisco concert was simply billed as the last on the Pistols' American tour. Before coming to the United States, the band had been a sensation in the United Kingdom for about two years as a kind of hybrid of a new form of music and the marketing campaign of Malcolm McLaren. At the time, the Winterland concert was viewed by many as the first major punk rock event in San Francisco, but it would quickly take on greater meaning than that because it turned out to be the last time the Sex Pistols performed together. Within a few weeks of that concert, Sex Pistols leader Johnny Rotten announced he was leaving the band. A year later, in February 1979, Sid Vicious died of a drug overdose in a New York City hotel room.

As the short but controversial and influential reign of the Sex Pistols came to an abrupt end in early 1978 in San Francisco, punk rock began to change. Until then, the phenomenon had been largely centered around the Sex Pistols, the Clash, and similar bands in London and around bands such as the Ramones, Television, and the New York Dolls in New York. No Bay Area band had yet made a real impression or impact on punk rock outside of California. That would soon change, as by the middle of 1978, San Francisco's punk scene had laid the groundwork for influencing the broader development of punk.

Stretch

On the day after Harvey Milk and Dan White were sworn in to the board of supervisors, Willie McCovey, the veteran slugger who had won the National League's Comeback Player of the Year Award after returning to the Giants in 1977, turned forty. The Giants were counting on the big first baseman, known as "Stretch" for his size and his stylish play at first base, to be a bright spot in what was likely to be another dismal year for the team. McCovey, who was by far the most popular player on the Giants, was a quiet man from Mobile, Alabama. He was an African American who had grown up in the Deep South, signed his first contract with the Giants organization when he was only seventeen years old, and begun his career with the Giants in 1959, going four for four against future Hall of Famer Robin Roberts in his big league debut.

· McCovey starred for the Giants for well over a decade but was traded to the Padres after the 1973 season. He then returned to the Giants as a free agent in 1977. During his first fifteen years with the Giants, McCovey established himself as one of the top left-handed sluggers in the game. He did this despite injuries and having to share playing time for many years with another slugging first baseman and fellow future Hall of Famer, Orlando Cepeda. McCovey led the National League in home runs in 1963, 1968, and 1969 and in slugging percentage from 1968 to 1970.[20]

For many years, McCovey was the best and the most-feared left-handed slugger in the league. He was big and hit the ball ferociously hard. Roger Craig, who later went on to manage the Giants to the pennant in 1989, had a 10–24 record in 1962 with a dreadful Mets team that finished sixty-and-a-half games behind the pennant-winning Giants. An exchange that Craig described between himself and the great Casey Stengel, who at that time was managing the Mets, demonstrates the respect most baseball people had for McCovey's power: "Casey always let the starting pitcher go over the other team's lineup, so the defensive guys would know where to play. I'm going over the Giants one day and I get to McCovey. I said, 'He's a low-ball hitter and a dead pull hitter. Play him to pull.' And Casey interrupts me and says, 'Mr. Craig, do you want the right fielder to play in the upper deck or the lower deck?'"[21]

At six feet four inches and just under two hundred pounds, McCovey was one of the biggest players in the game at the time. Although not exactly stocky, he was unmistakably muscular. Like many left-handed hitters, he had a clear but hard-to-define grace in his swing and in his presence on the field in general. He was never the kind of player who needed to say much, but during his second stint with the team (1977–1980), nobody doubted his role as the Giants' leader. As late as 1990, McCovey, not Willie Mays, was probably the most popular player in San Francisco Giants history. This only changed when the memories of both players began to fade. By mid-1978, McCovey would receive perhaps the ultimate San Francisco compliment when Mayor Moscone compared his status as a San Francisco institution to that of the Golden Gate Bridge and the cable cars.

Recognized as an all-time great, McCovey was elected to the Hall of Fame the first time he was eligible, was one of the best power hitters of his era, and from 1968 to 1970 was by far the most dominant hitter in the game, posting an OPS+ of 188 for that period, fully 27 points higher than his nearest competitor, Carl Yastrzemski.[22] However, McCovey also spent most of his career either playing only against right-handed pitchers, as he did in his first few years with the Giants, or losing time to injuries. Amazingly, during a career that spanned 22 seasons, more than a third of McCovey's career WAR came in the three years, 1968–1970, when he was the best hitter in the game.[23] McCovey was Rookie of the Year in 1959 as a twenty-one-year old but did not play 110 or more games in a season until 1963. Over the course of his career, he only appeared in 130 or more games ten times, and in 150 or more games only four times. Unlike catcher, for example, first base is not the most physically demanding position on the field, so making it to 150 games is not a tough goal to reach. McCovey was the best hitter in the game for three years, a very good player for seven, and a part-time player for most of the other twelve years of his career.

Stretch also played for many years in Candlestick Park, a pitcher's ballpark. Moreover, the middle to late 1960s, which should have been his best years, was an era dominated by pitching. McCovey had the additional misfortune of having the same first name and being from the same state as his team's more famous star, who was also African American. This made it more difficult for him to have a national profile that was not in the shadow of Willie Mays. Early in his career, McCovey had a chance for baseball immortality in the ninth inning of game 7 of the 1962 World Series when he came up to bat with two outs and the Giants down 1–0 with the tying run on third and the winning run on second. Again, luck was not on his side, as he hit a screaming line drive that was caught by Yankee second baseman Bobby Richardson.

In 2001, Bill James, one of the baseball's most respected analysts, ranked McCovey as the ninth-greatest first baseman ever, noting, "If he played in the 1990s with the DH and the modern parks, he'd hit 800 home runs."[24] McCovey never had the chance to do that, but he was still a legitimately great player whom San Franciscans saw as their first Giants star with no ties to New York, the city where the Giants had made their home before 1958. This was particularly true after Cepeda was traded to the Cardinals in 1966.

As great as McCovey was, the two greatest players in San Francisco Giants' history are Willie Mays and Barry Bonds. These two are also among the five best ballplayers ever. Babe Ruth is the only ballplayer who is broadly recognized as having been better than Mays. Barry Bonds's offensive numbers, widely believed to be inflated by the use of performance enhancing drugs late in his career, are even better than those of Mays. In the more than forty-five years since he retired, Willie Mays continues to be treated like the baseball legend that he is. This is particularly true in San Francisco, as the twenty-first-century Giants team has become very good at using the franchise's history to market itself. Nonetheless, the star centerfielder's relationship with Giants fans was always more complex that the adoration McCovey enjoyed from those fans.

Mays was recognized in San Francisco for being a great player, but he was not beloved by the fans in the way a player of his ability should have been. This difference was famously summarized by Hearst newspaperman Frank Coniff. During Soviet premier Nikita Khrushchev's 1959 visit to the United States, Harry Bridges, the radical leader of San Francisco's International Longshoremen's Association, mobilized his members to applaud Khrushchev's car as it drove into the city. This prompted Coniff to observe that San Francisco is "the damnedest city," where "they cheer Khrushchev and boo Willie Mays."

In a 1978 *Sports Illustrated* profile of McCovey, Ron Firmite reflected on why Mays was never embraced by Giants fans the way he might have been given that he was the best player of his time. "The premier ballplayer of his generation, Mays was never as fully accepted by San Francisco fans as Cepeda and McCovey were. There was much too much of New York about him, and while the younger players appeared publicly about town, Mays was virtually invisible away from the park. And yet he craved attention and was frequently peevish when others, obviously less deserving, received it."[25]

In mid-January 1978, with spring training only about a month away, the Giants had an interesting team, but their fans had little to be optimistic about apart from another year of watching their favorite aging slugger. The team that my brother and I were fans of in early 1978 and with whom many other young San Franciscans would fall in love by the end of the year was not in great shape. The previous year had been the fourth year in a row in which the Giants had lost more games than they had won. Giants fans, the few of us who were still around in early 1978, did not have much reason to believe the coming season was going to be any better. The team that finished in fourth place in 1977, twenty-three games behind the first-place Dodgers, had made no big trades or signed any major free agents between the end of the season and spring training of 1978. They had drawn 700,056 fans in 1977, fewer than any team in the big leagues except for the Oakland A's across the bay. However, that 700,056 was better than the Giants had drawn in any year since 1973. From 1974 to 1976 they averaged fewer than 600,000 paying fans. Things got so bad that by 1976 it was widely believed the team would be leaving San Francisco for Toronto. In January 1976, even the San Francisco papers were reporting that: "It may sicken a few folks between Market Street and Reno, but the Toronto newspapers are already running stories comparing the Giants, by position, to other teams in the division.... They behave as if the kidnapping has already been accomplished."[26]

At the last minute, local businessman Bob Lurie and Bud Herseth, a wealthy meatpacker from Arizona, purchased the Giants and pledged to keep them in San Francisco, so the Giants were still in San Francisco as the 1978 season approached. However, the Giants' long-term future in San Francisco was far from guaranteed. The most widespread speculation in spring of 1978 was that one of the Bay Area teams would move and the other would find a way to split its home games between Candlestick Park and the Oakland Coliseum.

Sinking attendance, losing baseball, anonymous players, and a dreadful ballpark were not out of place in a city that, like many in America during those years, suffered from declining population, rising crime, and a shrinking industrial base. For most of those years, few people in San Francisco paid any attention to the Giants. Other than intense baseball fans and some kids, few seemed aware of the Giants during the mid-1970s. They were a team devoid of stars, playing in the southeast corner of the city in front of very few fans.

Attendance figures do not entirely capture the way the relationship between the Giants and the city where they played felt as 1978 began. The year 1977 had been the team's twentieth since moving to San Francisco from its longtime home in Manhattan. The novelty of big league baseball had worn off by the late 1960s. Sentiment toward the Giants soured further when they traded away Willie Mays midway through the 1972 season. When Mays was sent back to New York to finish his career with the Mets, the Giants lost their best-known player, who had been the face of the franchise for a generation. A number of younger players, most notably Bobby Bonds, had the opportunity to replace Mays in that capacity, but none were up to the daunting challenge.

By the mid-1970s the Giants were a bad team with no real identity play-ing in a freezing and cavernous ballpark. They were also playing in a city that had changed probably more than any other in the country in the twenty years since they had moved west. While the city underwent dramatic social and cultural change, the Giants remained far from the center of the city, lit-erally and metaphorically. After winning the National League West in 1971 and then losing in the National League Championship Series to the Pitts-burgh Pirates, they rarely contended, had few broadly recognizable players, and did not invest in reaching out to the rest of the city.

San Francisco 1978

Despite its extraordinary physical beauty, growing progressive political tradition, and increasingly important place in American cultural and social history, San Francisco was struggling by the late 1970s. The 1980 census would reveal a population of 678,974, down by more than 95,000, or about 13 percent, over a thirty-year period beginning in 1950. This was the first time the population of the city had dipped below 700,000 since 1940.

The San Francisco of the late 1970s was influenced by the economic changes and policies that began in the 1960s. The city that nurtured the Summer of Love, became a global center of gay rights, as the movement was known at the time, and where punk rock married left-wing politics, was made possible because of its unique history going back, in some respects, to the days of the Gold Rush, but also to the more recent past. Fitzgerald's account of this transition explains the changes San Francisco had experi-enced in the fifteen or twenty years preceding 1978:

> In 1960 San Francisco was a commercial and industrial city with a wide variety
> of manufacturing enterprises. Its population was heavily blue collar, and
> though racially and ethnically diverse, the city was not truly integrated. It
> was . . . a city of its neighborhoods, each with its own main street, its own
> shops and restaurants. . . . Its WASP establishment was more than a little stuffy,
> and its police and politicians, being largely Irish or Italian Catholics, had no
> respect whatsoever for "diverse lifestyles." . . . The flight of manufacturing
> emptied the factories and warehouses South of Market Street; the flight of
> blue-collar workers in its wake emptied the ethnic neighborhoods, among

them the Haight-Ashbury and the Castro. It emptied the Irish and Italian neighborhoods, and it thinned the black population in the Fillmore District and the Hispanic population in the Mission District. Great tracts of the Fillmore District were razed to the ground and never rebuilt. . . . This was ideal for the tribes of sixties children who came to live on the fringes of the economy.[27]

Some of Fitzgerald's assertions are probably overstated. The Mission was still substantially Latino in the late 1970s; western San Francisco was similarly heavily Irish and working-class at that time. However, in general she captures the feeling of the city then, and the set of conditions that facilitated the important events in 1978. Her description of neighborhoods still applied in 1978 and contributed to some of the political division and contestation at the time. One of the most important words Fitzgerald uses is. "emptied," because San Francisco in 1978 was much more sparsely populated than it is today. That emptiness and sense of space helped define the city in 1978. There was also an underside of life in San Francisco in those years that was fed by difficult economic times, racial divisions, tensions between the old and new San Francisco (for which Dan White and Harvey Milk were powerful symbols), and a drug culture where psychedelics and flower power had given way to heavier and more dangerous and powerfully addictive drugs.

In the decades since 1978, San Francisco has become known for being the most progressive major American city and also, incongruously and more recently, for being at the epicenter of the ongoing tech boom that has made the area from Silicon Valley all the way up to Sonoma County one of the wealthiest regions in world history, but a few decades ago San Francisco was a very different place. While the gay liberation movement was beginning to gain momentum after winning a major victory with the election of Harvey Milk in 1977, there were still many strong pockets of working-class white conservatism, most notably in the western part of the city and the Excelsior District, whose voters had sent Dan White, a former policeman, to the board of supervisors in 1977. Less dramatically, there were powerful real estate and business interests that were not happy about George Moscone's radical agenda. The events that would rock the city later in 1978 were a reflection of that contestation. Ultimately, although an enduring and relatively peaceful, although still frequently contested, compromise or hybrid emerged, neither San Francisco won a definitive victory.

In 1978 that outcome was not at all inevitable or even easily predictable. It is obvious now that San Francisco is a global center, and even a model, of tolerance, but it was not clear in the 1970s that Harvey Milk's San Francisco would win out over Dan White's in that regard. In the introduction to his 2012 work on San Francisco during those years, David Talbot writes, "San Francisco values did not come into the world with flowers in their hair; they were born howling, in blood and strife. It took years of frantic and often violent conflict—including political assassinations, riots, bombings, kidnappings, serial race murders, antigay street mayhem, the biggest mass suicide in history, a panic inducing epidemic—before San Francisco finally made peace with itself and its new identity."[28]

Charles A. Fracchia Sr., the San Francisco historian, described San Francisco in 1978 to me as a city going through difficult economic and social times. "It was a tough period of time," he said, citing economic problems including inflation and gas lines but also adding that "there was a feeling that things were not right."[29] Political consultant Rich Schlackman echoed these sentiments when we spoke in 2017: "There was no business here [in San Francisco]. . . . It was slowly dying."[30] Music critic Joel Selvin, however, gave me a different view by arguing that at the time "people thought that life in San Francisco was pretty f**king peachy. There wasn't an enormous amount of discontent in the vast bulk of the white middle class."[31] The difference in Selvin's and Fracchia's perspectives is partially generational. Fracchia grew up in pre-1960s San Francisco and was more aware of, and concerned about, the changes to his city that began in the late 1960s. Selvin is half a generation or so younger and recalls the era from that perspective, while having less of a memory of the earlier San Francisco where there were fewer hippies, less social conflict, and more good-paying blue collar jobs. These two perspectives are a reminder that even now, more than forty years later, the San Francisco of the mid-1970s is still occasionally contested.

My 1978

Other than two trips to the East Coast to visit my grandparents and other family members in New York, and one or two journeys to Marin County or down the Peninsula, I spent all of 1978 in San Francisco. I have distinct memories of many of the events that made 1978 so significant. I remember the day of the assassinations, hearing the news from Jonestown, many ballgames at Candlestick Park, driving through Harvey Milk's Castro district with my mother, and overhearing the more conservative parents of many of my friends reflect on their changing city. I was too young to hang out at punk rock shows in 1978, but I remember seeing those early punks and the reactions they got from older San Franciscans. These memories are vague and inconsistent, and were initially experienced by a child, so, for example, I can remember the concession options and prices from Candlestick Park, but I have no real recollection of the Peoples Temple before hearing about Congressman Leo Ryan's trip to Jonestown in November 1978. Nonetheless, it is unavoidable that my memories and perspective frame much of this book.

I am and always have been both a San Francisco insider and a bit of an outsider. I am a Jew who was born in New York and who has lived most of his adult life in that city. During my childhood and youth, my background made me stand out from my peers, most of whom had deeper roots in San Francisco and very few of whom were Jewish. I have no 49ers, early pioneers, University of California graduates, Dust Bowl refugees, or immigrants from Central America or Asia in my family background, although my forebears' shtetl credentials are pretty strong. I left San Francisco at twenty-two and have never lived there since, but because I spend at least a month or two there every year, I still believe I understand the vibe of the city pretty well.

I still know the best places for Asian food in San Francisco's Richmond district, remember what the city felt like in the 1970s, can discuss the changes to the city as well as anybody, have seen many of best local bands of the 1970s and 1980s, know the fastest driving shortcuts around the city from my days delivering pizza while in college, wake up every morning in baseball season no matter where I am and check to see if the Giants won the night before, and have both a grade school and high school diploma from schools within the forty-nine-square-mile boundary of San Francisco. The grade school I attended is part of the city's vast and once almost all-encompassing network of Catholic schools. I have a visceral dislike for all things related to Los Angeles, especially the Dodgers—even though it turns out Los Angeles is a pretty cool town. For me, like all real San Franciscans, there is still only one city on the west coast of the United States.

2

San Francisco in 1978

....

Today, 1978 in San Francisco is largely remembered for two things that happened only a few weeks apart late in the year. The first was the horrific mass murder in Jonestown, Guyana, by deranged Peoples Temple leader Jim Jones. This was followed fewer than two weeks later by the assassination of Supervisor Harvey Milk and Mayor George Moscone by former supervisor Dan White. Those two events had a huge impact on San Francisco and created psychic scars for almost everybody who lived in the city. Most of us, regardless of age, ethnicity, sexual orientation, or neighborhood, can remember precisely where we were when we learned of both tragedies, as well as the discussions and feelings that followed, how our political views and positions informed our interpretations of the events, and the sense for many months afterward that something had gone badly wrong in the city we loved so much.

The horror in Jonestown solidified San Francisco's reputation in the eyes of the rest of the country as a place that was not just slightly crazy, but also dangerous. It was different in San Francisco because this terrible event was very much a local story. In our city, Jonestown was not just an abstraction or a warning about counterculture excesses. It was a tragedy that resonated deeply in parts of the city. Many San Franciscans, particularly African Americans, had friends, family members, or acquaintances who died in Jonestown. We saw the empty Peoples Temple building on Geary Street for a long time after the killings. Until he left San Francisco in mid-1977, Jim Jones had been a presence in San Francisco's religious and political life.

The killing of Harvey Milk helped make the San Francisco supervisor a civil rights icon and brought national, and even global, attention to Milk's role as a leader of the gay liberation movement. However, George Moscone's death also had a tremendous impact on San Francisco, as the mayor who had been elected on a historic progressive platform, and had sought to govern that way, was replaced by a probusiness centrist. In this regard, the long-term impact of the assassinations on San Francisco itself, therefore, has not always been adequately recognized in the subsequent decades.

Because of the enormity of these two historical events, much else about what made 1978 such an unusual, important, and fascinating year in San Francisco, and that contributed to the city being what it is today, is frequently similarly overlooked. That year marked the point punk rock broke through in San Francisco, as bands such as Crime, the Nuns, the Avengers, and others forged San Francisco's punk rock identity. Forty years later, the band that remains most identified with San Francisco's unique punk rock scene, with its strong emphasis on radical left-wing politics, is Dead Kennedys. Dead Kennedys formed and played their first show together in 1978, which was the year that the United Kingdom's most famous punk rock band, the Sex Pistols, played their last show, also in San Francisco. San Francisco, even in its current wealthy techie iteration, retains a strong connection to the 1960s, the Summer of Love, and the music and politics of that era; the punk scene that came along in the late 1970s, however, is rarely given its due. At the time, it was a surprisingly important musical and youth movement that ensured San Francisco would retain its reputation as an important place for youth culture and music into, and well beyond, the 1980s.

If you talk to middle-aged men who were born between about 1964 and 1972 and who grew up in San Francisco about their memories of 1978, they will acknowledge, of course, the significance of Jonestown and the assassinations, a few may even mention going to one of their first punk shows, but a surprisingly large number will mention baseball. One such man is John Maschino, who was an eleven-year-old boy in 1978 but now has a PhD in American history and teaches in Southern California. Maschino, who lived in Marin County just across the bridge from San Francisco, describes himself as having been "absolutely captivated with this [1978] team" and traces his lifelong passion for the Giants to 1978, the year his father gave him the "I hate the Dodgers" T-shirt that Maschino still occasionally wears.

The San Francisco Giants did not even make it to the playoffs in 1978, but it was still a very significant year for the team and its relationship with its city. The Giants finished in third place in 1978 but drew more fans than in any season since 1960, their first in Candlestick Park. At the time, that was the second-highest attendance in franchise history, going back to the nineteenth century in New York. The Giants generated more excitement in 1978 than they had since at least their division-winning 1971 season. Young stars such as Jack Clark, veterans such as Vida Blue and Bill Madlock, and the not quite ageless Willie McCovey helped a new generation of fans fall in love with the Giants in the middle of what would prove to be the roughest decade and a half in their very long history.

The year 1978 was also when Proposition 13 became law in California, dramatically limiting social services over the following decades, and when Proposition 6, which would have stripped gays and lesbians of some basic civil rights, was defeated. It was also the year that Winterland, Bill Graham's legendary San Francisco concert venue, closed for good and the year that Pier 39 opened, kicking off the modernizing of the city's eastern waterfront.

In short, there was a lot going on in San Francisco in 1978. It may be coincidence or just a quirk of history that so many memorable events occurred in one calendar year in that city, but few cities experience as much turmoil, upheaval, tragedy, and new beginnings in a decade as San Francisco did in that one year or even in the one month of November 1978. The events of 1978 not only were dramatic, colorful, exciting, tragic, and frightening, but they also created the foundation for twenty-first-century San Francisco. There are several different possible storylines that reveal 1978, but there was only one San Francisco, and for those of us who lived there, it was all happening at one time in our town.

The State of the City

On December 11, 1975, a *New York Times* article outlined the urban problems that most American cities were facing during the mid-1970s: "There are many tears shed here. Many are poor. Many are threatened. Some are being crowded out. Interests still battle interests, and the weak are crushed. Change has come rapidly; it is ill understood, and badly dealt with by community leaders. What once was a city filled with a thriving middle class has been abandoned by families seeking better schools, better homes and the fundamental security of personal safety."[1] The writer, Wallace Turner, was not describing New York, Detroit, Cleveland, or any other big city in the Northeast or the Midwest, but San Francisco, where on that day the mayoral runoff between George Moscone and his conservative Republican opponent, John Barbagelata, was occurring. Turner sought to explain further to his New York readers how bad things were in San Francisco in the long piece he wrote that day that included subheadings such as "Heroin Problem" and "Unemployment Up." Turner concluded on the less-than-upbeat note that "Wilson Riles, the state superintendent of schools, had said San Francisco's [schools] are the worst of any city in the state."[2] An article in the *San Francisco Examiner* two days later echoed these same sentiments about the dire state of the city that the new mayor would inherit: "In short, Moscone will find a city afflicted with ailments common to most American cities and with its resources badly depleted and great chunks of its citizenry discontent."[3]

As suggested by Turner's article, crime and security were significant concerns for San Franciscans throughout the mid-1970s, when San Francisco averaged about 130 murders a year.[4] Given that San Francisco had a population that was less than one-tenth that of New York, it had approximately the same murder rate as that city, where between 1,500 and 1,700 murders occurred each year in the late 1970s.[5] By contrast, the number of murders in San Francisco has not exceeded 100 since 1997; more recently, it was fewer than 50 in 2013 and 2014, 53 in 2015, 58 in 2016, 56 in 2017, and 48 in 2018.[6]

The relatively high crime rate in San Francisco during the 1970s is sometimes overshadowed by the nature of the crimes that occurred in the city during that decade. While the data suggest that San Francisco was a dangerous place to live in the 1970s, popular culture and most memories stress that as far as crime is concerned, it was both a dangerous and a weird place to live. Today, most non–San Franciscans only remember Jonestown and the Milk and Moscone murders when they think about crime in the city during the 1970s, but those were only two of the jarring and vivid killings that plagued San Francisco throughout the decade. Patty Hearst and the Symbionese Liberation Army—half cult, half radical political movement—robbed the Hibernia Bank in the Sunset District in 1974, and the Zebra Killings terrorized San Francisco in 1973–1974. The Joe Boys shot the Wah Ching in a Chinatown gang murder in the Golden Dragon Restaurant in

1977. These high-profile crimes helped solidify San Francisco's reputation as a city where the Summer of Love of 1967 had given way to the crime, violence, and chaos of the 1970s.

These crimes not only frightened many San Franciscans, but they hardened some political positions and contributed to the polarization of the city, as many San Franciscans believed more aggressive policing was needed while others, particularly racial minorities, believed such approaches violated civil liberties. The investigation into the Zebra Killings, known as Operation Zebra, included a stop-and-frisk policy that resulted in many innocent African American men being stopped and searched by police, frequently in ways that were time consuming, humiliating, and in violation of their civil rights. However, many white San Franciscans supported this, seeing it as a necessary crime-fighting tactic. Christine Lamberson notes, "The murders stood at the nexus of multiple problems facing U.S. cities during the 1970s. Cities like San Francisco were experiencing rising crime rates, continued radical violence and persistently low confidence in law enforcement officials."[7]

The clash between supporters of the police and minorities concerned about civil liberties has remained a big part of the politics of many cities. As recently as 2013, Bill de Blasio was elected mayor of New York City, winning huge shares of the African American and Latino vote in the Democratic primary and general election, in substantial part because of his opposition to stop-and-frisk policies. Conservative mayoral candidates over the last four decades have frequently supported these or similar policies. In San Francisco in the 1970s, the conflation of African American crime and African American radicalism made these issues more complex, but for many white people it was a distinction without a difference, as both, in their view, required a strong law-and-order response.

In some other respects, San Francisco in 1978 looked a lot like the rest of urban America. The city had been losing shipping and manufacturing jobs for over a decade, leaving unemployment and large swaths of unused warehouses and factories in the wake. A 2002 San Francisco Planning Department document states, "By the 1980s, the bulk of the larger manufacturing and distribution businesses had left San Francisco as suburban locations proved more attractive and affordable."[8] The same report indicates that the number of manufacturing jobs in the city declined from 69,000 in 1953 to about 45,000 in 1975.[9] This is a substantial change for a city the size of San Francisco. Among the poorest neighborhoods in San Francisco that were

Table 2.1
San Francisco Population by Decade,
1950–2010, 2016

Year	Population
1950	775,357
1960	740,316
1970	715,674
1980	678,974
1990	723,959
2000	776,733
2010	805,235
2016 (estimate)	870,887

SOURCES: For 1950–2010, data is from "Population by County 1860–2010," BayAreaCensus.Gov. The 2016 estimate is from "American Fact Finder," U.S. Census Bureau.

most affected by this economic downturn were Hunters Point and Bayview. In the western part of Hunters Point lay a small peninsula called Candlestick Point, where about fifteen years earlier the city had built a ballpark named Candlestick Park.

As shown in table 1, San Francisco's population according to the 1980 census, a reasonably good measure of San Francisco in 1978, was the lowest of the postwar period.

The 2010 census, which does not account for the considerable growth since that time, shows the population of the city as 805,235. While this is not radically more population growth than some other cities have experienced, because San Francisco is surrounded by water on three sides and mountains on a fourth, population growth is felt very acutely by residents. The low population figures in 1978, on the other hand, meant that the city had many unused industrial spaces and underpopulated residential areas where landlords could not be too picky about tenants and where rents remained cheap. Many of these spaces have now become the sites of highly sought after condominiums and live work spaces for people in the tech sector, but in the late 1970s and into the early 1980s, they became incubators for San Francisco's burgeoning punk rock culture.

There are very few cities that remain stagnant after forty years, or in some respects even recognizable, but even in that context, the changes that San Francisco has experienced in the last forty years are startling. One of the most significant ways the city has changed during this period is that it is much more crowded today. Due to years of economic decline, San Francisco in 1978 was defined not by crowds, traffic, or a lack of parking places, but by being underpopulated, even feeling empty. The change represents a victory not for Moscone and Milk, but for the downtown and real estate interests who supported their opponents, including the man who would become their killer. This began, or was reinvigorated, during Dianne Feinstein's progrowth mayoralty, which lasted nine years.

This growth is at the core of the city's twenty-first-century identity and has put a strain on its infrastructure, driven up housing costs, and forced San Franciscans to spend more time than ever before stuck in traffic or looking for parking. There are positives to this as well. The city is safer; has an exciting and vibrant feel; is filled with an unprecedented number of excellent restaurants, professional opportunities, and recreational venues for those with money; and has a stronger tax base. More abstractly, the city has a very different vibe than it did in the 1970s. The increased population has made it a less viable destination for young adults with limited funds and not a lot of conventional professional ambition, such as those who flooded into San Francisco in the 1960s and 1970s. It is no longer a place where space for starting a band, building a political movement, or just hanging out with one's friends is cheaply available. That too has changed the feel of the city.

A closer look at the census data, as shown in table 2, shows some other key differences between 1980 and 2010. Most evidence suggests that the trends in this table have accelerated since the 2010 census.

The San Francisco of 1978 was much whiter than it is today, but it still had a substantial African American population. By 2010, the percentage of African Americans had almost been cut in half, while the proportion of white San Franciscans declined as well. Most of this was made up by consistent growth in the city's Asian American population and slight growth in the Latino proportion.

Racial politics in San Francisco followed quite a bit from these demographics. For example, George Moscone was, in the context of the mid-1970s, a very progressive mayor, but he was also white. At the time Moscone was elected mayor in 1975, numerous American cities had elected African American mayors, including Cleveland (Carl Stokes in 1967), Newark (Kenneth Gibson in 1970), Cincinnati (Ted Berry in 1972), Detroit (Coleman Young in 1973), Los Angeles (Tom Bradley in 1973), and Atlanta (Maynard

Table 2.2
San Francisco Demographics, 1980 and 2010

	1980	2010
White	59.2%	49.7%
African American	12.7%	7.8%
Latino	12.4%	14.1%
Asian/Pacific Islander	22%	31.3%
Children under 17 (19 in 1980)	133,621	112,802
Median household income (2010 dollars)	$47,654 (1979)	$71,745
Living below poverty level	13.7% (1979)	12.5%

SOURCE: http://www.bayareacensus.ca.gov/counties/SanFranciscoCounty70.htm.

Jackson in 1973). In the same year Moscone was elected, Walter Washington, who was African American, became the first elected mayor of Washington, D.C. Within a few years, cities such as San Antonio would elect a Latino mayor, while a few miles south of San Francisco, San Jose would elect an Asian American mayor.

Moscone's election meant that the thirty-seventh mayor of the city would be like thirty-five of his thirty-six predecessors—that is, a white Christian man. Only Adolph Sutro, who was Jewish and served as mayor from 1895 to 1897, did not fit that mold. Additionally, other than Dianne Feinstein, who had run unsuccessful campaigns for mayor in 1971 and 1975, there had never been a major candidate for San Francisco's top office who had not been a white male. Since Moscone, three of San Francisco's mayors have been white men: Art Agnos, Frank Jordan, and Gavin Newsom. A fourth, Mark Farrell, served as mayor for part of 2018 after being appointed by the board of supervisors, but he never sought election to that office and relinquished it in the middle of 2018. The other four post-Moscone mayors include Feinstein, Willie Brown (African American), Ed Lee (Chinese American), and London Breed, an African American woman.

San Francisco's demographics in 1975–1980 were different from those of many American cities in that the white proportion of the voting population was higher than in cities such as Cleveland, New York, or Detroit, while the nonwhite vote was divided among several different groups. Additionally, much of the progressive vote in San Francisco at this time was white due to years of progressive whites, gay and straight, moving to the city. As mayor, Moscone succeeded in bringing together a very diverse group of San Franciscans to run the city, but racial politics there remained complex.

By the mid-1970s, the Bay Area was one of the corners of America where radical politics on the part of African Americans, Chicanos, Asians, whites, and even Native Americans had gained a foothold. Although today Berkeley in the 1960s has become almost a catchword for the radicalism of that era, there was much more to late 1960s and early 1970s Bay Area radicalism than just Berkeley. The Black Panther Party got its start in Oakland. From November 1969 through June 1971, Native Americans took over Alcatraz, the island in the middle of San Francisco Bay that was once a federal prison and is now a popular tourist destination. The Chicano liberation movement, which had strong roots in San Francisco, rose to national, or at least regional, prominence during this period as well.

San Francisco State University (SFSU), while not as academically prestigious or elite as UC Berkeley, was one of the most radicalized major campuses in America during those years. From late 1968 through early 1969, students at SFSU, led by the Black Students Union and the Third World Liberation Front, engaged in a strike against the university. The five-month-long strike was the longest in the history of American higher education.[10] In the years following, groups representing Asian American, Latino, and African American students continued to have a large and radical presence on campus.

In the 1970s, elements of new progressive politics (most notably gay rights), neighborhood-oriented quality of life issues, and environmentalism were beginning to become part of the city's political discourse. These concerns that were just emerging then continue to have a lasting impact on the politics of San Francisco. However, in the 1970s economic and racial issues were still central to city governance and politics and were at the core of progressive concerns. San Francisco's African American community, while much larger than it is today, had seen the Western Addition, one of the major centers of African American population, fragmented by a development project that turned Geary Boulevard into a multilane thoroughfare, almost like a highway, cutting through the heart of the community. Latinos in the Mission shared the concern felt by African Americans regarding police brutality and excesses. The loss of shipping and manufacturing jobs had hit the city's nonwhite population hard as well. Additionally, the city's historically large Asian American community still had very little political power.

By 1978, there was also evidence that at least some progress was being made. In January, Gordon Lau became the first Chinese American elected to the board of supervisors, and after emerging as the progressive candidate to become its president, he narrowly lost that competition to Dianne Feinstein. Willie Brown, an African American who represented much of San Francisco in the state assembly, had been elected to his seventh term in 1976 and was soon to become speaker of that body. Things were changing, and Moscone was helping steward that change.

Another line of table 2 tells an often overlooked but essential part of the story of San Francisco's demographic change. In the late 1970s and early 1980s, the city had many children and youth. By 2010 that had changed. The census data here is a little unclear, as children were defined differently in the two census reports. Nonetheless, even if that 2010 number is increased to 125,000, it would still represent 16 percent of the overall population, compared to 20 percent thirty years earlier. In general, the people who lived in San Francisco in 1978 were more likely to be white or African American and more likely to be children than the San Franciscans of today.

Beyond the census, San Francisco was a city that, as would become tragically apparent by year's end, was deeply divided. It was in the midst of a transition that had begun just over a decade earlier and would continue for a few more years into the early 1980s. One way to understand this is that in 1964 the Republican party nominated Barry Goldwater for president in a raucous convention that pitted the liberal faction of the party, led by Nelson Rockefeller, against the more conservative faction of the Republican party, represented by Goldwater. That convention was famous for Goldwater's spirited, if wordy, defense of his own extremism during his convention speech: "I would remind you that extremism in the defense of liberty is no vice! And let me remind you also that moderation in the pursuit of justice is no virtue!"

During Rockefeller's speech opposing Goldwater and calling for the Republican Party to support civil rights, a white delegate tried to physically assault an African American delegate who was cheering for Rockefeller. Fortunately for the white man, his wife held him back. Picking a fight with Jackie Robinson, fewer than eight years after retiring from the Brooklyn Dodgers, would not have ended well for the paunchy racist in question. That convention did not take place in Dallas, Phoenix, or anywhere else in the Sun Belt or the South, but in the Cow Palace, a multiuse facility in the southern part of San Francisco.

Twenty years after the Republicans nominated Goldwater at the Cow Palace, the Democratic Party held its convention in San Francisco. At that convention, they nominated a pair, Walter Mondale and Geraldine Ferraro, that would go on, like Barry Goldwater and Bill Miller in 1964, to be soundly drubbed in the general election. Some pundits speculated that by holding the convention in San Francisco—where left-wing protesters, punk rockers, and others, myself among them, demonstrated outside the convention hall entertained by, among other bands, Dead Kennedys—hurt the ticket because it made the Democrats vulnerable to charges of being too liberal. Thus, the city that the GOP saw as an appropriate convention site in 1964 was only two decades later too radical for the Democrats.

In 1964, San Francisco still was politically a lot like many other major American cities. The biggest differences to an outsider visiting San Francisco would have been the city's sizable Chinese American community and the sheer natural beauty of the place. Some things do not change. However, other than that, San Francisco was a heavily white Catholic city whose political leadership was made up mostly of Irish and Italian Americans. It was a union town like New York, Boston, or Chicago. Its African American community was concentrated in two low-income neighborhoods, the Fillmore–Western Addition and Bayview–Hunters Point. In many elections San Franciscans supported Democrats, but almost always white straight male ones who were rarely great progressives. Every mayor since John Shelley was elected in 1964 had been a Democrat, but for the three decades before that, San Francisco was governed by Republican mayors.

By the last years of the twentieth century, San Francisco would become a synonym for tolerance and progressive politics. It was the global capital of the LGBT movement, a city of astounding ethnic diversity and one where politicians such as Nancy Pelosi—on the national level a symbol of liberal political views—were viewed by many locals as too conservative. Beyond politics, late-twentieth-century San Francisco was a place where alternative lifestyles of all kinds were celebrated and where everything that was still thought of as kind of weird in much of the country, from organic food to yoga, was part of the fabric of everyday life. In 1978, however, the city was still transitioning between the two San Franciscos. The tragic events that occurred later in that year may have tipped the balance toward the future, but it was not exactly apparent at the time. Charles A. Fracchia Sr. described the political climate at the time as one where in San Francisco there was "a transition from a relatively moderate or conservative political situation to one which got very radical."[11]

Quentin Kopp, who was first elected to the San Francisco Board of Supervisors in 1971 after moving to San Francisco from the East Coast, echoed

Fracchia's sentiment about the transition in early 1970s San Francisco during a 2018 interview: "During that period, '71 to '75, you had the aftermath of what happened in Haight-Ashbury, starting about 1967. You had the hippies, the flower children, and then in the Haight-Ashbury you had some radical, left-wing young people . . . who incidentally liked firearms." Kopp added, "It felt like San Francisco had changed completely. It was an unsettling feeling to me."[12]

Conservative politicians such as John Barbagelata, who very narrowly lost the 1975 mayoral race, and Supervisor Dan White were able to rally popular support among working-class conservative white voters through their positions on gays, hippies, and punks and on other social issues. In this regard, longtime San Francisco political consultant Rich Schlackman observed in 2017, "Out in Dan [White's] district, they thought the whole world was changing in front of them. It's like the Trump voters now."[13]

The transition Fracchia, Kopp, and Schlackman described occurred not only within San Francisco but nationally with regard to perceptions of San Francisco. In the mid-1960s, San Francisco could still pass as a normal American city. It was run by the business community and labor unions who frequently shared the prodevelopment goals of the business leaders because more building meant more jobs. The major voting blocs were Irish and Italian. The nonwhite population was on the fringes of political life. The city had better than average cultural institutions, a football team, and baseball (the Giants) and basketball (the Warriors) teams it had recently lured from New York and Philadelphia, respectively. As late as 1970, much of this remained true, with the caveat that the Summer of Love had occurred and there were a few neighborhoods with a lot of hippies. By the end of 1978 that had changed forever, as San Francisco settled into its role as a hub of either tolerance or left-wing excess, depending on your political views.

George Moscone's San Francisco

This transition was real, but much of the politics in the 1970s was fueled not just by social issues but by economic issues as well. Moscone was not a threat to the city's business interests because he thought gay people should be treated fairly or because he wanted the city to be governed by people that reflected the diversity of San Francisco. He and Milk were seen as threats to those interests because of their views on issues such as rent regulations, taxation, business regulations, and land use. Moscone and many of his voters opposed what was then referred to as the "Manhattanization" of downtown San Francisco, which referred to the accelerated development of the Financial District and of some of the underused spaces around that part of San Francisco. As the decades have gone by, the memory of Moscone's progressive credentials has faded. He is now seen by many largely as the straight career politician who was killed minutes before Harvey Milk, but the impact of Moscone's death on San Francisco was enormous. In a work examining the relationship between gay politics and urban politics, Robert Bailey argued that

> most lesbians and gay men remember November 27, 1978, as the day Harvey Milk was assassinated, but for the history of San Francisco, it was George Moscone's murder that more truly altered the city's future. Moscone had put together a coalition of neighborhood and community groups, minorities, and new immigrants—gay men and lesbians among them—to confront the local effects of San Francisco's rapid economic change. The neighborhood effects of urban change included a rapid rise in the cost of residential and commercial space, the destruction of much of the lower-income (albeit inadequate) housing near downtown, the displacement of its population and the loss of manufacturing jobs.[14]

Richard DeLeon concurs with Bailey's assessment of the importance of Moscone and places Moscone's mayoralty in the bigger picture of late-twentieth-century politics in San Francisco. "Moscone also aspired to be the city's first progressive mayor, not merely a liberal mayor. . . . He widened the doors of City Hall to let more people in. . . . His appointments pierced established bureaucracies and transfused new blood and progressive ideas into city government. . . . He challenged the conservative establishment and the downtown business elite. At the very least he made progressive government thinkable."[15]

Along with Willie Brown, the longtime assemblyman from San Francisco who went on to become speaker of that body and who later served two terms as mayor of San Francisco, Moscone was one of the first straight politicians who actively supported gay rights. For example, these two smart and savvy legislators managed to get California's antisodomy law repealed in 1975. This was a major victory for gay Californians at the time and in the 1970s, even in San Francisco, was considered radical.

Moscone married this vision of a San Francisco where policy would be made that preserved and improved the livability, or in later parlance, quality of life, with the left-of-center politics of the era, thus representing a major break and new direction for San Francisco. That vision began with his campaign. DeLeon described the significance of Moscone's 1975 campaign:

> Moscone's campaign was a dramatic departure from San Francisco's political traditions. In building his grass-roots electoral coalition, he reached out for the support of neighborhood activists, high-rise opponents, African Americans, Latinos, Asians, gays and lesbians, and other community groups previously neglected by establishment politicians. He attacked the pro-growth policies of the Alioto administration and promised to end the Manhattanization of San Francisco. . . . He promised unemployed workers and low-income renters that he would give a high priority to creating jobs and affordable housing for residents. A strong gay rights advocate and civil rights liberal, Moscone committed his administration to eliminating homophobia and racial prejudice in city departments and agencies.[16]

Moscone's press secretary, Corey Busch, described the campaign and the early months of Moscone's mayoralty as "a really difficult time, a time of transition, and a time of wresting power away from a group." Busch fleshed this out by describing Moscone's efforts to bring San Francisco's diversity into its government: "bringing people into city government that represented parts of the city that had never been represented before, ever . . . women, minorities, gays."[17]

In the 1975 mayor's race, Moscone was one of three major candidates. The charismatic and ambitious state senator had explored running for governor the previous year before deciding against the idea. Moscone easily won the first-round balloting with 31.52 percent of the vote but was well short of the majority needed to avoid a runoff. For the first time, mayoral candidates in 1975 needed a majority rather than a simple plurality in the first round. Dianne Feinstein, a member of the board of supervisors who sought to chart a moderate course in a rapidly changing city, was widely expected to finish second and challenge Moscone in the runoff, but she came in third, 1,196 votes behind John Barbagelata, a conservative Republican member of the board of supervisors. Feinstein's weaker-than-expected showing raised the question of whether she and her brand of centrism had a future in a rapidly polarizing San Francisco, while also ensuring that the next mayor would not be a compromise-oriented centrist but either an unabashed progressive or the candidate of conservative backlash.

Moscone's runoff opponent in 1975 was the candidate of reaction against the changing San Francisco, a torch that by 1978 was most visibly carried by newly elected supervisor Dan White. John Barbagelata was a successful real estate broker who had first been elected to the board of supervisors, along with Dianne Feinstein, in 1969. Barbagelata was astute enough to understand that in the first round Feinstein, not Moscone, stood in his way. The Republican supervisor had little chance of stopping Moscone from making the runoff or of persuading progressive supporters of Moscone to vote for him. Instead, Barbagelata approached the first round as a battle with Dianne Feinstein, as well as several other lesser candidates, for the moderate and conservative vote. Additionally, Feinstein, at first glance, seemed like the more formidable runoff opponent for Barbagelata. She would be able to take some of the probusiness vote from him while also consolidating the progressive vote, as she was to the left of Barbagelata on most issues. However, against Moscone, Barbagelata would have a much better shot at consolidating his conservative base and a necessary share of the more centrist vote.

Barbagelata's friend and political ally Quentin Kopp recollected how "Barbagelata ran a campaign against one person, Feinstein. He paid no attention to Jack Ertola. He paid no attention to Milton Marks, who's a fellow Republican. He paid no attention to George [Moscone]. He put out pieces that had his voting record on one side, hers on the other."[18] Barbagelata's strategy worked and landed him in the runoff.

Kopp had a good sense of Barbagelata's political strengths and weaknesses, describing him as "a good real estate broker and salesman." Kopp continued: "But he's like a guy who just doesn't know government or appreciate it.... [But] John knows how to sell. He treated a campaign like selling a house."[19] Barbagelata appealed to a very different San Francisco than the one that voted for Moscone. Former San Francisco mayor Art Agnos described the contrast between the two candidates in that runoff:

[Barbagelata] was not a neighborhood person. He was a business guy. He was wealthy—a well-to-do realtor on the west side. A very conservative, religious man. Decent man ... was close to his family, was a classic conservative Catholic businessman, and reflected those kinds of attitudes. ... That was the old traditional San Francisco that always controlled the city, and he was just the latest manifestation of that kind of political philosophy. Moscone was the new. He was into civil rights. He supported Cesar Chavez. He was a Kennedy guy. He was the face of the changing city.[20]

The runoff between Barbagelata and Moscone was one of the great mayoral races of modern American history. Only the Dinkins-Giuliani races in New York in 1989 and 1993 were as close and as ideologically polarizing as the mayor's race in San Francisco in 1975. Unlike most hard-fought mayor's races of the era, this one was not, at least on its surface, primarily about race. Like many San Francisco politicians in the thirty years or so after World War II, including Joe Alioto, the mayor they were seeking to replace, Moscone and Barbagelata were both Italian American and Catholic. They both came from modest backgrounds and had built successful careers in the 1960s and 1970s.

Despite this, the election was extremely polarizing, pitting representatives of two very different political views against each other for an office that had been dominated by centrists and for which highly competitive elections had been a rarity in recent decades. Barbagelata ran as a prototypical big-city conservative of the era, attacking Moscone as being a profligate spender of taxpayer money: "Moscone favors a new citywide income tax. . . . Moscone supports sharp increases in City business tax. . . . Moscone's answer to the City budget is . . . MORE TAXES." At the same time, Barbagelata touted his own positions and record as "100% OPPOSED to a city income tax. . . . Barbagelata's answer to the budget: LESS SPENDING."[21] On crime, Barbagelata's campaign asserted in the same flyer, "MOSCONE HAS THE WORST VOTING RECORD IN THE STATE ON CRIME," while reminding voters that "Barbagelata has consistently voted to give police the laws, tools and manpower to do the job," and promising, "Barbagelata opposes selective enforcement of laws. Prostitution leads to organized crime . . . gambling . . . heroin . . . and worse."[22] Archie Bunker lived in Queens, not the Outer Sunset, but Barbagelata was speaking to angry, middle-aged white voters like Archie. The racial message in Barbagelata's campaign, while rarely explicit, was hard to miss. In the 1970s, like today, pledges of support to police were understood to be appeals to conservative white voters.

Moscone ran a very different campaign, presenting himself as both the voice of new, progressive San Francisco and also of the neighborhoods, which in the parlance of that era was understood to be in opposition to downtown real-estate and business interests. One piece of campaign literature told voters that "Moscone wants the people of San Francisco to have the major voice in making the decisions that affect their lives—the City's neighborhoods, the City's family, the City's people."[23] In another piece of campaign material, Moscone described his campaign as being "run by the people of the City, for the people of the City—so that we can have at last a city government in which you can and want to take part, make your voice heard and know that you really matter . . . I know too—as you do—that these problems can't be met by a City Hall that ignores the City's neighborhoods, the City's families, the City's people."

Moscone did not exactly run a relentlessly positive campaign either. A Moscone campaign newspaper called the *Election News* that was published in advance of the runoff election included two crudely drawn cartoons, one of which showed a hapless Barbagelata as a marionette being controlled by a giant hand with the five fingers labeled "downtown," "GOP," "real estate," "builders," and "speculators." A second cartoon, in case some people found the first one too subtle, showed a somber-looking Barbagelata riding on top of a tank labeled "Republican Machine." The tank's gun was pointed toward the ground the tank was about to run over. The ground had the words "the neighborhoods" written on it.

The election divided the city along political, ethnic, and geographical lines. Reporting on the runoff results the day after Moscone defeated Barbagelata, the *Chronicle's* Michael Harris described how "the election results last night revealed a split city, with George Moscone capturing the eastern part of San Francisco and John J. Barbagelata winning the west. It was, finally, the votes of San Francisco's ethnic minorities that provided Moscone with his narrow margin of victory."[24]

An article that same day in the *Examiner*, at the time San Francisco's afternoon newspaper, reported results from a handful of precincts that reflected these divisions. This included Burnett School in the heavily African American Hunters Point neighborhood, where Moscone drubbed Barbagelata 230–38, and a polling place in the Haight where Moscone won by an equally impressive margin of 177–27. Meanwhile at the Sunset Clubhouse, deep in the working-class and largely white Sunset District, Barbagelata won by an overwhelming 222–36 margin. At the El Drisco hotel in the heart of Pacific Heights, one of the city's wealthiest neighborhoods, Barbagelata's margin was a very comfortable 108–44.[25]

The 1975 election swept a progressive slate into office. In addition to electing Moscone mayor, voters in San Francisco reelected Richard Hongisto as sheriff and elected Joseph Freitas to be district attorney. Hongisto and Freitas won handily, but Moscone's race was decided in a runoff against John Barbagelata by fewer than 4,400 votes, a difference that amounted to about 2 percent of the overall vote. When you win or lose an election by such a small margin, there are many things that, had any of them gone the other way, would have changed the outcome of the election. A poor debate performance, a campaign flyer that didn't resonate with voters, the failure to secure a key endorsement, or missing a few days on the campaign trail because of an illness are just some these small things that change the outcomes of close elections.

In 1975, Moscone's huge margin among African American voters was one of the things that helped propel him to victory. To help get a big turnout in African American communities in the Fillmore and the Bayview–Hunters Point section of San Francisco, Moscone needed volunteers to knock on doors, put up posters, hand out literature, and the like. Even today, people who can produce large numbers of these kinds of volunteers in big-city elections are extremely valuable. When Moscone needed help in the African American community, among the people he turned to was a powerful minister who, despite being white, had a strong presence in African American San Francisco and claimed to be able to provide the needed volunteers. The Reverend Jim Jones did not disappoint. He provided hundreds of volunteers to help get out the African American vote for Moscone. Moscone benefited from the high African American turnout and became mayor. Jones also provided similar support to Hongisto and Freitas in their easy election victories. It would be an exaggeration to simply say that Moscone owed his victory to Jim Jones, but Jones was one of many small and medium-sized factors that helped make Moscone mayor. The new mayor recognized this by appointing Jim Jones to the San Francisco Housing Authority in late 1976.

There is a lot of evidence to suggest that Jones did more than simply mobilize volunteers for Moscone, but that he registered voters in San Francisco, some of whom actually lived outside of the city, so that they could vote for Moscone.[26] If this occurred, it is a relatively unambiguous example of voter fraud. It is unlikely that such voter fraud made a difference in the final election result, but it is nonetheless very probably the case that Jones committed voter fraud as part of his effort help Moscone.

By 1978, Moscone was in the third year of his mayoralty and looking toward a reelection campaign in 1979, most likely against Supervisor Quentin Kopp. Moscone's first two years in office were not easy, as divisions from the election remained, leaving him without a progressive majority on the board of supervisors. By early 1978, however, Moscone had picked up progressive support on the legislature and had come tantalizingly close to an enduring 6–5 majority that he could have used to remake the city in earnest.

Transforming San Francisco to reflect these burgeoning progressive cultural and political values was never going to be easy, but if anybody could do it, that person was Mayor Moscone. He was a skilled legislator but also a committed progressive. He was capable of soaring rhetoric and principled stances, but he also had grown up politically alongside Phil Burton and Willie Brown and knew how to play political hardball. Moscone was also uniquely well suited to the political moment, as by the time he became mayor he had deep roots in traditional Catholic San Francisco as well as strong credentials with the emerging progressive city.

Busch described Moscone to me as a particularly well-positioned progressive San Francisco politician: "Native son, raised by a single mom, didn't have any dough [growing up], impeccable liberal credentials, proven leadership ability with what he got done in the senate. . . . On top of that, he was as good a retail politician as there was. He knew everybody in town."[27] Rudy Nothenberg, who served as Moscone's deputy mayor, said that despite the anger many on the right felt toward Moscone, "people had no reason to fear him." Nothenberg continued: "[He was] deeply committed to civil rights, deeply committed to civil liberties—otherwise a liberal Democrat and progressive economic policies. . . . George loved this city. He grew up here, was a playboy. He was not a radical."[28]

In the 1970s, most major American cities were still governed by mayors who, regardless of race or ethnicity, rarely sought significant changes to economic, development, or land-use policies. In this regard, other big-city mayors of the era, such as Abe Beame and then Ed Koch in New York, Sam Yorty and then Tom Bradley in Los Angeles, and Richard J. Daley and then Michael Bilandic in Chicago, were much more conservative and conventional in their politics than Moscone.

Moscone was very different from those other mayors in that from the beginning, through his appointments to boards and commissions as well as to high-profile positions such as chief of police, he brought in a new group of people and threatened the power structures that had long run the city. Powerful business interests or landlord associations had little reason to care if gay people were allowed to congregate in bars in the Castro, if police did not always crack down on hippies smoking pot, or even if African American and Chicano elected officials advocated for greater civil rights. However, slowing down development or removing tax breaks for their projects was not something they could tolerate. As Busch told me, "The polarization was not around anywhere near the surface gay-straight issues. The polarization was really around who's gonna run the city, and breaking up the power structure, and giving power to the neighborhoods."[29] Busch accurately noted one of Moscone's most significant accomplishments:

> Up until [Moscone's] election, the city had been completely dominated politically, socially, business-wise by white men. . . . A lot of Irish and Italian, but all white men. . . . The first pillar of what he wanted to do in his vision of governance was he had to break that up. He had to bring into city government and the halls of power people that represented the true diversity of the city, not just in terms of ethnic diversity but political diversity, gender sexual orientation. . . . He couldn't do anything else unless government represented the diversity of the city.[30]

Moscone was mayor for just under three years, but he changed the face of city government in a way that has proven to be irrevocable, even when the policies pursued by later mayors have been less than radical.

While Milk and Moscone's legacy on issues of tolerance and diversity is clear, the rest of their agenda has not done as well. The progressive mayor and supervisor had a vision for San Francisco in which economic development and other questions would be addressed from the perspective of the neighborhoods, and downtown business and real estate interests would not be central to policy making. That vision has not come to fruition. Instead, San Francisco has been both a tolerant city while also being friendly to business and real estate. The city has strong residential rent-control laws but also widespread real estate speculation, vacancy decontrol, and no commercial rent control. The downtown skyline is almost unrecognizable even when compared to 1990, as new skyscrapers have gone up rapidly to keep pace with the tech boom in the Bay Area.

Since Moscone's assassination, almost every mayor of San Francisco, regardless of gender or ethnicity, has shared the centrist, probusiness, relatively-liberal-on-social-issues positions of Dianne Feinstein, the woman who became mayor when Moscone was killed. The only possible exceptions were Art Agnos and Frank Jordan. The former was a Moscone-like progressive who served one term from 1988 to 1991. The latter was, in San Francisco terms, a probusiness social conservative who also served one term after defeating Agnos in 1991.

It is not possible to know what would have happened if George Moscone had been able to finish out his term or if he had gotten reelected in 1979 and served a full second term as well, but it is a pretty good bet that San Francisco would have looked a lot different in the 1980s and 1990s. Thus, the bullets from Dan White's police-issued handgun radically changed the trajectory of San Francisco, helping to make it what it is today.

San Francisco's Diversity

San Francisco in 1978 was a contested and even divided city, but it was more than that. Though a small city, for its size it was an extraordinarily diverse one. Racial diversity was an important part of this, as San Francisco was one of the few cities in the country with sizable African American, Latino, Asian, and white populations in the late 1970s. New York, by contrast, widely understood to be the most diverse city in the country, had an Asian population of fewer than 4 percent in the 1980 census.[31]

The different neighborhoods of San Francisco also gave the city a very diverse feel. Compared to those of New York or Chicago, the Financial District in the eastern part of San Francisco was very small, but it still felt, at least for a few blocks, a bit like midtown Manhattan or Wall Street. Men, most of whom were white, wore suits and carried briefcases. Women dressed in similar business attire. There were few hippies or punks walking around the Financial District on most days even though it was less than a ten-minute walk from North Beach, which was where the Mabuhay Gardens and most of the punk scene was based. There were, naturally, a number of gays and lesbians working in those banks and law firms, but many were not out at their offices.

Just north and west of the Financial District was Chinatown. Generations of tourists have visited Chinatown, bought cheap tchotchkes, and eaten in Chinese restaurants there, but Chinatown has also always been a neighborhood where people live, work, and raise children. San Francisco's Chinatown is one of the oldest and most famous in the Western Hemisphere. Even in the middle of the twentieth century, San Francisco stood out from other American cities because of the size of its Chinese community. For decades, one of the cultural highlights of the year in San Francisco has been the Chinese New Year celebrations. In addition to the famous parade, the various Chinese civic organizations sponsor other events, including banquets. Some of these draw high-level politicians eager to court the Chinese American vote. In February 1978, Mayor Moscone was attending the Miss Chinatown USA contest, the kind of San Francisco event that was easy for a gregarious politician like George Moscone. However, the mayor left the event early with his security detail. Herb Caen later reported that Moscone "had just rec'd a death threat deemed 'serious' by police. It was the same day he had appointed a black sheriff. . . . Thirty percent of George's appointments have been black' says a Moscone aide, 'and every time he makes one there is a reaction.'"[32]

This threat demonstrates the extent to which Moscone's attempts to create a municipal government that looked like San Francisco itself was causing a reaction from more-conservative elements. Hostility to Moscone's appointments was particularly acute in the law enforcement community, where many believed, rightly, that Moscone was trying to change the way policing was done in San Francisco, with more of an eye to protecting the rights of all citizens.

To the south of Chinatown and the Financial District was South of Market, not yet known as SOMA. In 1978, South of Market was a rundown neighborhood that had not recovered from the departure of thousands of shipping and manufacturing jobs. It was home to cheap SROs, largely empty warehouse spaces, and low-budget bars, restaurants, and retail outlets.

In the western half of San Francisco, neighborhoods such as the Sunset and Richmond were still largely working-class and more conservative, but with pockets of hippies grateful for the low rent. There were also a few affluent areas such as Sea Cliff out by Baker Beach or St. Francis Wood. Many who could afford to live elsewhere avoided the neighborhoods in the western part of San Francisco because they were cold and foggy almost year-round. However, these were vibrant functioning communities with schools, churches, and a handful of streets with businesses that met most of the needs of the communities around them. Thus, even the Sunset and Richmond felt like a collection of small villages. If you lived on Anza or Cabrillo around Thirtieth or Fortieth Avenue, you likely did most of your shopping and other household-related consumption on a strip of Balboa around Thirty-fifth Avenue. If you lived a few blocks to the north, you likely shopped on Geary.

In the northern part of the city, Pacific Heights had many large single-family homes where many of the wealthiest San Franciscans lived. These quiet, tree-lined streets were on top of a hill overlooking the Cow Hollow and Marina districts, where George Moscone had grown up, and then the bay to the north. Many homes in Pacific Heights had views of one or both bridges and bay windows where rich residents could look out at Marin County, Alcatraz Island, and the boats in the bay.

In 1978, the Mission was still heavily Latino. The non-Latinos who lived there did so largely because of economic necessity, as the neighborhood had not yet become a destination for young, mostly white people. There were no upscale restaurants or boutiques along Valencia Street as there are now. Instead, the community was substantially Mexican American and working-class.

Many other San Francisco neighborhoods had their own distinct character, such as the African American areas in the Fillmore and Bayview–Hunters Point, the still heavily Italian American neighborhood of North Beach, and affluent areas such as Jordan Park, Nob Hill, Russian Hill, and others. Almost all of these neighborhoods had their own character, feel, shopping areas, and often even climate.

This was the complex and diverse environment in which the events of 1978 occurred. Many people then (as now) spent much of their time in their own neighborhoods or in similar ones. Upper-middle-class people who commuted from, for example, Pacific Heights or Sea Cliff to the Financial District every day rarely would have found themselves in Bernal Heights, the Mission, or Potrero Hill. Punks hanging out at the Mab and in North Beach rarely made it out to the western half of the city unless their families happened to live there. Kids who went to neighborhood public schools, seniors with limited mobility, mothers caring for children, and people running small businesses in their own communities also were not deeply familiar with many of San Francisco's neighborhoods other than their own. This sometimes exacerbated distrust, unfamiliarity, and suspicion between different communities that belied San Francisco's progressive reputation.

3

Spring Training

••••••••••••••••••••••

Spring training began in February 1978 with the Giants looking very much like the team that had finished the previous year in fourth place, twenty-three games behind the division-winning Dodgers, and with a .463 winning percentage. The team was hoping for a bounce-back year from ace pitcher John "The Count" Montefusco and for continued improvement from Bob Knepper, who seemed poised to become an impact starting pitcher. Terry Whitfield had hit .285/.329/.433 in 1977, providing some hope that he would join Jack Clark, who was clearly on the verge of stardom, to improve the Giants offense.[1]

Most observers predicted that either the Dodgers would repeat as champions of the National League West, or that the Reds, who finished in second place in 1977, would edge out Los Angeles and take the division. These two teams, after all, had combined to win the National League West every year since 1971, which was the Giants' last division title. The Dodgers, led by sluggers Dusty Baker, Ron Cey, Steve Garvey, and Reggie Smith, and with a deep starting rotation that included Don Sutton and Tommy John, had won the division by ten games in 1977 and had essentially the same team ready to go in 1978. In Cincinnati, Johnny Bench, Joe Morgan, Pete Rose, Davey Concepcion, Ken Griffey, and George Foster had all been part of the core of the dominant 1975–1976 Big Red Machine. Tony Perez, another key piece, had been sent to Montreal, but the rest of the nucleus was still there.

By most measures, the Giants were outgunned as their players reported to Arizona to prepare for the regular season. In 1977, they had scored 673 runs, tenth best in the twelve-team National League. That was ninety-six fewer runs than the division-winning Dodgers and fully 129 runs fewer than the second-place Reds. They were better at preventing runs, having given up only 711, seventh overall in the league. The Dodgers, however, gave up only 582 runs, the fewest in the league in 1977, while the Reds, who were known mostly for their offense in those years, gave up only fourteen more runs than the Giants. The Reds had improved their pitching midway through the 1977 season by picking up Tom Seaver in a June trade with the Mets and had been in the running to get Vida Blue, whom the A's had been trying to move. Candlestick Park was a pitcher's park, so the Giants' hitting was better, and the pitching not quite as good, as these raw numbers suggest.

Given that all three of those teams, as well as the Houston Astros, who finished third in the National League West in 1977, came to spring training in 1978 with most of the same key players as they had in 1977, few people predicted the Giants to contend. The 1978 edition of *The Complete Handbook of Baseball*, one of the most widely read and respected baseball preview books of the era, predicted the Giants to finish fifth. Its one-line description of the Giants, in the division prediction section that was modeled on a horse-race betting sheet, was "fades early and dies." The handbook predicted the Reds, "a big stakes winner," to win the division, and the Dodgers, "experienced horse, knows course," to finish second.[2] The handbook summarized the Giants' outlook this way: "It is going to be a long hard climb for the Giants. The pitchers will only be able to shoulder the burden so long and another quality hitter is needed in the lineup. Even then, the Giants are likely to give up as many runs as they score just on their defense alone."[3]

For baseball fans in early 1978, the biggest questions facing the Giants were not so much how they would play on the field during the season, but where they would play and whether or not they would be able to find a way to stay in San Francisco. Since the A's had moved to Oakland from Kansas City in 1968, the Bay Area had struggled to support two baseball teams. By the mid-1970s, it was almost axiomatic in the baseball world that the Bay Area was not big enough for two teams. The words of Glenn Dickey, who covered sports in the Bay Area, during spring training of 1978 reflect this: "Almost from the moment the A's first arrived in Oakland a decade ago, it has been obvious that the San Francisco Bay Area could not support two Major League Baseball teams."[4]

As the 1978 season approached, it was not clear the Bay Area could even support one team. In 1977, the Giants and A's had drawn a combined total of 1,195,655 fans to their games, finishing twenty-fifth and twenty-sixth in attendance for all of Major League Baseball's twenty-six teams. That total for the two teams was less than the attendance for the Angels, Rangers, Cardinals, White Sox, Dodgers, Red Sox, Padres, Royals, Mariners, Orioles, Expos, Reds, Pirates, Tigers, Phillies, Cubs, or Yankees. In other words, well over half of the teams drew more individually than the Giants and A's combined. In 1977, the Dodgers, Reds, and Phillies each drew more than twice the number of fans as the two Bay Area teams did together.

There was broad agreement that something had to give with regard to the two Bay Area teams, but it was less clear what. The Giants' move to Toronto had fallen through in early 1976 when Bob Lurie and Bud Herseth bought the team at the last minute and agreed to keep the Giants in San Francisco, but other rumors persisted. Putting that bid together and making sure the National League approved it rather than a competing bid by the Toronto-based brewery Labatt required round-the-clock work and negotiations by San Francisco's new mayor. As one local paper reported, "There is no question, in looking back now, that Moscone's presentation before a closed meeting of National League owners . . . is what made Bob Short and Bob Lurie owners of the Giants in San Francisco instead of Labbatts [sic] Breweries in Toronto."[5]

At various times in late 1977 and early 1978, the Giants and A's were both thought to be moving to Denver. Washington, D.C. was another rumored destination for the Giants. Most intriguing were the various ideas that involved the Giants playing some of their games in Oakland, sometimes as part of a deal to replace the A's after they moved, sometimes as part of an effort for the Giants to push the A's out of Oakland. By early 1978, the A's were in even worse shape than the Giants, having finished with the worst attendance in baseball while managing to finish in last place in the American League West behind the expansion Seattle Mariners. All of the stars from the great 1970s teams had been traded or left via free agency except for ace lefty pitcher Vida Blue, whom most baseball people thought was not long for Oakland either. This helped the idea of the A's leaving and the Giants splitting their home games between Oakland and San Francisco become popular in many places around baseball—but not in San Francisco.

This was a question of logistics, baseball, money, and civic pride. If Giants games were played in the Oakland Coliseum, the city of San Francisco would lose revenue. Moreover, the idea of the Bay Area Giants splitting their time between two ballparks would, in the long run, have been impractical and made it harder for the team on the field. Baseball teams can create a home-field advantage if the players learn their field well and the team management can design a team to take advantage of the particularities of their ballpark. This is much harder to do if a team has two home fields. Additionally, as bad a ballpark as Candlestick was, the Coliseum was only slightly better.

There was also a more symbolic side to this. By the late 1970s, San Francisco had long ago lost any claim on being the largest or most important city on the West Coast. The economy was in very bad shape, population was dwindling, and the dreams of the Summer of Love had, in too many cases, been run over by drug addiction, crime, and a general sense of sleaziness in some parts of the city. Losing the Giants, even the post–Willie Mays Giants who played in a mostly empty, dreadful ballpark and in most seasons lost more games than they won, would have been a big psychic blow to San Francisco.

Few people were more aware of this than Mayor Moscone. The one-time star athlete who had given up a powerful position in the California State Senate to become mayor almost certainly knew that if the Giants left town, he would always be remembered as the mayor who let that happen. He was also probably aware that such a political defeat, particularly if it came early in his term, would have made the rest of his time in office much less effective and his chances for reelection considerably slimmer. He was also opposed to rebranding the team anything other than the San Francisco Giants: "There's no way I'd personally agree to change the team's name in any manner shape or form. I think it's critical that they remain the San Francisco Giants."[6]

Giants principal owner Bob Lurie, the man who was credited with saving the team from a move to Toronto the previous off-season, evinced a willingness to explore having his team play some games in Oakland, but San Francisco's mayor saw it differently: "I'm keeping my door open and we're willing to see any creative suggestions or solutions that they [i.e., MLB] might have . . . [but] we don't see any advantage in it for us. Why should we have to split the franchise with Oakland?"[7]

Moscone was speaking from the heart. As a lifelong San Franciscan and sports fan, he knew the value of the Giants to many in the city. The mayor was also engaging in smart politics. As a progressive mayor in a divided city, he was happy to grab onto an issue that could unify the city. Moreover, by supporting the local baseball team, this Italian American son of Cow Hollow and the city's Catholic schools was signaling to conservative and moderate voters that he wasn't so different from them. However, the stakes were high. If Moscone had failed to keep the Giants in San Francisco, his political fortunes would have suffered. Rudy Nothenberg confirmed this, telling me that "in terms of the politics of it [i.e., losing the Giants], we were very, very fearful."[8]

Despite this, even Moscone gradually recognized that it was inevitable for the Giants to play at least some of their games in Oakland. In late March, Eugene Friend, president of the San Francisco Recreation and Parks Commission, the city agency with jurisdiction over Candlestick Park, drafted a memo outlining the conditions for the agreement. Some of these conditions included "at least one more than ½ of the 'home' baseball games the San Francisco Giants . . . shall in fact be played in San Francisco. . . . The name of the team shall be the San Francisco Giants as to games played in the United States, Canada or anywhere else in the world, except for games played at the Oakland Coliseum. As to such games the name of the team shall be 'the Giants.'"[9] The tone of the memo is unmistakably that of a representative of a city doing what it can to hold onto its team and with it the stature associated with being big league.

As the season approached, the obstinacy of the owners of the Giants and the A's as well as the hesitation of city officials on both sides of the bay over any agreement to share facilities meant that the status quo would continue for another year. As spring training wound down, both the Giants and A's learned they would not be moving, at least not until after the 1978 season. This gave their fans a chance to focus more on the game itself as Opening Day approached.

Although San Franciscans were spared the indignity of having to share the Giants with Oakland, there was another reason for Giants fans to fear that 1978 might be the last year for their team in San Francisco. In February, as spring training was beginning, Quentin Kopp, a conservative member of the board of supervisors generally assumed to be planning to run against Moscone for mayor in 1979, suggested that Moscone had made a secret agreement with the National League that made it easy for the Giants to leave after the 1978 season.

Moscone disputed the extent to which the deal had been secret, telling Kopp in a letter that "the subject of my March 3 [1976] letter to Mr. Feeney [the President of the National League] was a matter of public above-board discussion."[10] The specific clause that concerned Kopp, and many other San Franciscans once they became aware of it, was Moscone's support for Feeney's request: "That if, after the first three seasons of baseball [beginning with the 1976 season] the Giants failed to attract an average attendance of one million persons per year, the result of which was that the new owners were then desirous of selling to an entity that would remove the Giants from San Francisco, the City and County of San Francisco would not seek to enjoin such sale."[11]

Moscone's pledge to Feeney did not mean the Giants would leave if they could not average one million or more fans from 1976 to 1978, but it did mean that he would not stand in their way if they tried to leave following three seasons in which they could not draw enough fans. This was generally understood to mean the Giants would very possibly leave if they could not meet that attendance threshold. Given that the team had drawn a total of only 1.3 million fans in 1976 and 1977; few thought the Giants had any chance of drawing fully 1.7 million fans in 1978. If they failed to do that, Moscone would have signed away his right to try to stop the Giants from moving to Denver, Florida, or elsewhere.

On the Field

Spring training in the late 1970s had a very different feel than it does now. Many players came to spring training needing some time to get in shape, so the players took longer to get in regular-season form. There were fewer fans who went to spring training and fewer events catering to those fans. Additionally, ordinary fans had much less access to information back then, so the prospects in spring training were often not well known, and the beat writers had to introduce them to fans during spring training.

As spring training opened, the Giants were counting on four players to lead their offense. Three were either in the middle of, or would go on to have, very long and productive careers and are members in good standing of the Hall of Very Good. Bill Madlock had led the National League in hitting in

1975 and 1976 while with the Chicago Cubs and was traded to the Giants before the 1977 season for Bobby Murcer. He brought a combination of strong hitting, moderate power, and some speed to the Giants.

Darrell Evans was one of those players who was never fully appreciated while he was playing. The 1970s were a time when batting average was still the primary way that hitters were evaluated. Evans could do a lot of things as a hitter, but hitting for a high batting average was not one of them. Over the course of a twenty-one-year career that spanned from 1969 to 1989, Evans only hit .248. His highest batting average in any season was a very respectable but not great .281 in 1973. Evans, however, had an extraordinary batting eye and drew 1,605 walks over the course of a career. His on-base percentage, now recognized by many as a more valuable tool for evaluating hitters than batting average, was a very impressive .361. He drew a 100 or more walks in a season five times in his career.

Evans was not just skilled at reaching first base; he had power as well. When he retired in 1989, his 414 career home runs were good enough for twenty-second on the all-time home run list. Evans's combination of power and patience would have been much more valued in the twenty-first century, but in the 1970s, his low batting average prevented many from understanding his true value. Even among Giants fans, Evans was generally seen as a useful player, better than a journeyman but not quite a star. In reality, he was an extremely good player for a very long time.

Evans was a soft-spoken man who by all accounts was a good teammate, but a few years after that 1978 season he solidified his credentials as one of the more unusual players in baseball history when he claimed that he had seen a UFO outside of his home in the East Bay. He later described his feelings at seeing the UFO to *Sports Illustrated*: "It was so strange. It was as if they wanted us to see them. It was as if they had singled us out. At least, I wanted to think that. I guess I'd always hoped there'd be something like this, something that would come in peace. I think we knew from the start what it was."[12]

Following his strong rookie season in 1977, Jack Clark seemed ready to become the next great Giants slugger. Since the late 1960s when Willie Mays began to show his age, the Giants had looked for that next star outfielder, but it had never worked out. Dave Kingman, Gary Maddox, Gary Mathews, Bobby Bonds, and George Foster were among the better-known outfielders the farm system produced in those years and who the team hoped could help cement the Giants' relationship to San Francisco's somewhat fickle baseball fans. Some of these young outfielders, such as Bonds and Matthews, played very well with the Giants before being traded away or signing with other teams as free agents. Others, such as Foster, only broke through after being traded away from San Francisco. Many of these players did not do well enough in limited chances with the Giants. Kingman couldn't field. Maddox didn't impress the Giants enough with his hitting, but his defense was great. Mathews and Foster never became the stars the Giants had hoped they would. Only Bobby Bonds developed into a star with the Giants, but he was unable to consistently perform at a high level and so was traded away as well.

Because they came up in the Giants system, all of these good young out-fielders were inevitably compared to Willie Mays, which was always unfair and put undue pressure on many Giants prospects. This was particularly true if a player—like Bonds, Foster, Matthews, and Maddox—happened to be African American. Of these Giants, Bonds felt that comparison the most acutely, but he had some very good years with the Giants before being traded away to the Yankees. Almost twenty years after that trade, the Giants would sign Bobby Bonds's son as a free agent. Barry Bonds came closer to being the next Willie Mays than anybody else, including his own father.

Jack Clark looked like he might be different. As a nineteen- and twenty-year-old in 1975 and 1976, Clark had appeared in thirty-four games for the Giants. He had not played particularly well, but very few players are able to play at all at the big league level at that age. By 1977, Clark had become the Giants regular right fielder. His .252/.332/.407 slash line was very impressive for a twenty-one-year-old rookie, but not yet star quality. Clark would go on to have a fine eighteen-year career that included 340 home runs and a .267/.379/.476 slash line, but he never quite broke through as a true superstar.

When the Giants brought McCovey back for the 1977 season, many fans thought it was just a goodwill gesture to an aging slugger who had always been popular with the fans, but McCovey surprised a lot of people by having a great year. He hit .280/.367/.500 with twenty-eight home runs and won the National League's Comeback Player of the Year Award. The Giants were hoping McCovey could hit as well in 1978, so manager Joe Altobelli penciled the suddenly ageless slugger into the first base job and the cleanup spot.

The rest of the lineup looked unremarkable. Marc Hill and Mike Sadek shared the catching. Neither could hit, but both were adequate defensive backstops. Larry Herndon and Derrel Thomas were both speedy centerfielders and decent hitters. Either Rob Andrews or Thomas was likely to emerge as the starting second baseman during spring training. Neither was likely to be an impact player. The two remaining starters, while not great players, were in their own way intriguing. Terry Whitfield turned out to have a career year in 1978, which was also one of only two years of his ten-year career when he played full-time. Coming into the season, the Giants hoped they could get Whitfield's usual solid defense and a bit more from his bat. That is exactly what they got. Whitfield was also one of a handful of players on that team who brought an energy and excitement to his game that quickly made him a fan favorite. His distinctive batting stance, in which he lifted his right heel up so that the only part of his front foot that made contact with the ground was the tip of his toes, was imitated by kids throughout San Francisco's sandlots that year, particularly by those of us who, like Whitfield, batted left-handed.

Four players started games at shortstop for the Giants in 1978, but Johnnie LeMaster started eighty-five, more than half of the team's games, at that position. Rob Andrews, Vic Harris, Roger Metzger, and LeMaster were all light-hitting types. Unfortunately, none of them, other than Metzger, were consistently strong with the glove either. LeMaster was the Giants' starting shortstop from 1978 to 1984 and was a subpar fielder and weak hitter for almost all of those years. The 1978 season was no exception. By the 1980s, LeMaster had become a symbol of the ineptitude of the Giants of that era. He was the kind of player who was booed mercilessly, but not entirely unaffectionately, by Giants fans. For a game or two in 1979, he actually came out of the dugout with his usual number ten and the word "Boo" instead of his last name on the back of his jersey.[13] The fans appreciated LeMaster's ability to laugh at himself, but they probably would have preferred a shortstop who could hit and field a little.

During his time with the Giants, LeMaster was a somewhat polarizing figure for Giants fans. Many booed him aggressively and could only see his faults as a player. Others felt he was treated unfairly by the fans and was a fine fielder whose anemic bat would have been less conspicuous on a better offensive team. One of the latter is Charles A. Fracchia Jr., the son of the prominent San Francisco historian, who was thirteen years old during that 1978 season and still occasionally wears a replica Johnnie LeMaster "Boo" jersey when he watches the Giants now. Of LeMaster, Fracchia told me, "I liked him. I felt he was kind of a glue on the infield." But even Fracchia, whose passion for the Giants has never wavered, conceded, "They stuck with him for far too long."[14] John Maschino, who followed that 1978 team closely as an eleven-year-old and remains a Giants fan forty years later, had a less charitable view toward LeMaster, one that was likely the majority view among Giants fans at the time: "He should have been released several times over. Even at the age of eleven just starting to understand baseball, I knew that . . . Johnnie LeMaster was the last guy you wanted up in a key situation. . . . Defensively, the only thing I remember about him is the countless times I saw balls roll through his legs in the ninth inning with men on base."[15]

The LeMaster story, however, is a bit more complicated than that. The skinny shortstop was a devout and conservative Christian. His faith remained part of his life long after he quit playing baseball. This meant that in the late 1970s, his religious views clashed with much of the political climate of San Francisco. That became apparent with regard to the burgeoning gay liberation movement that was increasingly centered around San Francisco. At some point during his playing career, LeMaster made remarks to the media in San Francisco that revealed his less than tolerant views toward gays and lesbians. This contributed to his unpopularity with the fans and gave the constant booing a political angle as well. The problem with this story is that if you were there at the time, you know it doesn't quite ring true. I booed Johnnie LeMaster enthusiastically for his entire career and was a pretty knowledgeable baseball fan and political progressive at the time, but I did not even know about LeMaster's views on gay people until long after he retired. Moreover, by the early 1980s, I was paying enough attention to boo players such as Eric Show, Dave Dravecky, and Mike Armstrong who had been revealed to be members of the John Birch Society. I was firmly in that space in the Venn diagram where political radicalism and obsessive interest in the Giants overlapped, but I was not aware of this LeMaster story at the time. I have also spent hours online trying to find primary sources with LeMaster's comments and have been unsuccessful, so the anecdote may not be true at all. LeMaster has long been active in his church, so it is possible the story is true. The evidence, however, is not easy to find. We booed LeMaster because he couldn't hit; for that matter, he couldn't field much either. His intolerant views may be an added post facto justification, but they were not the prime mover.

Additionally, in the San Francisco of 1978 and even the early 1980s, the tolerant consensus that has defined the city for decades had not yet emerged. While there were certainly fans who would have booed a player who espoused right-wing views, they were a small minority of those who went to ballgames. In those days, ballparks, even in San Francisco, did little to make gay fans comfortable, and few straight people would have booed somebody for making antigay statements.

As spring training began, the Giants lineup was therefore set at some positions, but a handful of big questions remained. Who would claim the role of swingman and fifth starter behind a starting four of John Montefusco, Bob Knepper, Jim Barr, and Ed Halicki? Could one more big year be coaxed out of beloved slugger Willie McCovey? The biggest question Altobelli had to answer was how to get all of his big bats in the lineup at the same time. Darrell Evans's ability to hit for power from the left side and draw enough walks to offset his low batting average was important for the team, but his natural positions were third base, where Bill Madlock had always played, and first base, the only position the aging McCovey could play. In 1977, Evans had spent a lot of time in left field, but Altobelli wanted to free up left for Terry Whitfield, who had hit well in 1977 and was a much better defensive outfielder than Evans.

Altobelli also had to sort out his second base/centerfield problem. Rob Andrews, a light-hitting (.264/.345/.303 in 1977) second baseman, came into camp as the favorite to hold that job, but centerfielder Derrel Thomas could also play second and was being squeezed for time in center by Larry Herndon. The Giants needed to find a way to play Evans, Madlock, and McCovey every day and to get the most out of Whitfield, Herndon, Andrews, and Thomas while also figuring out how to get spare parts like Gary Thomasson and Gary Alexander enough playing time.

These lineup and roster problems seemed daunting as spring training went on, but they were not new to Altobelli, who had spent much of 1977 trying to figure out these same challenges. It turned out that was time well spent, although it had made for a rough year on the field, as described in the *San Francisco Bay Guardian*:

> Because so many of the 1977 Giants were either untried or questionable, Altobelli juggled his lineup almost every day. . . . The outfield was shaken up so often that it looked like an occidental version of the Chinese Central Committee: with Jack Clark, Randy Elliott, Terry Whitfield, Derrel Thomas, Gary Thomasson, Darrell Evans and Larry Herndon rotating in and out of the lineup from day to day, and sometimes from inning to inning. Thomas and Evans also made it into the infield from time to time as did shortstops Johnnie LeMaster and Vic Harris, second baseman Rob Andrews and back-up first baseman Skip James.

[Altobelli] slipped catchers Marc Hill, Mike Sadek and Gary Alexander in and out of the lineup in no readily apparent pattern.[16]

By the time spring training of 1978 began, Altobelli had figured some things out. Jack Clark had to play every day in right field—neither Derrel Thomas nor Randy Elliott hit enough to be full-time outfielders—but there were still too many third basemen and a weakness at second. Rarely do managers come into spring training, move a few players around, make a couple of trades, and come away with a different, more stable, and considerably better team, but that is what the Giants did in February and March 1978.

As of September 15, 1977, Bill Madlock had played 555 big league games and had never taken the field at any position other than third base, but for the last six games of 1977 Madlock played second base. Early in spring training in 1978, Altobelli made it clear that Madlock would be the team's second baseman. This meant that Evans would slot back into third, Whitfield would take over left, and McCovey would be the primary first baseman.

That move solved some problems, but one more remained—specifically, what to do with Thomas and Andrews, especially as Herndon was emerging as the likely centerfielder as spring training went on. With much of the lineup set, Thomas and Andrews were vying for a reserve infielder role. The problem was particularly acute because in 1977, before moving to center, Thomas had made it clear he did not want to "play part time to Rob Andrews," describing that possibility as "sickening, simply sickening."[17] Presumably Thomas felt the same way about backing up Larry Herndon in centerfield and Bill Madlock at second. The Giants were able to solve this problem by a trade of unhappy ballplayers, with both teams hoping that a change of scenery would help. At the end of February, the Giants sent Thomas to the Padres for Mike Ivie. Thomas got in 128 games for the Padres in 1978, playing all over the diamond, and settled into a career that kept him employed, ironically, as one of the top utility men in the game until 1985.

Ivie, initially a highly touted catching prospect who had been the first overall pick in the June 1970 draft, came to the Giants with no clear place to play. After the Padres realized Ivie was not a catcher, it became apparent that first base was his strongest position, but McCovey was the Giants' first baseman. Ivie could also play third, although not well, so he was not going to push the dependable and better defensive player Darrell Evans for playing time there. Nonetheless, Ivie was clearly poised to help the team both as a powerful bat off the bench and as a starter in place of Stretch against tougher left-handed pitchers who frequently gave the big left-handed hitter problems.

As March came around, the Giants' everyday lineup seemed sorted out. It was a nice, solid lineup, but not, at least on paper, ready to compete with the Dodgers or Reds. Opening Day was scheduled for April 7, but the Giants were not through yet. For Giants fans, the most important day of the year turned out to be a few weeks before Opening Day. March 15 was the day that it became possible to hope that this Giants team might be able to contend.

On March 15, the Giants pulled off the kind of trade that armchair general managers dream about. They packaged a bunch of second-tier prospects, established mediocrities, and some cash in exchange for a proven twenty-eight-year-old star. In those days, trades were not made with much of an eye toward contract status or years remaining before a player became a free agent. Instead, trades were made and evaluated based simply on the talent that changed hands. By that measure, this was a great trade for the Giants.

Gary Alexander, Dave Heaverlo, Phil Huffman, John Henry Johnson, Gary Thomasson, Alan Wirth, and Mario Guerrero are names that few baseball fans remember. None went on to significant big league careers. Most were out of the game by the early 1980s. Gary Thomasson went on to some notoriety in Japan, where he failed to hit in 1981 and 1982 despite being very well compensated by the Yomiuri Giants. (The word "Thomasson" has become an obscure Japanese slang term for an object that, despite having no clear value or use, is well taken care of.) By sending Thomasson and these others across the bay, the Giants got the last great player from Charlie Finley's A's, the team that had dominated baseball in the early 1970s. By the end of 1977, Reggie Jackson and Catfish Hunter were playing with the Yankees, Rollie Fingers and Gene Tenace with the Padres, Sal Bando with the Brewers, and Bert Campaneris with the Rangers, with other A's of that era scattered around the big leagues. But Vida Blue remained in Oakland, toiling away for a truly terrible A's team.

Through 1977, Vida Blue had built a very impressive baseball resume. He had played on three All-Star teams and three World Series winners, had won one MVP award and one Cy Young Award and had finished in the top ten in Cy Young voting four times. He was a three-time twenty-game winner who regularly pitched 250 innings a year. He was the kind of ace a team could build around, and that is precisely what the Giants hoped to do with Blue.

Vida Blue was also one of those players who was bigger than the numbers. He had burst onto the baseball scene in 1971, his first full season, when he went 24-8 with a 1.82 ERA and 301 strikeouts. That year he won the MVP and Cy Young Awards and started the All-Star Game. He was a dynamic, media-friendly star who did not shy away from controversy. After his great 1971 season, Blue sought more money for 1972 than the A's were willing to pay him, leading to a nasty dispute between Blue and the A's. At one point during that standoff, Blue briefly retired to take a job at a pen company.

The owner of that Oakland A's team, Charlie Finley, was unconventional, irascible, cheap, and impatient, and he knew how to build a winner. He was a less wealthy and more innovative earlier iteration of George Steinbrenner, but in a green sports jacket rather than a white turtleneck. One of Finley's many gimmicks to try to raise interest in his players was to give them colorful nicknames and frequently back stories as well. Jim Hunter became Catfish. John Odom became Blue Moon. Finley wanted to give Blue a similarly colorful nickname. Somehow Vida, unusual and catchy in English, and Spanish for "life," wasn't good enough for Finley. The owner called Blue into his office and proposed that Blue change his first name to "True," even offering him two thousand dollars to go along with the idea.

Blue, who was actually Vida Blue Jr., was outraged by the idea, in part because his father had died only a few years earlier. Blue refused and, according to baseball lore, told Finley, "Why don't you change your name to 'True F**king Finley'?" The A's owner did not follow the suggestion of his star southpaw. Blue made his feelings toward Finley clear in an interview shortly after he was traded to the Giants: "I once would have played for nothing—and did until Mr. Finley had me sign on that crooked line. . . . Hey, I didn't mean that. I meant the dotted line. And then things changed."[18]

In coming to the Giants, Blue remained in the same media market and came to a team whose fans were already familiar with his pitching exploits and his personality. The Vida Blue trade was not only major because of Blue's pitching prowess, but it was also a statement trade. *San Francisco Chronicle* columnist Glenn Dickey captured this in the first paragraph of his March 17 column about the trade: "There are a lot of things that can be said about the Giants trade for Vida Blue, but the most important is this: The trade shows that the Giants are serious about building a contending team." Dickey also presciently added that "Blue's quality is almost as important at the gate as on the field."[19]

Blue had been trying to get out of Oakland for a while, and Finley had tried to get rid of Blue in the past. He tried to sell Blue's contract to the Yankees midway through the 1976 season, at the same time as he tried to sell Joe Rudi and Rollie Fingers to the Red Sox, but commissioner Bowie Kuhn voided that deal. After the 1977 season, the A's put together a deal to send Blue to the Reds for $1.75 million and a slugging first base prospect named Dave Revering. Kuhn, who was increasingly unable to figure out how baseball in the age of free agency and big money was going to work, voided that deal as well.

Blue was immediately projected to be the ace of the Giants rotation. He would join three other pitchers—John Montefusco, Ed Halicki and Bob Knepper—all of whom were also under thirty, as the Giants frontline starters. In those days, most teams still employed a four-man starting rotation. Jim Barr, who with Blue on the squad became a swingman and occasional fifth starter, had just turned thirty a few weeks before the Giants acquired Blue. Montefusco, who was usually called simply The Count, was the best-known of those pitchers. He had been the National League's Rookie of the Year in 1975 but had struggled a bit in 1977. Halicki was a solid veteran who had been an effective pitcher in the previous three years. He had even thrown a no-hitter against the Mets in 1975. Halicki was also, by the standards of that era, extremely tall. He stood 6 feet 7 inches, thus earning the nickname "Ho-Ho," the catchphrase of the Jolly Green Giant of frozen vegetable fame. The Giants even had a promotional day when they gave away full-size posters of Halicki that young fans could use as growth charts. Few ever got as tall as Ho-Ho. The fourth man in that rotation was another lefty, who had gone 11–9 with a 3.36 ERA as a twenty-three-year-old rookie in 1977. If Bob Knepper could improve on that strong rookie season, the Giants could expect to have the best left-handed starting pitching in the league.

The Blue trade had an immediate impact, as the Giants, who had entered spring training as also-rans, were now perceived to be contenders. In a *Sports Illustrated* baseball preview just before the beginning of the season, Ron Firmite wrote, "So now after months of haggling and with Bowie [Kuhn]'s blessing, Blue has been sent to the San Francisco Giants for seven able bodies and much less moolah; as a result, what figured to be another two-team race in the National League West looks more like a three-team affair. With the addition of Blue, the Giants have a pitching staff superior even to the Dodgers."[20] W. A. Van Winkle, a partisan Giants fan writing for the *San Francisco Bay Guardian*, offered a similar view of the trade in an article written in June 1978, by which time Blue had already made his presence felt at the 'Stick, as many Giants fans referred to the cold and cavernous ballpark: "On March 15, 1978 came the stroke that shot the Giants into contention and sent a rumble through the National League West. Vida Blue, the 1971 Cy Young winner, owner of one of the most fearsome fastballs in the league and a veteran of three World Series winning teams during his days with the Oakland A's, crossed the Bay to San Francisco."[21]

Hank Greenwald, the longtime Giants announcer, believed Blue's impact on the Giants was strong, positive, and almost immediate: "Vida coming over was a spark. . . . It said to the fans we're serious about maybe trying to turn things around. . . . Vida was an effervescent guy. He bubbled over with enthusiasm. He showed a love of the game, that he was happy to be playing baseball."[22] Greenwald's analysis sums up how many fans felt at the time as well. In the early 1970s, the Giants were the team that traded away or sold future Hall of Famers, such as Mays, Gaylord Perry, Juan Marichal, and McCovey. Fans also were dismayed that the team had been on the wrong end of many other trades in recent years. For example, as spring training of 1978 began, the reigning National League MVP, George Foster, was a former Giants prospect who had been sent to Cincinnati in a trade that brought the Giants essentially nothing. The Blue trade was a very different direction for the Giants. Looking back on that trade, John Maschino spoke for many Giants fans: "When he [Blue] came to the Giants, I was very excited. He'd been an integral part of that A's team [the 1972–1974 World Series winners]. . . . There was something about the man, the way he carried himself, that resonated. There's something about this guy. He stands tall. He's proud of who he is. He takes no shit on the field, and he deals. . . . I don't think there's any question that the team was suffering from morale or however you want to put it, so to have this star who actually wanted to play for the team come over with that kind of swagger . . . I think it was powerful."[23]

Blue, for his part, was pleased with the trade. Dickey told me that Blue "was very happy to get away from Finley. He just hated Finley. . . . He was happy to get away and come to the Giants. The Giants welcomed him."[24] Dickey's memory thirty-nine years after the trade is accurate. Once Blue came to the Giants, he brought an energy and focus that the Giants badly needed. His winning pedigree and happiness at being traded from a franchise in disarray to a contender allowed him to provide veteran leadership while also keeping the younger players relaxed and not too tense. Blue was a top starting pitcher, and a very famous player, but despite the excitement around the trade, adding Blue was not really enough to make the Giants the kind of team that could, on paper at least, win a division. Firmite conceded as much in the *Sports Illustrated* article when he added, "The Giants overall talent does not compare with that of the two leading contenders."[25]

The Gay Rights Ordinance

A few weeks after the Vida Blue trade, Harvey Milk demonstrated that he was more than just a groundbreaking political figure, but that he could be an effective legislator as well. In doing so, he also made good on his promise to use his position on the board of supervisors to protect the rights of gays and lesbians in San Francisco. On March 21, Milk's gay rights bill, which prohibited discrimination based on sexual orientation in employment, housing, or public accommodation, was voted into law by the board of supervisors.

It is somewhat extraordinary that a year or two before the bill passed, the idea of even having a gay person on the board of supervisors in San Francisco would have surprised many, but the bill passed easily by a vote of 10–1. The only dissenting vote came from Dan White, the socially conservative first-year legislator. In voting against the bill, White broke with his most influential supporter on the board, as Dianne Feinstein, the board's centrist president, joined Milk and the rest of the majority in supporting the bill.

Feinstein's position here is significant because it further demonstrated the balance she had long sought to preserve in her political life. In 1971, during her first term as supervisor, Feinstein had won some attention, as well some mockery, for probing the rise of pornography in San Francisco. Among her critics on this issue were the Mitchell Brothers, whose businesses she had singled out, thus earning Feinstein their lasting enmity along with that of many gay San Franciscans who took exception to her assertion that pornography "promoted homosexual cruising." However, Feinstein had also told a group of gay activists in 1971, "The gay community has provided a tremendous richness to San Francisco. I'm proud to be your representative and to help bring your community into the mainstream of life here." For the time, those remarks were very pro-gay. Feinstein, even in the very early years of her long career, did more than just talk about gay issues. In 1965 while serving on the state parole board, she voted against a proposal to make gay relationships or liaisons automatic parole violations. She also supported Willie

Brown and George Moscone's legislative efforts to expand gay rights and successfully authored a bill banning discrimination against gay people in the workplace.[26]

White's vote was more significant, however, because it was part of a fissure that was evolving between White and Milk. The two first-term supervisors, although from different ideological ends of the city legislature's spectrum, had crafted a good working relationship and had even made efforts to get to know each other personally during the first two months that both had been on the board. But on March 12, about a week before the vote on Milk's gay rights bill, their relationship began to fray.

On that day, a vote came up about whether a facility for troubled and criminal youth would be opened in White's district. The facility, known as the Youth Campus, was to be run by the Catholic Church. White was Catholic, as were many of his constituents, but he opposed the project, believing it would bring problems, including violence and crime, to his district. The church was advocating for the project and putting pressure on White, but White was steadfast in his opposition and set about finding the six votes he needed on the board to stop the project.

Based on a discussion the Friday before the Monday vote, White believed Milk was with him, but when the vote was called on Monday, Milk voted against White and for the facility. Milk had voted with his liberal colleagues rather than with White. This meant that the Youth Campus proposal passed by a vote of six to five, with Milk joining other newly elected progressive members Carol Ruth Silver, Ella Hill Hutch, and Gordon Lau in the majority. Feinstein and Kopp voted with White in the minority. In a 2008 interview with the *SF Weekly*, Ray Sloan, a senior aide to White at the time, described the impact of what White perceived to be a betrayal: "That was it. Harvey was no longer a friend, and it wasn't any fun anymore. It was all 'no' votes on the parades and anything else Harvey wanted."[27]

Sloan's view on this is powerful because as a gay aide to White, he was uniquely positioned to understand both supervisors' thinking on these issues. This view, that the Youth Campus vote was the turning point in the relationship between the two new supervisors, has some real elements of truth to it. White was clearly furious with Milk and indeed felt betrayed by his vote for the Youth Campus, but White's campaign rhetoric and identity as a social conservative cannot be completely ignored here either. It is possible that had Milk supported White's opposition to the Youth Campus, White would have voted with Milk on the gay rights ordinance, but we can never know that. In the bigger picture, White's vote on Milk's bill didn't matter because Milk already had ten votes, whereas White needed Milk's vote to stop the Youth Campus.

While the vote on the Youth Campus received no attention outside the city, Milk's bill was national news. Reporting from San Francisco, Les Ledbetter of the *New York Times* described how "the growing political power of homosexuals here and their co-existence with many others in this historically tolerant city were demonstrated last night when the Board of Supervisors approved a homosexual rights ordinance that many here consider the most stringent and encompassing in the nation."[28]

The article went on to quote Milk: "This will be the most stringent gay rights law in the country. . . . This one has teeth; a person can go to court if his rights are violated once this is passed." Milk's assessment was true, as was his description of San Francisco's gays and lesbians as "ecstatic" over the vote in the board of supervisors.[29] Gay activists in Milk's hometown who were reading their local paper that day could not have helped but notice that San Francisco had one more out gay person on its city legislature than New York had, and now San Francisco had one more strong gay rights bill than New York had. Later that fall, Ken Sherrill became the first out gay elected party official in New York when he was elected district leader in the Sixty-Ninth Assembly District, but New Yorkers would have to wait until 1991 before there was an out gay elected official, City Councilman Tom Duane, in their city. The only other San Franciscan supervisor mentioned in the *Times* article was Dan White, who, speaking as a representative of the forces of fear and intolerance, "said he feared that many San Francisco residents who were already upset by the 'demands' of 'large minorities' . . . would either leave the city or react punitively if the proposed ordinance goes through."[30]

Shortly after the board of supervisors voted on the bill, Mayor Moscone, as widely expected, happily signed the bill into law. Moscone's alliance with Milk made support for the bill easy, but Moscone had also been one of the first big city mayors to embrace gay rights. This was partially out of political necessity. Even before running for mayor in 1975, Moscone's state senate district included most of San Francisco, which beginning in the 1970s had a large gay vote. Because he was a progressive Democrat, Moscone needed the support of those gay voters. However, Moscone's support for gay rights was not simply transactional. As a legislator and later mayor, Moscone always supported civil rights and equality. Gay rights was part of that.

For example, as mayor, Moscone was a visible supporter of the Golden Gate Business Association (GGBA), an organization of gay businesspeople. In a letter of support for their 1978 dinner, Moscone lauded the organization: "Year after year, the members of this organization have made significant contributions to the health and strength of our community. . . . The active representatives of this group have played a major role in preserving San Francisco's economic foundations as well as the ambience of its neighborhoods."[31] These comments are significant and reflect the era not least because they demonstrate the reticence of even a pro–gay rights mayor to use words like "gay" when referring to a gay business organization. Moscone's recognition of the GGBA's impact on neighborhoods also shows that the mayor was a smart politician who was always able to return back to his core message of neighborhoods.

Moscone displayed a comfort with gay San Franciscans that went beyond politics. The April 24 edition of the 1978 *San Francisco Gazette*, a newspaper serving the city's gay community, featured a large photo of the mayor wearing khakis, a patterned shirt, and a knit tie while tossing out the first pitch of the city's gay softball league's season. The accompanying story described how "an estimated crowd of 2,000 saw Mayor George Moscone officially open the 1978 Community Softball League season by throwing out the first ball."[32]

Two thousand people seems like an enormous crowd for an amateur softball game. In fact, six times the previous year the Giants had failed to draw that many fans to a game at the 'Stick, but softball was a big deal in gay San Francisco in the late 1970s. It brought the community together and put the lie to the stereotype of gay men being weak and unathletic. From 1973 through 1978, an annual softball game was played between the police department softball team and the winner of the Community Softball League. In 1979, the ranks of gay San Francisco softball were bolstered by the addition of Glenn Burke, an Oakland native and former standout prospect in the Los Angeles Dodgers system who had not made it in the big leagues and whose sexual orientation undoubtedly cut short his big league career.

The ten members of the board of supervisors who voted for Milk's gay rights ordinance and the mayor who supported it placed themselves on the right side of history. Many of these politicians supported Milk because they believed it was the right thing to do. Moscone was a Milk ally who had supported gay rights in the state senate. Hutch, Lau, and Silver were progressives who wanted to stamp out bigotry in their city. Feinstein and also Ron

Pelosi, Lee Dolson, Quentin Kopp, and John Molinari voted for the bill despite scant public records on gay-related issues.

The reason for their support was less likely to have been based on great concern for gay people, but more about politics. Milk's election was a victory for gay San Francisco, but he won in a district that had been drawn so that a gay candidate could win, and he defeated other gay candidates in the election. The passage of this bill was different. Supervisors who had little connection to the Castro or other gay areas of town realized that if they angered San Francisco's gay community, they would have little citywide political future. This was an important political moment for gay San Francisco, as it moved gay politics out of the gay ghetto of the Castro. From that moment on, gay rights became part of the core of progressive politics in San Francisco. It was not the last time in 1978 a San Francisco politician would make an important decision with an eye on the gay vote in a citywide election.

In 1974 or even 1976, you could call yourself a progressive and equivocate on gay rights, even in San Francisco, but after Milk's gay rights bill passed with such broad support, that was never the case again in San Francisco. This was a very important achievement for gay San Franciscans, who have remained at the center of progressive coalitions in the city ever since. It only took another twenty to thirty years for progressive America as a whole to catch up with San Francisco.

Much of that credit goes to Milk himself, who quickly understood how legislatures function and the incentives that drive the behavior of politicians, and to Moscone, who brought gays and lesbians into his progressive coalition. In getting this bill passed, Milk not only delivered something for his political base, but made it clear to anybody who was paying attention that he was a smart political operator who knew how to play the game.

4

Heading to the 'Stick

●●●●●●●●●●●●●●●●●●●●●●

The transitions San Francisco was experiencing in the late 1970s had a particular impact on its young people. Regardless of who our parents were, we were growing up in an unusual time and in an increasingly unusual city. In some cases, this meant that the reaction and anger felt by adults—frequently targeted at ethnic minorities, gays and lesbians, hippies, and other symbols of the new city—was passed on to their children. Some embraced these biases; others rebelled against them. Asian, Latino, and African American youths were also targets of this rancor as many of their parents worked to make San Francisco a different and more tolerant city. There were also kids, like my brother and me, whose parents were newer San Franciscans helping to bring these new values to their adopted hometown.

With some exceptions, in San Francisco in the late 1970s and early 1980s you could tell a lot about a child's family background by what music they listened to as they moved into adolescence. The first division was race, as African American, Latino, and many Asian kids tended to listen to soul, disco, various Latino genres, and rhythm and blues. Among most white and some nonwhite kids, the divisions broke on class and education lines as well. White kids from more socially conservative working-class families who did not rebel against the views of their parents were drawn to what was then known as hard rock but that soon evolved into heavy metal. In this period, if you saw a kid, usually a teenage boy, with a Led Zeppelin or Pink Floyd T-shirt, there was a very good chance he or she was white, although some were Latino or Asian Americans, and a pretty good chance his parents were not professors, civil rights attorneys, or social workers. These kids often lived in the Sunset, Richmond, or Excelsior districts or other white working-class areas of the city. They frequently could be identified by the uniform of much of working-class San Francisco back then—a Derby jacket, Ben Davis pants, and a hooded sweatshirt. These kids were known as WPODs for "white punks on dope," a phrase that became a song by the San Francisco punkish band the Tubes. It was this demographic in which the "Disco sucks" movement, with all its racist and homophobic overtones, was strongest.

The children of liberal, educated, white San Franciscans tended to be more drawn toward old hippie music and attire, or more conventional pop music, but punk rock was beginning to make inroads among these kids as well. There is no data on these generalizations, but if you were under twenty and lived in San Francisco, or most other cities in America at the time, you knew this social and musical cartography, perhaps not even consciously. Although many sons and daughters of middle-class professionals were drawn to punk to the point where in some sense they were overrepresented in the punk scene, most punks were from working-class backgrounds and grew up either in the same neighborhoods as the WPODs or in working-class areas that surrounded the Bay Area, including parts of Alameda, San Mateo, Contra Costa, and Marin Counties. Regardless of where most punks were from, punk was never enormously popular. It was considered an oddity in 1978. East Bay Ray (née Raymond Pepperell), the guitar player from Dead Kennedys, described young fans of punk to me as "the people in high school who didn't fit in anywhere else . . . socially awkward people that found something in common."[1] There were also young people, primarily young white people, for whom music simply wasn't that important or who were drawn to the arena rock and New Wave (a kind of sanitized punk rock), the two genres that were heard on mainstream radio stations much of the time.

It would be nice to say that all of us, regardless of our backgrounds or musical tastes, were united by the Giants, but that would be an overstatement. In those years, the Giants did not play such an intense role in the lives and hearts of most San Franciscans, even younger ones. The team had moved to San Francisco in 1958, displacing a very popular team, the San Francisco Seals of the Pacific Coast League (PCL). The Giants played in a cold ballpark in a remote corner of the city. Even when they had good teams, as they had for most of the years from 1958 to 1971, they drew modest crowds and were peripheral to the gestalt of San Francisco. This was particularly true as the movements of the late 1960s began to change San Francisco.

There are some parts of the country where sports teams, frequently baseball teams, are deeply entrenched in the local culture. For example, in almost any story about growing up in New England any time since about 1900, the Red Sox, and the exaggerated pain of being a Red Sox fan, is a constant theme. For many New Englanders, the Red Sox have been a central pillar of their identity for decades. That is similarly true for Brooklynites who grew up in that borough between about 1900 and 1960. For those people, the Dodgers were a critical part of their childhood, and the departure of the Dodgers to Los Angeles following the 1957 season was a tragedy. For many Wisconsinites, the NFL's Green Bay Packers have been a central part of their lives for generations.

For San Franciscans in the 1960s and 1970s, and even later, this was not the case. While it was true that the Giants were San Francisco's team and most people there rooted for them when they thought about baseball, by 1974–1977 and probably earlier, baseball was not a driving passion for many San Franciscans, even young ones. Art Agnos, who first got elected to the state assembly in 1976 and became mayor eleven years later, told me, "Back then, they were just another baseball team that belonged to us, but there wasn't that imprint. There wasn't that chemical bonding we see today. . . . Back then, they were our baseball team . . . but there wasn't this bond."[2] Baseball and the Giants were one of the panoply of sports, music, drugs, and other forms of entertainment that competed for our attention. As 1977 turned into 1978, it was clear that baseball was not doing well in that competition. At that time, being an avid Giants fan was considered a socially acceptable but quirky thing, like collecting Asian art or cooking French food was for adults or being into photography or some weird kind of music was for kids.

Few San Franciscans have as much of a connection to both punk rock and to the Giants as Joe Dirt, who in the late seventies played guitar for bands such as Society Dog and the F**kups. In this century, Dirt has taken up almost permanent residence at the edge of McCovey Cove when the Giants are at home, where he tries to fish splash hits (home runs hit into the cove) out of the water before they sink. Dirt, whose outer-borough New York accent is almost as strong as Harvey Milk's was, grew up in Brooklyn rooting for the Yankees of the Mantle and Maris era but moved to San Francisco in 1971 and has been a Giants fan for decades. Even Dirt, despite his passion for baseball, conceded that in the late 1970s baseball "was a thing of the past for most people." However, when he told this to me, he then wistfully added, "I regret that I didn't get back into it sooner."[3]

The year 1978 was the twentieth anniversary of the Giants' move to San Francisco. In their two decades since moving west from New York, the Giants had developed a complex relationship with their city. They were initially greeted with enthusiasm and excitement, but even then, the feeling was not unambiguous. The Giants brought what we think of today as big league baseball to San Francisco, but the San Francisco Seals had been a beloved San Francisco institution for much of the twentieth century.

The Seals had been the best team in the PCL for much of that time. A number of Seals players had gone on to enjoy good to great careers with teams in the American or National League including Harry Heilmann, Ping Bodie, Frank Crosetti, and all three DiMaggio brothers—Vince, Dom, and Joe. Additionally, many Seals players, such as infielder Don Trower and pitcher Elmer Orella, were viewed as legitimate baseball stars in San Francisco but never played in the big leagues back east, despite in many cases having the opportunity.

For the first fifty or sixty years of the twentieth century, the quality of PCL baseball may have lagged behind that of the National and American Leagues, but many fans on the West Coast saw the PCL as essentially big league baseball. For most of that time there was little or no television, so fans on the West Coast rarely had the opportunity to see American or National League baseball. As a result, PCL teams and pennant races were followed closely by fans. Many players came from the West Coast and were well known by the fans. Because the Seals were usually one of the best teams in the league, this connection was particularly strong in San Francisco.

While some big league teams moved to cities where there was little significant memory of high-level baseball, or were begun anew as expansion teams in such cities, the Giants had to compete with the memory of a very well liked and very good PCL team. By the late 1970s this challenge had become even more difficult because, unlike the Seals, the Giants had yet to win a championship in San Francisco.

Charles A. Fracchia Sr., who was a college student in 1958 when the Giants came to San Francisco, described the historic move as "not a big thing." He continued: "George Christopher, who was mayor, definitely wanted the Giants to come, but the Seals were much beloved. . . . There were characters like Lefty O'Doul, . . . The advent of the Giants never replaced that. It has now [in 2017], but in the early years the connection was not made for the city."[4]

The Giants had some limited early success after they moved from New York, including a tough loss in the 1962 World Series to the Yankees. That World Series had one of the most dramatic endings in history, as slugger Willie McCovey, then in his fourth season with the Giants, lined out to second base with two outs in the bottom of the ninth. The tying and winning runs were on base, but the hard line drive hit by McCovey, one of the strongest men in the game, went right to Bobby Richardson, the slick-fielding Yankee second baseman, who caught it to preserve the Yankees' 1–0 win. During the following five seasons, the Giants contended regularly, finishing second in a ten-team league four times in a row from 1965 to 1968, but they never won the pennant. They had a fantastic nucleus of four future Hall of Famers—Mays, McCovey, and pitchers Juan Marichal and Gaylord Perry— and for some of those years, a fifth, Orlando Cepeda, but they could never make it back to the World Series.

Meanwhile, the Dodgers, who had moved to Los Angeles from Brooklyn the same year the Giants moved to San Francisco, won three World Series in their first eight years in their new home. This set the tone for the West Coast version of the rivalry between the two teams. The differences in the team's fortunes only got stronger in the 1970s. The Dodgers won pennants and frequently were first or close to first in attendance, while the Giants struggled to stay out of the cellar and to stay in San Francisco.

The Giants' failure to win another pennant in the 1960s despite the impressive collection of talent on their team dovetailed with other rapid changes in San Francisco. During the years the Mays-Marichal-McCovey Giants were finishing second every year, San Francisco was emerging as the center of a new global youth culture. Those were the years when the city became a magnet for hippies, other young people looking for something new and different, and eventually gays and lesbians. There were undoubtedly baseball fans among those new San Franciscans, but they did not seem very interested in the Giants.

Almost no histories of San Francisco in those years ever mention baseball, focusing instead on the drugs, music, social change, and hippies. That is probably natural given how extraordinary the developments in San Francisco must have felt at the time, but it demonstrates the bifurcation in San Francisco. Baseball in general, and the Giants in particular, was something that belonged to an older San Francisco. Those young people who kept rooting for the Giants were likely to have grown up in the city and were not hippie migrants. As the team stopped contending around 1972, even those fans lost interest, leaving the Giants with a troublingly small fan base. Over time this meant that the Giants had little connection to the new city. The Giants played in the same city that became a symbol of the late 1960s, but the city the Giants played in and the city where the hippies made their presence felt most strongly seemed to have little connection to each other at the time.

By the mid-1970s, the hippies, the gays, and others were not big Giants fans. The upper deck of Candlestick Park may have frequently smelled of marijuana, but by then it was not just hippies who were smoking pot. Younger fans by this time had never known a winning Giants team, while fans old enough to remember the 1940s and 1950s frequently pined for the days before the Giants, when the Seals were still San Francisco's team. The combination of a bad Giants team and the lingering Seals nostalgia among many San Franciscans made it tough for the Giants in the mid-1970s. During spring training of 1978, Herb Caen noted how the shadow of the Seals still made life difficult for the Giants: "Glenn Dickey, the sports columnist, observes shrewdly that the Giants and the A's have no nostalgia going for them. When old baseball fans get together—are there any young ones?— they talk about the Seals and the Oaks and the Sunday double-headers, the morning game in one city, then a rollicking ferryboat ride and the second game across the Bay."[5]

Caen may have been overstating the power of Seals nostalgia somewhat and by the late 1970s, there was also ample nostalgia for the Mays-Marichal-McCovey Giants of the 1960s, but memories of the Giants did not go back any further than that. For anybody over thirty-five years old in the Bay Area, childhood memories, the strongest source of nostalgia, were still of the Seals and of the Oaks, the PCL team that had played in Oakland from 1903 to 1955.

Those 1976 and 1977 Giants were a genuinely uninspiring team, winning seventy-four and seventy-five games while drawing 626,868 and 700,056 fans. Moreover, because only about twenty Giants games a year were televised, people who did not attend the games rarely had a chance to see the Giants. In 1976 and 1977, they weren't missing much. The pitching, led by Montefusco and Halicki, was decent, but even after adding Evans in 1976 and Madlock and Clark in 1977, the offense was not very powerful, especially in a division that featured the famous Big Red Machine in Cincinnati and a very strong Dodger team in Los Angeles.

The Giants' ballpark also played a major role in their misfortunes. During the four decades from 1960 through 1999, the Giants played in Candlestick Park, a huge multi-use stadium. The stadium was known for being extremely cold and windy at night. My brother and I would attend night games there wearing the same clothes we wore for our annual December trip to New York to visit family. During night games, kids sipped hot chocolate to stay warm, while many adults spiked their coffee from flasks of liquor they had snuck into the park under their heavy layers of clothes in an effort to stay warm and maybe to dull the pain of those mid-1970s Giants teams.

Candlestick Park was not just cold. It was also a pretty dreadful place to watch a baseball game. Because it was built for both baseball and football, many seats, particularly those in the upper deck beyond third and first base, offered less-than-ideal views of the game. In the 1970s and 1980s, Candlestick had a seating capacity of just over 59,000 for baseball and over 60,000 for football. The sheer size of the place meant that many fans were far from the action.

The weather at Candlestick Point was often warm during the days, but even sunny days had their quirks. On otherwise pleasant sunny days, as soon as the shade hit, the temperature would drop very quickly, as much as what felt like ten to twenty degrees in an inning. Moreover, many of the lower deck reserved seats behind home plate or in the infield fell under the shade of the upper deck and received little or no sun. Thus, on warm days, the best seats were usually in the upper deck. Experienced fans knew that the upper deck seats around home plate were a bargain because they had good views of the action, were warm, and were cheaper than seats in the lower deck.

Candlestick Park was also a no-frills kind of place in the 1970s. The food was basic ballpark fare. There were no garlic fries, tropical drinks, ethnic dishes, main courses (other than hot dogs or hamburgers that more often than not were cold), or anything else interesting to eat. However, you could buy an extra-large hot dog known, for no discernible reason, as a Polish sausage. There were few souvenir shops, little entertainment other than the baseball itself, and only a handful of promotional giveaway days. For real baseball fans, this was ideal, but for casual fans it only further limited the appeal of the ballpark and the team that played there.

Visiting players hated coming to Candlestick to play, but the cold and wind did not discriminate between the Giants and their opponents. In the

1961 All-Star Game, the wind was so strong that it blew Giants reliever Stu Miller off the mound. By the 1970s, enclosing the outfield grandstand with an upper level may have cut down on the wind a bit, but it was still windy enough most evenings to turn home runs into fly outs and for little whirlwinds of hot dog wrappers and other ballpark detritus to be constantly blowing about.

Unfortunately, the disdain visiting players had for Candlestick Park did not translate into a home-field advantage, because most players on the Giants didn't like playing there either. This sentiment was particularly acute among position players, because the wind that blew in off the bay not only chilled fans and players from both teams but made the 'Stick a very tough park for hitters. Pitchers probably liked this, but even for them it didn't compensate for the cold.

Calling Candlestick Park home also made it difficult for the Giants to compete for good players, particularly once the age of free agency began in the late 1970s. Free agents who could choose between several teams rarely signed with the Giants. Longtime Giants announcer Hank Greenwald recollected, "By and large guys hated playing there, and I'm not just talking about visiting players. . . . I can't see any way you can step up to the plate as a hitter and be calling time out to step out and rub your eyes and get the dirt that's been blowing in your eyes and try to clear your vision to face a ninety-five-mile-per-hour fastball."[6] This is one of the reasons why in the early days of free agency the Giants almost never signed top-tier free agents, settling instead for useful players such as Bill North or overpaying for less-than-useful players such as Rennie Stennett. Players with clauses in their contracts that allowed them to veto trades to some teams often exercised that veto rather than play eighty-one games a year in Candlestick Park.

Charles A. Fracchia Jr. is the son of the San Francisco historian and an extremely devoted Giants fan of many decades. In his view, the Giants ballpark "defined baseball in the city in a negative way . . . in a horrible way. It was hard to get fans. It was kind of a miserable place to go."[7] Glenn Dickey, the longtime columnist for the *San Francisco Chronicle*, similarly attributed the sometime disconnect between the city and its baseball team to Candlestick Park: "It was just a terrible park. . . . What was supposed to be the best seats downstairs were mostly in the shade. . . . And it was really brutal to watch a game down there."[8] This is more significant than it first sounds. While knowing that the slightly cheaper seats upstairs offered a better viewing experience allowed young fans like me to save a few dollars and enjoy better seats, it meant that the ballpark had no chance of becoming a popular place for politicians, local celebrities, and business leaders to be seen, as AT&T Park has become in the twenty-first century and Dodger Stadium has been since the 1960s. Most celebrities had no interest in going to a ballpark where they had to sit far away from the action and cameras at night to avoid freezing.

Candlestick Park was not only a cold and unpleasant place for night baseball, but for many San Franciscans it was difficult to get to as well. The 'Stick was located on Candlestick Point in the southeast corner of the city not far from the airport. For the residents of Bayview–Hunters Point, the ballpark was relatively close by, but for the rest of the residents of San Francisco, it was out of the way. Candlestick Park was accessible by car, and because the Giants in those days were not very good, there was usually ample parking around the ballpark. This is largely because Horace Stoneham, the owner of the Giants when they moved from New York to San Francisco, felt that the franchise had failed in New York in the decade or so following World War II because there was no parking in the northern Manhattan neighborhood in which the team played. Therefore, a precondition for any ballpark that would be built for the Giants was 10,000 parking spaces. At Candlestick, Stoneham got his parking spaces, but he also got a ballpark so cold and cavernous that by the mid-1970s the parking lot was mostly empty on many game days.

These parking spaces, however, were of little help to kids who were too young to drive and who wanted to see their team play. It is a cliché to contrast the amount of unstructured free time children had in the 1970s with the heavily structured lives of many children in the twenty-first century, but it is true. Moreover, children in San Francisco of that time—particularly those whose parents were caught in the maelstrom of making a living, divorcing, finding themselves, and recovering from the hangover of the 1960s—were in many respects uniquely unsupervised. The confluence of all the ills of the inner city, as well as a large segment of middle-class San Franciscans who were single parents, meant that not only did the San Francisco of the late 1970s have a higher proportion of children per capita than it does today, but those children had less parenting and more time on their hands than most young people today. For many of us, beginning when we were quite young, going to the ballpark was not a family ritual or opportunity for father-child bonding, but something done with our siblings and friends.

The city's transit authority, universally known as Muni, short for Municipal Railway, solved this problem, sort of, by creating a network of buses, collectively called the Ballpark Express, that took fans from various parts of the more northern and western parts of the city to the 'Stick. This made the Giants accessible for kids and seniors who had a lot of time on their hands and either did not want to or could not drive.

Opening Day and Concerned Relatives

When the Giants began their 1978 season on April 7 against the San Diego Padres in front of 36,000 fans at Candlestick Park, there was little reason to think much was going to be different or that either of those two teams would contend. The Padres had gone 69–93 in 1977 and were not expected to be much of a factor in the National League West in 1978. Zander Hollander picked them for fourth place in the division, noting that they were "improving, could surprise."[9] Hollander's prediction turned out to be somewhat accurate, as the Padres ended up with a respectable fourth-place finish, going 84–78 in what turned out to be a very competitive division.

Four of the men who men who played for the Padres that day ended up in the baseball Hall of Fame. Starting pitcher Gaylord Perry had begun his career sixteen years earlier with the Giants, and at age thirty-nine—in the first start of a season that would bring him his second Cy Young Award—he pitched six solid innings, giving up four hits and two runs while striking out eight and walking none. The last two innings of that game were pitched by Rollie Fingers, who had been the great reliever, and teammate of Vida Blue's, on the 1972–1974 World Series–winning A's. Fingers, like Perry, was in the middle of a Hall of Fame career.

The hitting star for the Padres in their first game of 1978 was the cleanup hitter, a twenty-six-year-old outfielder already beginning his sixth season with the Padres. Dave Winfield hit a single, a double, and a home run that day. Astute fans could have seen the Hall of Fame potential in Winfield, might have figured that with a few more good years Perry would be a candidate for the Hall of Fame, and recognized that if relievers were getting in, Fingers should be one of them. Even those fans probably would not have noticed the starting shortstop for the Padres that day, a thin, light-hitting infielder who seemed fine with the glove but was lifted for a pinch hitter in the sixth inning. However, that shortstop, Ozzie Smith, would go on to become the consensus greatest fielding shortstop ever and also get a plaque in Cooperstown.

The Giants were not quite at full strength as the season opened. Vida Blue was not ready to pitch yet, so the opening-day start went to John Montefusco. Bill Madlock was hurt, so he could not play. Rob Andrews filled in at second base and was the Giants improbable hitting star, with a double, two singles, and a stolen base. Montefusco left the game in the sixth with a 2–0 lead, but bullpen stalwarts Randy Moffitt and Gary Lavelle could not hold the lead, and the Giants lost 3–2.

On April 11, after the Giants took the remaining two games of the three-game set in San Diego, lefty Bob Knepper made his first start of the season against the Reds in Cincinnati. He held a very potent Reds lineup—which included Pete Rose, Ken Griffey, Joe Morgan, George Foster, and Johnny Bench—to six hits and two runs in six innings. Gary Lavelle added three scoreless innings in relief. The Giants offense was just good enough to win. Darrell Evans and Terry Whitfield both connected for home runs in the fourth off of Tom Seaver. Jack Clark hit another against reliever Dave Tomlin in the eighth to put the Giants ahead for good by a score of 3–2. It was only the fourth game of the season, but Giants fans were pleased to see their team with a 3–1 record.

On the same day back in San Francisco, a flyer was distributed to the media, political leaders, and others provocatively titled, "The Nightmare Is Taking Place Right Now: Will You Help Us Free Our Families." The image on the flyer was what appeared to be an undernourished and sad-looking child peering out from behind prison bars. The flyer was distributed by a San Francisco–based organization called Concerned Relatives and Citizens. The purpose of the organization was made clear in the first paragraph of text: "We are individuals having only one thing in common; relatives isolated in the 'Jonestown' jungle encampment in Guyana, South America, under the total control of one man, Jim Jones. . . . Our only concern is for our families. We are bewildered and frightened by what is being done to them."[10] The group also appeared at the Peoples Temple headquarters on Geary Street to present their concerns directly. They were met by Peoples Temple attorney Charles Garry, who spoke to the press falsely, and less than eloquently, dismissing the charges as "a lot of bullshit."[11]

In the ten months since Jones had left San Francisco to join several hundred of his followers in Guyana, the Peoples Temple had retained a physical presence in the city. The headquarters, on Geary near Steiner, remained

active, while many Temple members were still in the United States attending to church business or otherwise going on with their lives. In some cases,
they were planning departures to Jonestown. Rumors about abuses of the
kind enumerated by Concerned Relatives and Citizens—including "no dis-
sent permitted," "armed guards are stationed around Jonestown to prevent
anyone from leaving," and "mail is censored"[12]—had surfaced in San Francisco periodically. However, Charles Garry was not the only San Franciscan either anxious to dismiss these rumors or hoping they weren't true. Many
powerful politicians, including the mayor, the lieutenant governor, and Willie Brown, a very influential state assemblyman who represented part of
San Francisco in the legislature, had benefited from a good relationship with
Jim Jones and were not inclined to believe the worst about him.

It is easy to be shocked that San Franciscans were not more outraged by
the rumors around what Jim Jones was doing in Guyana, or to be perplexed
as to why the mayor, or even ordinary citizens, did not demand investiga-
tions earlier. Those sentiments seem reasonable from the perspective of the
twenty-first century, or even from the 1980s, but the feeling at the time was
very different. In the 1970s a lot of very strange things were occurring in San
Francisco, most of which were beyond the ken of even progressive politicians such as Willie Brown, Harvey Milk, or George Moscone. Almost all
the people who ran San Francisco, regardless of their political views, were
old enough to be somewhat overwhelmed by the pace of change in their city
over the previous decade. Drug users, cult members, hippies, gays, and others
had all been part of that fast-moving story. For many ordinary San Franciscans, particularly older ones, these groups were all weird—almost inter-
changeably so. To be for traditional values at that time meant to be against
cults, gays, civil rights, drugs, and hippies (and later punks), but not neces-
sarily to differentiate between them.

The Zebra Killings, a series of murders of white people by radical African Americans, had disrupted the city a few years earlier. The Zodiac Killer,
another serial killer who struck mostly in Northern California, had been
active for much of the previous ten years or so. For over a decade, teenagers
had been coming to San Francisco and disappearing into a maelstrom of
drugs and the counterculture. During those years, communes and cults of
all kinds had sprung up. This was the broader context in which the Concerned Relatives had made their plea. Given all this, it is apparent why all
of San Francisco was not yet ready to stop in its tracks because of what some
said was occurring in Jonestown.

Jim Jones's sojourn in San Francisco was relatively brief, but he had been involved in the Peoples Temple or its antecedents since the late 1950s. Like many leaders who occupy the space somewhere between cult, religion, and hucksterism, Jones mixed ideas that were very good with some that were destructive and some that were bizarre. For example, Jones's commitment to civil rights, going back at least to the 1950s was, by all measures, sincere. He understood and seemed genuinely to believe, long before many other white people did, that all people are indeed equal regardless of the color of their skin, and that a just and fair society would reflect that. That noble view was balanced by Jones's notion, which grew stronger over the years, that pretty much everybody around him, regardless of race, was there to serve him, whether by working for him for almost no compensation, turning over their life savings to him, or satisfying his sexual desires. By the 1970s, progressive politics notwithstanding, Jones was also becoming unhinged, frequently asserting his own divinity and believing that he should dictate virtually every aspect of his followers' lives and that his followers should be willing to die for him. However, he had managed for the most part to conceal that side of himself from San Francisco's political leaders.

Jones did not have longstanding ties to San Francisco but was from rural Indiana, where he had been raised in a conservative and traditional environment by a father who was quite ill and a mother who was not happy and often overwhelmed by having a sick husband, a son, and rarely enough money. As a young man, Jones moved to Indianapolis and began working as a minister before starting his own congregation. Jones began building his Peoples Temple, originally called the Community Church, in the 1950s in Indianapolis. Due to his strong emphasis on civil rights and equality—which was quite progressive, even radical for the time—most of Jones's early congregants were African American. Additionally, his congregants, regardless of their ethnic background, were largely from lower-income backgrounds and did not have much education. Given the nature of Jones's sermons (including his flimsy grasp of history and current events), suggestion of his own godlike qualities, and reliance on tricks such as fake faith healings, he naturally had a much stronger appeal to people who were less educated. Over time, this began to be a problem, as Jones needed people with education and training to do things such as help him in his legal battles, write newsletters, and even liaise with public officials. Nonetheless, Jones's early followers were extremely hardworking and dedicated, and they often possessed skills such as carpentry or car repair that were helpful to the Peoples Temple and to Jones.

As Jones continued his work in Indianapolis, the Peoples Temple grew increasingly strange. Conventional Christian theology gave way to frequent suggestions, and later assertions, of Jones's divinity. Jones's sermons became longer, often requiring congregants to spend almost their entire Sunday listening to him. Followers were asked to devote more and more of their time and resources to the Peoples Temple, and those who resisted generally faced punishment from Jones. During these years, Jones retained his strong views on civil rights while openly advocating for socialist policies, something not too many white ministers in the Midwest were doing in the 1950s or early 1960s.

From his early days in Indianapolis, Jones understood the importance of local politics. He built relationships with local politicians, praising them and offering them support if they did things he liked. He also became directly involved in city government, chairing the city's human rights commission. Jones used his role on the commission to advocate aggressively for civil rights but also to promote himself and to demonstrate to his followers that he was an important player in Indianapolis. However, although it had a significant African American population, Indianapolis was too conservative for the political messages that were beginning to dominate Jones's preaching.

By the early 1960s, Jones's peripatetic nature, growing tension between him and many in Indianapolis, and the dwindling size of his Peoples Temple contributed to his decision to leave Indianapolis. During that decade, he explored the possibility of moving his congregation to Brazil, and he even lived there with his family during most of 1962 and 1963. This was the first but not the last time that Jones explored the idea of leaving the United States. Although Jones was unable to get any traction in Brazil, that idea never really went away. Jones ultimately decided to move the Peoples Temple in 1965 to Ukiah, California, a rural community about 115 miles north of San Francisco. A few hundred of Jones's most loyal followers came with him. Ukiah, an overwhelmingly white, socially conservative town whose economy was centered around agriculture, was not an obvious place to establish the headquarters for what by the mid-1960s was a cultish church group whose members were largely African American and urban and who believed in civil rights and socialism.

Despite this, the Peoples Temple was based in Ukiah for roughly a decade. Those years were a period of great growth, and the organization expanded throughout California. The successes enjoyed by the Peoples Temple in these years did not come easily and were the result of Jones's vision and ability as well as the extraordinary hard work and sacrifice of many of his congregants. However, these were also the years when the Peoples Temple became unambiguously a cult and when Jones began to descend more profoundly into madness and delusional thinking.

From Ukiah, Jones built a cult that looked like many others both before and since. The leader convinced his followers of his divinity, or at the very least, his special relationship with God. He used this to demand that his followers devote their lives to him, forcing them to live in very spartan conditions while he enriched himself, became addicted to amphetamines, and slept with many of his followers. The Peoples Temple commitment to civil rights and a corresponding involvement in politics buoyed by Jones's considerable ambition continued during this period. Members were used as resources for friendly politicians, often filling halls for rallies or volunteering on campaigns and other activities.

Jones's political interests eventually led him to explore leaving Ukiah for a bigger and more politically relevant community. He contemplated moving the Peoples Temple to several cities before deciding on San Francisco. By the early 1970s, San Francisco was the perfect American city for a left-wing cult leader with a strong concern for civil rights who also sought to exploit African Americans. San Francisco offered a large African American population, progressive politics, and even by then a reputation as a place that was hospitable to hippies, gays, and others outside of the American mainstream. San Francisco was offbeat enough that another cult leader, or a radical church, would not be too unusual.

One of the reasons Jim Jones was drawn to San Francisco, and that he was able to build political relationships during his years there, was that this was a time when there were many preachers who could mobilize large numbers of African American volunteers, were a little bit unconventional, and had left-of-center politics. Jones was unusual because he was one of the very few white ones, and was stranger than most, but at least in some respects, people like him were part of the fabric of much of urban America—and San Francisco more than most cities—in the 1970s. Corey Busch, Mayor Moscone's press secretary, conceded that he remembered thinking of Jones as "one weird dude" but also added in reference to Jones's political presence in San Francisco, "This was a city in the seventies where you have Glide Memorial and Cecil Williams doing the kinds of things he was doing. You had John Maher and Mimi Silbert doing Delancey Street and the things Delancey Street was doing. So for a Jim Jones and Peoples Temple, this was not out of character for what was going on and bubbling, beginning to really take root in this town at that time."[13] Rich Schlackman echoed this sentiment: "I didn't see any difference between Arnold Townsend [an African American activist of the time] and Jim Jones. . . . You had ten names going to the [heavily African American] Western Addition. You called them."[14]

Carol Ruth Silver, who had been a Freedom Rider in the 1960s and described herself to me as being "radicalized by the civil rights movement," said that she viewed the Peoples Temple "as very similar to churches in the South." She continued: "They had a charismatic minister—in this case, a white one. . . . He could get people to march."[15] Silver's recollection of the Peoples Temple in San Francisco helps explain why, at least when they were active in San Francisco, they did not draw much scrutiny. The abuses and increasingly strange behavior of Jones were noticed by some, but much of it remained hidden. Thus, it is entirely plausible that in the context of the time, the Peoples Temple was genuinely understood by many to be a slightly weirder-than-average church that was deeply involved in progressive politics.

San Francisco may not have created Jim Jones, but it appealed to him because it was less conventional than most American cities. Additionally, its small size and space for left-of-center politics gave Jones an opportunity to be more than a gadfly. Most major American cities in the early and mid-1970s were still either too conservative for Jones's kind of radical politics or too large for the Peoples Temple to make much of an impact. San Francisco was different. In San Francisco, Jones used many of the same tactics he had used in Indianapolis, Ukiah, and elsewhere to ingratiate himself and his organization with local politicians. He provided bodies to fill half-empty halls for speeches and to volunteer on campaigns, made buses available to move his people to events as needed, ensured that his members, regardless of whether they were legally eligible, all voted for candidates he supported, wrote warm letters to politicians who supported his interests, and otherwise sought to build a political machine of sorts.

San Francisco proved to be a very receptive place for Jones's appeal and welcomed the work his church did in providing social services to needy people. As Busch remembered, "When Jones first got to San Francisco . . . everybody was taken in by what they perceived to be a tremendous amount of good that he was doing—with poor people . . . and all kinds of things."[16]

By the mid-1970s, a broad range of progressive San Francisco politicians associated with Jones, including state senate majority leader turned mayoral candidate George Moscone, praised Jones publicly and valued his support during campaigns.

During the 1976 presidential campaign, Jones sat next to Rosalyn Carter, the wife of Democratic nominee Jimmy Carter, at a campaign event in San Francisco. Tim Reiterman and John Jacobs describe a gala in the fall of that year at the Peoples Temple: "The head table was filled with familiar faces—Lieutenant Governor and Mrs. Dymally, Assemblyman Willie Brown, Mayor George Moscone, District Attorney Joe Freitas and others. ... The guest list read like a register of the city's luminaries—Democrats, Republicans and radicals."[17]

It is easy to characterize San Francisco's liberal political elite as being naively captivated by Jones, but there was more to it than that. Willie Brown's comments at that gala event—"Let me present to you a combination of Martin King, Angela Davis, Albert Einstein . . . Chairman Mao"[18]—suggest more than little bit of irony. Brown, at the very least, was aware of Jones's high regard for himself and need for flattery. Similarly, although the role that Jones played in Moscone's 1975 election victory cannot be ignored, Moscone also had concerns about Jones. That is why he waited so long to reward him for his campaign efforts and then only gave him a spot on the housing commission. Jones had expected something bigger. This also may be why Jones's time in San Francisco's political life was brief. He only served on the housing commission for about a year, and by mid-1977, fewer than two years after Moscone's election, he had relocated to Guyana, never to return to San Francisco.

Although the Peoples Temple had not yet entirely abandoned San Francisco, by mid-1978 few in the city were paying much attention to the cult. Most of its members had left. Jones himself was no longer serving on the housing authority or living in San Francisco. The Peoples Temple was beginning to look like another of the odd detritus tossed up by the turmoil of the 1960s that was quickly fading into the jungle of South America and into history.

When you mention 1978 in San Francisco today, if people remember anything it is the assassinations and Jonestown, but in the middle of the year, Jones himself was looking more like a strange footnote to local history. According to the historian Charles A. Fracchia Sr., even the exposé in *New West* and the various reports of abuses in Jonestown were "not a huge thing."

Political consultant Rich Schlackman, who had worked on Moscone's mayoral campaign, said of Jones that by 1978, "I forgot him. I literally forgot him."[19] Corey Busch, George Moscone's press secretary in 1978, described the attitude by many in the city toward Jones as "out of sight, out of mind," adding for context that "there was a lot of shit going on in the city at that time."[20] Political life in San Francisco had, at least for the moment, moved beyond Jim Jones. Many San Franciscans were beginning to turn their attention to some more positive news from the southwest corner of the city.

First Place

The Giants and most of their fans were among those not paying too much attention to Jonestown in mid-April 1978. Bill Madlock was able to get back in the lineup on April 16 when he played second base and went two for four while batting third. On April 26, the Giants lost their fourth in a row, 6–1 to the Braves. On that same day, the A's bested the Twins 9–8 in twelve innings to push their record to 14–3. At that point in the season, the A's, not the Giants, looked to be the big baseball story in the Bay Area.

In that game against the Braves, Joe Altobelli changed the batting order as part of an effort to shake up a struggling lineup. Instead of leading off with Larry Herndon, who as a fast centerfielder was a prototypical leadoff hitter but had not done so well in that role up to that point in the season, Altobelli put Madlock in the leadoff spot. Madlock didn't have Herndon's speed, but he was very good at getting on base. Additionally, with Evans, Clark, and Ivie or McCovey in the middle of the lineup, Madlock's medium-level power was not needed in one of the RBI spots.

Through 1977, Madlock had posted a .388 career on-base percentage (OBP). That was the eighth-highest in all of baseball from 1973 to 1977. Herndon came into the season with a much lower .324 OBP, a big drop-off from Madlock. Herndon had begun the season in the leadoff spot because he looked like a leadoff hitter. He was a speedy outfielder without much power who could steal bases. Altobelli's view that speed was less important in the leadoff spot than the ability to get on base was considered almost radical in 1978, but he went with it. It seemed to work, as the Giants were a sub-.500 team before that move and played better than .500 baseball the rest of the way.

Ironically, from a statistical angle, Altobelli gave up most of the advantage he got from moving Madlock into the leadoff spot by tinkering with his number-two hitter as well. While Herndon was leading off, Darrell Evans had been batting second, but on April 26 Altobelli moved Terry Whitfield into the number-two hole, where he stayed for more or less the rest of the season. Whitfield looked like a number-two hitter in the way that Herndon looked like a leadoff hitter. The left-handed-hitting Whitfield hit for a decent batting average, was reasonably fast, and didn't have much power. In 1977, the first season in which he got significant playing time, Whitfield hit an impressive .285, but that is about all he did. His OBP was only .329, and he only had seven home runs. Evans, on the other hand, was only a .248 hitter over the course of his nine-year career going into 1978, but he had a very impressive .368 OBP. In 1978, he would post a .360 OBP compared to .335 for Whitfield. Batting Evans instead of Whitfield second would not have made a very big difference for the Giants and would have probably led to only a few more runs over the course of the season. Altobelli was ahead of his time in finding a leadoff hitter, but he could not see the value of Evans in the number-two position. In any case, from that point on, the top of the Giants batting order was set. Clark, the first baseman, Ivie or McCovey, Evans, and Herndon would make up the middle of the order, while the light-hitting Hill and LeMaster would, along with the pitcher, make up an anemic bottom third of the order.

On May 12 in a Friday night game at the 'Stick, Madlock and Whitfield showed what they could do at the top of the lineup. That night they combined to go five for eight with three RBIs. The RBIs came on back-to-back home runs in the fourth. Madlock's came with one on, and Whitfield followed with a solo shot. The three-run fourth came after the Giants had scored one in the first and four in the third, giving them an 8–1 lead. Despite giving up ten hits, Vida Blue struck out five on his way to a complete-game win. The win improved Blue's record to 5–1 with an ERA of 2.77. The lefty who had come across the bay during spring training was not disappointing his new team or their fans. That win also improved the Giants' record to 17–12, putting the team in first place. It was the first time they had been in first place that late in the season in five years.

Less than a quarter of the season had passed, so it was still relatively early, but for a franchise that had been struggling the way the Giants had in recent years, making it to first place in mid-May was no small accomplishment. With the exception of those of us who were very young and unlearned in the ways of Giants collapses, few fans that night thought the Giants could hold on to first place for more than a few days, let alone win the division.

5

Harvey Milk

● ●

There are few local politicians over the last fifty years anywhere in the United States, perhaps in the entire world, who are as well known and celebrated as Harvey Milk. Since his death, Milk has become a civil rights hero only one or two steps below Martin Luther King in the minds of many twenty-first-century American progressives. There have been books and movies about him. Schools and community centers are named after him. In 2016, the U.S. Navy named a 677-foot ship after Milk—a man who would have been summarily dismissed from the Navy during the time that he served if his sexual orientation had become known to the brass.

If anybody had told you in January 1977 that Harvey Milk would be commemorated that way, you would have not have believed them, even if you were optimistic about the future of LGBT equality. Milk at that time was a failed politician and an unlikely symbol for future generations of LGBT Americans. He had lost three previous races, finishing tenth in a field of thirty-two in a race for five at-large seats for the board of supervisors in 1973, and seventh, but a somewhat distant seventh, in a race for six at-large seats in 1975. In 1976 Milk was defeated in a Democratic primary for the state assembly by future San Francisco mayor Art Agnos. Milk would eventually be elected to the San Francisco Board of Supervisors in November 1977, but it is nonetheless striking that his entire career in elected office, a period just short of eleven months, occurred in 1978, and that in the only election he ever won, he received fewer than six thousand votes.

Milk made the most of his time in office, quickly emerging as a national figure in the gay liberation movement and becoming an important player in city and state politics. The significance of Milk, both as an openly gay man and a committed neighborhood-oriented progressive, was evident almost from the time he first got elected. Additionally, his close relationship with Mayor George Moscone increased his influence.

Milk's substantial political skills are easy to overlook in the larger story, but they were an important part of his success. Allen Bennett, the rabbi at Harvey Milk's synagogue, Sha'ar Zahav, had the opportunity to observe Milk in both political and nonpolitical settings: "He had a social skill . . . that was exceptional. He could not only read a crowd. He could read a person. As uncomfortable as he might make them, he would find some sort of commonality to build on."[1]

Although Milk advocated for neighborhood interests, he also had a unique profile, and responsibility, as the only openly gay elected official on the board of supervisors and one of only a small number of gay representatives in the whole country, none of whom had as high a profile. Thus, much the same way as in the 1940s through the 1960s member of Congress from the South Side of Chicago or Harlem were viewed as representing African Americans nationally, Milk became the spokesperson for gay San Francisco and to some extent for gay America. That was probably inevitable. Charles A. Fracchia Sr. summarized Milk's relationship with gay San Francisco succinctly: "He was a representative for the gays." Fracchia also was frank about how polarizing Milk was: "I remember Milk being detested by more conservative San Francisco—detested."[2]

During the late spring and early summer of 1978, Milk worked hard in his new position as a San Francisco supervisor. He was a consistent progressive voice on the board of supervisors, where the moderates still held a narrow 6–5 majority. Milk was generally a strong supporter of Mayor Moscone and was beginning to be respected as a hardworking representative and smart legislator, but other than the gay rights ordinance, he had yet to distinguish himself as a lawmaker in his first few months in office.

Ivie, Ivie

By the spring of 1978, Milk had begun to emerge as a symbol of the future of San Francisco, but the most beloved public figure in the city was more associated with the past. In 1978, the forty-year-old Willie McCovey was still the Giants primary first baseman, starting ninety-five games there, but he struggled with the bat, and by early in the season Mike Ivie was pushing him for playing time. Ivie was an excellent hitter who had no natural position after failing to make it as a catcher at the big league level. Ivie had played a bit of third, but the team already had two third basemen in Evans and Madlock, so Ivie only played four games at that position after he came to the Giants. He played twenty-two games in left field in 1978 but had neither the speed nor the fly catching ability to be a big league left fielder, so he usually played first against lefties and was used as a pinch hitter in thirty-nine games.

Ivie's best position in 1978 was hitter. His .308/.363/.475 slash line was good enough for second or third on the Giants in each category. Ivie was particularly effective against left-handed pitchers, hitting .319/.390/.507 when he had the platoon advantage. He was a valuable part of that 1978 team because he could hit lefties a lot better than McCovey could, and in games he did not start he was a very effective offensive weapon off the bench.

Ivie's career with the Giants was short and eventful. He played for San Francisco for parts of four seasons before being traded early in the 1981 season. During those years, he was never a full-time starter, but played a bit of both first base and the outfield. Nonetheless, in 1978 and 1979 he was an excellent hitter. He topped off his strong 1978 season with an even better 1979 season in which he hit .286/.359/.547, but he briefly retired in 1980 and was never the same player after that.

Mike Ivie is not well remembered by fans who were not around in 1978, because he did not play with the team long enough to make a big impression. His best year was 1979, a season that was otherwise very disappointing for Giants fans. However, Ivie had a strange career, one that provides rare insight into the emotional stress of being a big league ballplayer. Glenn Dickey described Ivie as "goofy . . . something wasn't functioning right there."[3] Dickey's tone during our discussion of Ivie was more charitable than his words sound on paper, suggesting compassion rather than disdain for the troubled slugger. Hank Greenwald indicated that Ivie had a difficult relationship with his father, whom he was perpetually unable to please, but also related an anecdote about how Ivie once told Greenwald that he was about to play his last game—before he had shared this information with his manager.[4]

During the fifteen-year period between 1972 and 1986 when the Giants did not appear in a single postseason game, there were not many memorable moments for the team. If one had to choose the greatest Giants moment during that period, some might point to Joe Morgan's three-run home run on the last day of the 1982 season that knocked the Dodgers out of the playoffs, the day after the Dodgers had done the same thing to the Giants. Morgan hit that home run, for a Giants team that eventually finished third, on October 3—thirty-one years to the day after Bobby Thomson's Shot Heard 'Round the World.[5] Morgan's home run was a great moment. It broke a 2–2 tie in the bottom of the seventh inning. I was among the more than 47,000 fans at Candlestick Park that day who cheered wildly not because our team was going to the postseason—they weren't, but because the Dodgers weren't going either.

Mike Ivie's moment felt bigger and was in many respects the true highlight of that fifteen-year run of Giants mediocrity. Perhaps it has been forgotten by many because Ivie was such a strange player and Morgan was an all-time great, or perhaps because as time passes the 1978 team looks like just another third-place team, but at the time and for many years after it was understood to be an important and exhilarating moment and the high point of that era.

The Giants and Dodgers had split the first two games of a three-game series in late May 1978. On Friday night, Bob Knepper had outpitched Doug Rau, winning 6–1 with the help of a three-run home run by Willie McCovey. Knepper held the Dodgers to six hits and two walks in a strong complete-game victory. The only Dodger run came on a solo shot by Ron Cey in the ninth inning when the game was already out of reach. On Saturday, Burt Hooton and Terry Forster held the Giants to two hits and one unearned run as the Giants, despite a strong outing by Vida Blue, lost 3–1, moving the Dodgers, still in third place, to within two and a half games.

More than 56,000 came to the series finale on May 28, the Sunday of Memorial Day weekend. My brother and I were among them. It was one of those rare day games at the 'Stick where a first-time visitor would not have believed the rumors about how cold the ballpark got at night. The crowd was in good spirits, as the young Giants team was in first place, school was almost out for summer, and everything, at least for the moment, seemed pretty good in San Francisco. Dodger ace Don Sutton had been struggling early in the season and was scheduled to go against The Count, John Montefusco.

Montefusco was well liked by Giant fans in 1978. The Count had made his debut in 1974, pitching in only five games, but in 1975 had brought some excitement and life to an otherwise struggling team. He also had pitched very well, going 15–9 with a 2.88 ERA, winning the National League Rookie of the Year Award, and coming in fourth in the Cy Young Award voting. He followed that up with a very strong 1976 season, going 16–14 with a 2.84 ERA while being the Giants' only representative on the All-Star team.

The Count was a good young pitcher on some pretty bad Giants teams, but he was more than that. He was a character who boasted about how good he was, promised to win games (often pitching well enough to make good on those promises), and never equivocated about his hatred for the Dodgers. All those things made Montefusco very popular at the 'Stick, but somewhat less popular a few hundred miles south in Dodger Stadium.

John D'Acquisto, a member of those mid-1970s Giants teams who briefly ran a bar and grill with Montefusco in San Francisco, described The Count's brashness when he made his debut at Dodger Stadium in 1974: "Count had a ton of confidence on the field. He had been at AAA Phoenix just six hours ago when he got the call to be at Dodger Stadium for the game. He was just itching for a moment like this. I was cocky, but Count . . . wow. Strutting out to the mound, ready for a fight, ready for his close-up on the major league stage."[6]

It didn't hurt Montefusco that he was Italian American in a town that still had a large Italian American population and where that community had strong connections to baseball. The San Francisco Seals of the old PCL had frequently featured high-profile Italian American players, including Frank Crosetti, Ping Bodie,[7] and three brothers from the North Beach section of San Francisco, just up the hill from the Cow Hollow where George Moscone grew up, who went on to become big league centerfielders of some note: Vince, Dom, and Joe DiMaggio. However, the San Francisco Giants had never had an Italian American star until Montefusco.

Following the 1976 season, Montefusco seemed well positioned to join the ranks of the top pitchers in the National League, but injuries limited him to only twenty-five starts in 1977. When he pitched that year, he was not as sharp as he had been in the previous two years. His 7–12 record and 3.49 ERA were a big step backward. By contrast, 1978 was beginning to look a little better. In his previous start, in Houston against the Astros, The Count had thrown six shutout innings to improve his record to 4–2 and lower his ERA to 3.12.

The Giants lineup behind Montefusco was set that afternoon with Madlock and Whitfield at the top of the order and Evans, McCovey, Clark, and Herndon in the middle. Shortstop Johnnie LeMaster and regular catcher Marc Hill were given the day off, as Vic Harris and Mike Sadek filled in for them. This was not much of an offensive drop-off, as none of those Giants catchers or shortstops could hit very much.

The Giants could do nothing against the future Hall of Famer Sutton for the first five innings and fell behind 3–0 as the Dodgers scored one in the third and two in the sixth. In the bottom of the sixth, a Whitfield double followed immediately by a single by Darrell Evans got the Giants on the scoreboard. McCovey struck out for the first out, but Evans could not score on singles by Clark and Herndon so the bases were loaded. Manager Altobelli now had a seal on every rock, with the light-hitting shortstop Vic Harris coming up. Altobelli had some options on the bench, but none of them were particularly good. Marc Hill and Johnnie LeMaster couldn't hit. Rob Andrews, who had filled in ably for Madlock when he was hurt, was not much better with the bat. Skip James was a left-handed hitter and so might have been an option, but he was on the team mostly to field and run for McCovey in the late innings and was only hitting .125 at that point in the season.

The best pinch hitter on the Giants bench, by far, was Ivie, but going to the best pinch hitter in the sixth inning would have left the Giants with no bats on the bench for the rest of the game. Moreover, Sutton was a righty, and Ivie was stronger against lefties. Orthodox baseball strategy suggested saving Ivie for an opportunity later in the game against left-handed Dodger relief ace Terry Forster. Despite this, the Giants manager decided to roll the dice with his best pinch hitter. Altobelli wanted to get those runs in and knew that the opportunity to get Ivie up against Forster in a big situation might never arise.

Candlestick Park was a pitcher's park, so when Ivie first connected it looked like he might just have a long sacrifice fly. Charles A. Fracchia Jr., who was at that game, describes what happened instead: "He nails that pitch over the fence. . . . The whole stadium rocks like it was an earthquake. The stadium shook. It was unreal. People hugging each other . . . such excitement. The only other time I've seen that much excitement [at Candlestick] was the 1989 playoffs."[8] Ivie had a huge grand slam, and the Giants had the lead

5–3. Few remember that the Dodgers tied the game right away in the top of the seventh, as Reggie Smith hit a two-run home run off a faltering Montefusco. Another Whitfield double followed by an Evans single in the eighth, however, gave the Giants the lead for good. Randy Moffitt pitched three scoreless innings of relief, giving the Giants a 6–5 win and a three-and-a-half-game lead over the third-place Dodgers and a one-and-a-half-game lead over the second-place Reds.

Ivie's grand slam was very early in the season to be considered a major highlight, but it was. I probably attended over two hundred games at the 'Stick, including the Giants' pennant-clinching game 5 against the Cubs in the 1989 National League Championship Series, to which Charles A. Fracchia Jr. alluded, and I never remember it being that loud. The crowd, at that time the largest to see a Bay Area big league game, was chanting "I-vie, I-vie" when the pinch hitter's name was announced. When Ivie connected, the drama only increased, because it was not clear the ball would go out. The collective ecstasy that followed was definitely unusual for a game in May, even a Giants-Dodgers one.

A home run—even a pinch-hit grand slam off a future Hall of Famer in a game between two historic rivals—that occurs in May for a team that ends up six games back in third place is rarely a truly memorable event. This one, however, was. Giants fans, myself included, may have reacted so excitedly to Ivie's grand slam because on some level we knew that 1978 was not the Giants' year. I was only ten years old, but it was evident to me that in the Giants' own division the Dodgers and Reds were better teams, and that in the American League East the Yankees and Red Sox, who ended up in a one-game playoff to decide what was probably the most exciting race of the four-division era, were probably better than any team in the National League. For these reasons, many of us had a sense of what was likely to happen over the next few months. Part of what made those months in first place in the summer of 1978 so exciting was precisely the knowledge that it wouldn't last, like a summer fling with that beautiful woman from school that you know will end when the richer, better-looking kids get back from vacation. Therefore, it was important to enjoy, even celebrate, every moment of it.

Perhaps it was something more than that—something to do with that moment for San Francisco. The excitement around Ivie's blast was an expression of hope that the young season would end well for this improbable first-place team, but most of us knew it would not. There was also a bit of misplaced optimism around the home run. Giants fans, particularly ones a few years or more older than me, who had seen the Giants miss out on the postseason for each of the last six years and go without a pennant for the previous fifteen years, had been disappointed by the Giants before. The 1978 Giants were a fun young team that seemed to hold much promise, but these older fans probably knew it couldn't last. Nonetheless, on that beautiful May day when the Giants were beating the Dodgers on the strength of a grand slam by a twenty-five-year-old slugger, all seemed right with our team and our city.

After the big win against the Dodgers that day, the Giants stood at 28–15, thirteen games above .500. With that victory, the Giants had begun to win back a city that had all but forgotten about them in the previous three or four years. In the middle of the following week, Herb Caen told his readers, "The team is indeed For Real. It's a miracle to see crowds at Candlestick. I walk a little straighter, knowing we is 'Numbah One!'"[9] None of us, not even Herb Caen, knew that game against the Dodgers would be the high point of the season. After beating the Dodgers in that series, the Giants went on to Houston, where they won the first two games of a three-game series to push their record to 30–15, good for a .667 winning percentage. That was the best percentage they would reach all season. From that point on they were 59–58, essentially a .500 team.

May 28 may have been the highlight of the year for San Francisco, as well as perhaps the most San Francisco day of the year. In addition to the dramatic Giants victory, thousands gathered downtown at the Civic Center Plaza for a rally supporting the Great San Francisco Marijuana Initiative, a ballot initiative instructing local law enforcement to stop arresting people for possessing, using, or growing small amounts of marijuana. The initiative, known as Proposition W, was approved by the voters but never honored by the police or city officials.

The rally, which included music and politics, was a reminder that in San Francisco the 1960s were alive and well. The band that headlined the rally was Moby Grape, an archetypical San Francisco band of the hippie era. One of the more well-known speakers that day was Paul Krassner, a journalist and writer most remembered for founding the magazine *The Realist* and for being one of the original Yippies. However, the rally was more than just a throwback to the previous decade. Leila and the Snakes, a punk band, also played the event. Other speakers included Assemblyman Willie Brown and Supervisors Carol Ruth Silver and Harvey Milk. These progressive politicians were placing themselves ahead of national views of marijuana, where legalization was still decades in the future, but in what was becoming mainstream opinion in San Francisco.

Another Giants Win and Another Warning

Probably the most notable thing about the Giants 2–1 victory over the Phillies in an afternoon game at the 'Stick on Wednesday, June 14, is that it lasted only 98 minutes. Those 12:30 midweek starts, usually on Wednesdays, were called "businessman's specials" back then. This conjured up an image of a businessman in a grey flannel suit sneaking out of his office at noon and returning at three or so after surreptitiously watching a baseball game and having a hot dog and a few beers for lunch. In the summers, however, those games drew mostly kids, some from day camps and others, like us, who went on their own.

The speed with which Vida Blue dismissed the Phillies made it possible for whatever businesspeople were among the crowd of just under 14,000 that day to indeed make it back to the office for a 3 P.M. meeting. Blue scattered five hits with only one walk and came within two outs of a complete game. However, after Blue gave up two hits with one out in the ninth, Altobelli brought in Randy Moffitt, who quickly struck out Philadelphia's two best hitters, Mike Schmidt and Greg Luzinski, to clinch the win for the Giants. Blue's record improved to 8–4 with a 2.60 ERA, making him one of the top pitchers in the National League with the season just more than a third over.

A few days earlier, readers of the *Sporting News* saw a cover that featured a beautiful shot of the Golden Gate Bridge with San Francisco in the background. In the foreground, clad in their orange Giants jerseys, were Bob Knepper and Jim Barr standing and Vida Blue and John Montefusco kneeling. The words "Prime Pitching" gave readers ideas of what the lead article might be. The *Sporting News* cover meant that the Giants' surprising run was becoming national news. The article lauded the Giants' excellent pitching, noting that ultimately the most important thing about the Giants was that "the team in game after game was winning and creating excitement in a city that some believed didn't care for anything except hippies and high-rollers."[10] That line summed up why many in the baseball world had not been hopeful about the future of baseball in San Francisco going into the 1978 season.

With that win over the Phillies, the Giants improved their winning percentage to .638, the best in the National League. The Reds were hanging tough as they trailed the Giants by only two games, but the Dodgers, despite beating the Mets that day, remained five games back and were beginning to look like they were on the periphery of the race. The Giants still lacked the firepower and the powerful hitting attack of the Dodgers or the Reds, but they were consistently finding ways to win. That Wednesday afternoon, the Giants had managed to win despite being held to four hits by Larry Christenson, a decent back-of-the-rotation pitcher, but nothing more. The Giants pitching, however, had been excellent.

That game against the Phillies occurred during the last week of school, so for those Giants fans who, like me, were children in 1978, it was a very good day. When attending games during that part of the season with the Giants stubbornly clinging to first place, we younger fans frequently heard older fans warning us of the inevitable "June swoon," which was occasionally followed by the even more ominous sounding "July die," but we were too young to be burdened by memories of the heartbreaking defeat in the 1962 World Series or the many second-place finishes in the 1960s, so we allowed ourselves a little hope.

On the same day that Vida Blue made such quick work of the Phillies, Deborah Layton, a former Peoples Temple member, sent a signed affidavit to several media and political figures. Layton had successfully fled the organization's outpost in Guyana only about a month earlier. Some of what she said in her affidavit was very troubling but not quite new information. Assertions such as "The Rev. Jim Jones gradually assumed a tyrannical hold over the lives of Temple members," or "The Rev. Jones saw himself at the center of a conspiracy," or "Rev. Jones insisted that Temple members work long hours and completely give up all semblance of personal life" were similar to what the Concerned Relatives had claimed a few months earlier. In that regard, Layton presented a chilling and frightening, if not altogether groundbreaking, vision of life in Jonestown.

Layton also described something called "White Nights" that occurred from time to time in Jonestown. It is an extraordinary coincidence that this term would be used in San Francisco almost a year later in reference to something other than Jonestown. However, in Guyana, "White Nights" were nighttime emergency meetings that were called by a panicked and paranoid Jones. These meetings sometimes took on morbid characteristics.

On page 9 of the eleven-page document, Layton made a very specific warning, one that seemed so outrageous that it was almost unbelievable. She asserted that Jones was planning to force all the residents of his embattled jungle encampment to kill themselves. Even to those who were concerned about what was occurring in Guyana, the idea that Jones was planning to become one of the worst mass murderers in history was probably hard to believe. To describe Layton's warning as prescient would be an understatement. In case the reader did not make it all the way to page 9, Layton and her attorney titled the document "Affidavit of Deborah Layton Blakey Re: The Threat and Possibility of Mass Suicide by Members of the Peoples Temple." Layton explained the basis for her warning:

> During one "white night," we were informed that our situation had become hopeless and that the only course of action open to us was a mass suicide for the glory of socialism. We were told that we would be tortured by mercenaries if we were taken alive. Everyone, including the children, was told to line up. As we passed through the line, we were given a small glass of red liquid to drink. We were told that the liquid contained poison and that we would die within 45 minutes. We all did as we were told. When the time came when we should have dropped dead, Rev. Jones explained that the poison was not real and that we had just been put through a loyalty test. He warned us that the time was not far off when it would become necessary of [for] us to die by our own hands.[11]

Layton had been a member of the Peoples Temple for seven years, had achieved a relatively high position within the organization, and had fled Guyana in a harried escape shortly before releasing this affidavit. This meant that she was in a position to know quite a lot about the Peoples Temple, but also that she may have had personal reasons for attacking Jones. Layton's complex relationship with the Peoples Temple partially explains why this affidavit, after being covered in a good-sized story in the *San Francisco Chronicle* the next day, was largely ignored for most of the summer.

In that *Chronicle* article, Layton's brother and sister, still in Jonestown, were quoted as saying, "These lies are too ridiculous to refute. . . . We are treated beautifully."[12] The author of that article was Marshall Kilduff. Kilduff was skeptical of the Peoples Temple, so although he, as a good journalist, sought those and other comments defending the Peoples Temple, the overall tone of his article suggested that something was, indeed, very wrong in Jonestown.

June 25: A Tale of One City

June 25 was a beautiful day for a ball game. The Giants were playing two that day, as they were home for a double-header against the last-place Braves. The Giants began the day three games ahead of the second-place Reds and hoped to sweep the Braves and increase their lead over both Cincinnati and Los Angeles. The first game was over relatively quickly. A couple of walks and two hits, including a two-run double by backup outfielder Jim Dwyer, gave the Giants a 3–0 lead in the bottom of the first. The Count was sharp that day, striking out eleven on his way to a complete game six-hitter. Home runs by Bill Madlock and Mike Sadek helped the Giants win a 9–3 laugher.

Until some point in the 1980s, doubleheaders were frequent events. They were usually scheduled on Sundays but occasionally on Friday evenings, when they were called "twilight doubleheaders." In those days, games were much shorter, so a doubleheader could easily be completed in under six hours if each game lasted roughly two and a half hours with half an hour between the games. The second game of the doubleheader that day went eleven innings, but the total time of the two games was still just six hours.

In game 2, starting pitcher Ed Halicki turned in a solid outing, giving up six hits and three runs in seven innings. Braves starter Mickey Mahler and a handful of relievers kept the Giants in check as the score after nine innings was 3–3. The Braves scored five runs while sending ten batters to the plate in the top of the eleventh and held back a Giants rally in the bottom of the frame to win 8–4. The Giants would have preferred to sweep the last-place team, but they nonetheless ended the day twenty games above .500 and two and a half games ahead of the second-place Reds. The Reds beat Los Angeles 5–4 that day, pushing the third-place Dodgers six games behind the Giants.

I don't remember if I went to the doubleheader that day. If I was in San Francisco, I probably did, but I don't save ticket stubs, and my memory is not that good. If I was there, I would have stayed to the end, enjoying a day of sun, baseball, and the warm hot dogs, stale popcorn, and flat soda that passed for food at ballparks during the 1970s. Although I would have been upset about the top of the eleventh in the second game, I would have left feeling good about the Giants and about San Francisco.

The real excitement in San Francisco that day did not occur at the ballpark but about three or four miles north and west of Candlestick Point in a very different neighborhood. The annual Gay Freedom Day parade, as it was known at the time, had been occurring since 1972, but this one was the biggest yet. Marchers would gather in the Castro and march down Market Street to the plaza outside of City Hall for speeches and a rally. The parade was front-page news in the next day's *San Francisco Chronicle* with an above-the-fold photo of the huge crowd and a headline that stated "240,000 at Gay Parade." The accompanying article opened, "There were, of course, the usual number of campy queens and the usual number of sternly disapproving tourists from Omaha.... But, hanging over it all for many gays who have seriously thought about their situation was the visage of Assemblyman John Briggs (Rep-Fullerton) and the hot Biblical rhetoric of Anita Bryant, the twin chief adversaries of the nation's homosexual rights movement."[13]

The article noted that the annual San Francisco event had been growing and becoming more important politically. Now for the first time ever, the parade was led by an out gay elected official. Technically Harvey Milk represented a few square miles in the center of San Francisco, but he was the councilman for all of gay America that summer and that day. Milk rode in the front of the parade on the top of a convertible with a lei around his neck, a big smile on his face, and a sign reading, "I'm from Woodmere, N.Y."

The parade was a celebration of growing gay political power. The community that had elected Milk the previous year had played a big role in electing Moscone in 1975 and was increasingly recognized as essential to any progressive San Francisco coalition. However, many gay people in San Francisco were also concerned about political attacks on their community by ambitious and bigoted politicians who saw antigay activism as a route to political power. The specter of Proposition 6—a statewide initiative and brainchild of a conservative Southern California legislator named John Briggs that would have made it legal to fire any teacher who was gay or even suspected of being gay—was on the minds of many marchers.

There was more to the parade than politics. It was also a celebration. Drag queens, muscle-bound gay men and women in all manner of costumes, scantily clad men and women enjoying the warm day, and people on motorcycles and roller skates were all part of the festivities. If you look carefully at photos of that day, or find some footage on YouTube, you will see a multicolored striped flag that is now almost universally recognized as the Pride flag. The San Francisco Gay Freedom Day parade of 1978 was likely the first time that flag was part of a public event.

McCovey and Clark

Five days after the historic Gay Freedom Day parade in San Francisco, the Giants found themselves playing the Braves in another doubleheader. This one was in Atlanta on a Friday. The Giants began the day three and a half games ahead of the Reds and five up on the Dodgers. The Braves, for their part, were in last place in the National League West, seventeen games behind the Giants. This seemed like a good opportunity for the Giants to build on their lead while beating up on the weakest team in their division. The Giants didn't quite manage to do that. Instead, they ended up losing three of four to the Braves, beginning by being swept on Friday night.

The first game of the doubleheader was one the Giants could have won. John Montefusco was shaky but effective in the first six innings, giving up only two runs, while the Giants scored six. However, The Count could not get an out in the seventh inning. The Braves scored four runs in both the seventh and the eighth to go ahead. The Giants scored three in the top of the ninth, but that wasn't enough as the Braves held on to win 10–9. Despite this tough loss, two Giants did important things in game 1.

The Braves started two lefties that day: Jamie Easterly in game 1 and Mickey Mahler in game 2. Platoons weren't always as strict in those days before big baseball data, so Joe Altobelli decided to give McCovey a start in one of the games rather than sit him for the whole day. Even though he was struggling at .224/.313/.396, McCovey was in his usual cleanup spot in game 1.

His great comeback season in 1977 notwithstanding, it was reasonably evident by early 1978 that McCovey was no longer the best candidate to bat fourth on the Giants. The best power hitters on that team were Jack Clark, Mike Ivie, and Darrell Evans, but McCovey was, and remains, San Francisco Giants royalty, so he usually batted cleanup. Additionally, the fans still loved McCovey and wanted to see him repeat his 1977 performance. As Matt Johanson and Wylie Wong succinctly put it, "No Giant was ever more popular than 'Stretch,' the lanky left-hander who routinely whacked baseballs over Candlestick Park's right field fence."[14] In 1978, McCovey started 113 games, batting cleanup in all but four of them. In those he batted fifth.

McCovey made his manager look smart that evening by hitting a home run to lead off the top of the second inning. That home run tied the game for the Giants, but more importantly it was the five-hundredth of the aging slugger's career. Today, largely because the steroid era sluggers of the 1990s and early 2000s racked up huge home run totals, there are twenty-seven members of the 500 home run club. Some of these players are not well remembered today, even though they retired just a few years ago. For example, only pretty intense fans know a lot about the careers of players such as Gary Sheffield or Rafael Palmeiro. However, when McCovey hit that shot off of Jamie Easterly, he became only the twelfth player in baseball history to reach five hundred home runs, so it was a much more significant event.

The powerful first baseman sought to downplay the importance of the home run: "I was anxious to get the 500th behind me because I was starting to have a lot of distractions. . . . That's why there was this sense of relief when I hit it. I really wasn't excited, but all my teammates came out of the dugout and acted as if we had just won the pennant or the World Series."[15] McCovey would never again be a great player, or even a good one, although he would have some big pinch hits as late as 1980, but that home run was significant for the franchise. It helped undo the damage from the 1972–1974 period when the Giants had traded or sold Mays, McCovey, and Marichal and gotten almost nothing in return. By severing their links to three of the greatest players in the franchise's San Francisco history, and in the case of Mays one of the greatest ever, the Giants' management alienated fans, did not meaningfully improve the team, and showed an ugly, callous side. Unlike Marichal and Mays, McCovey came back to San Francisco, thus giving younger fans a chance to see one of their team's legendary stars at the twilight of his career. John Maschino described what this meant to him and the close friend with whose family he attended many games in 1978: "Dave and I didn't get to see Mays play, but we got to see McCovey play. That was meaningful. We wish we could have seen both of them play, but at least we got to see one of them play and that was important."[16] Fans the age of Maschino and I had not seen McCovey at his best, but we had some sense of what he could do. That five-hundredth home run created a connection to the past for us younger fans because McCovey hit it not while bouncing around with the Padres or DHing for the A's, but while wearing the orange and black where he belonged.

Maschino further described what McCovey meant to Giants fans in 1977–1980, particularly to those of us who never had the chance to see Mays play:

Whenever I talk to friends of mine who are roughly my age and who grew up in San Francisco or Marin County or the Bay Area, . . . [McCovey's] the first person that's mentioned as a favorite player. Vida Blue will come up in that conversation too, but McCovey is the first one. I can think of several close friends right now off the top of my head who would tell you that Willie McCovey is their all-time favorite ballplayer, myself included. He looms larger than life. For me at the time, as someone who didn't know a lot yet about the history of the game, . . . McCovey obviously was this player who was much older and had a long track record, so when he came over, . . . here was this guy who had this resume, and I was just starting to pay attention to things like statistics and career records. . . . I know for sure I saw him hit several home runs that year. . . . Those were above and beyond in terms of exciting moments. My friend Dave and I lost our minds. He was such a hero.[17]

The historic home run by the aging franchise icon overshadowed an excellent day for Jack Clark. Going into the game, Clark was having a good year, hitting .303/.366/.521 with nine home runs in his team's first seventy-four games. Those were very good numbers for a twenty-two-year-old spending only his second full season in the big leagues and toiling for a team that played in a pitcher's park. They were good enough for Clark to draw a lot of attention around baseball, including a spirited write-in campaign for the All-Star Game. In July the *Sporting News* had recognized that "as the Giants began their climb to the top, Clark was stunning the ball and leading the way."[18]

Clark's first at bat in the first game of that doubleheader did not go well, as he grounded into a double play to end the first inning. Another ground out in the third inning, this time to first, suggested that this was not going to be a good game for the young right fielder. However, Clark led off the sixth with a solo home run to put the Giants ahead 2–1. After flying out in the seventh, Clark came up again in the ninth, this time with one aboard and his team trailing 10–7. Clark hit another home run to bring the Giants within one run, but then Jim Dwyer, who had pinch run for McCovey earlier, flew out to end the game. Clark hit yet another home run in the first inning of the second game of the doubleheader, which the Giants also lost. Three home runs and four RBIs is a good night even if your team gets swept, but Jack Clark was only just getting started.

Clark went on to hit safely in the Giants' next twenty-four games. The twenty-six-game hitting streak set a franchise record, for the post 1900 era, that still stands today. During this period Clark was perhaps the best hitter in baseball. He slugged .368/.420/.689 while driving in twenty-nine runs, more than one per game. The Giants had a 47–27 record, were twenty games above .500, and were in first place by two and a half games when the streak began, and they were 61–40 and in first place by two games when the streak ended. Clark's hot hitting kept the Giants in first place when the Dodgers and Reds were winning regularly. On July 26 when the streak ended, those teams were beginning to close in on the Giants. Without Clark's torrid slugging, the Giants would probably have been out of first place by mid-July.

Jack Clark had a long, and by most measures, very good big league career that took him, after he left the Giants, to the Cardinals, Yankees, Padres, and Red Sox. He retired with a career .267/.379/.476 slash line and 53.1 WAR. He hit 340 home runs in his career and was a four-time All-Star. At the time of his retirement, fewer than thirty players in history had drawn more walks than him. There are a handful of Hall of Fame sluggers who, like Clark, played outfield, first base, and DH, and who accumulated fewer WAR over the course of their careers, including Jim Rice, Orlando Cepeda, Ralph Kiner, Chuck Klein, and Hack Wilson. On balance, though, Clark did not have a Hall of Fame career, and he fell off the ballot after only one year of eligibility.

Although he had an excellent career and for many years was among the most productive hitters in the game, there was always a sense of disappointment around Clark, particularly while he was with the Giants. Much of this was because he would never again be as good as he was in 1978, when he was twenty-two. Clark struggled with injuries throughout his career, playing in 150 games or more in only three seasons, including 1978. His 5.9 WAR in 1978 was a career high. By more conventional measures, Clark's failure to improve after 1978 was also unmistakable. His .306 batting average in 1978 was the highest of any full year in his career. His 181 hits, 46 doubles, 318 total bases, and 15 stolen bases in 1978 were also career highs. In 1978, Clark looked like the kind of ballplayer around whom the Giants could build a contending team for the foreseeable future, but it didn't work out that way. Clark was a very valuable player the entire time he was with the Giants, but never as good as he was in 1978.

Clark played eight full seasons with the Giants, and parts of two others. From 1977 to 1984 he was a solid contributor in some years, a star in others, and he wrestled with injuries for most of 1984. During his almost decade long stint with the Giants, Clark was the team's best player, but his time with the Giants was complicated. Like many who are the best players on under-performing teams, Clark received more than his share of blame for the

Giants' failures. He was rarely booed by fans, but he was never universally beloved either. From 1977 to 1980, McCovey was by far the most popular Giant. By 1982, Chili Davis had supplanted Clark as the exciting symbol of the future.

Clark was an excellent hitter, but he was also a frustrating player for fans to watch, as he never seemed to stay healthy long enough to put that great season together. The closest he came was 1978, which was only his second full season in the big leagues. The slugging right fielder also never quite seemed to live up to his potential even when he was healthy. Although he was fast and had a powerful arm, he never made himself a great defender and eventually had to move to first base due to injuries. He also had occasional mental lapses, including in one game when he caught a fly ball for the out, tossed it to a fan, and began jogging into the infield before realizing it was only the second out of the inning. For some fans, including John Maschino, Clark's foibles only made him more human and thus more likeable: "The famous moment [was] Jack Clark forgetting how many outs there were in the outfield. Other players have done that. That's nothing new, but because Jack Clark did it ... everybody made fun of him ... but I think kind of in an endearing way, because that's the kind of thing Jack Clark would do. . . . It made it feel like Jack Clark is like us. These ballplayers are kind of super-human, but Jack Clark is a forgetful doofus, just like I am." Referring to 1978, Maschino added, "Ultimately Clark was the guy who drove that team offensively. . . . Clark, he was the man. . . . We loved him. We loved Clark. I remember being absolutely heartbroken, devastated several years later when he was traded away. I couldn't really forgive the team for that."[19]

During his time with the Giants, Clark never seemed happy or content. For most of the last three years or so he was with the team, trade rumors frequently swirled around him as did occasional, and misplaced, suggestions that he was not playing his best. Hank Greenwald, who announced Giants games for most of the time Clark was there, offered an explanation for why fans never cottoned to Clark and why the slugger rarely seemed happy with his role on the Giants: "Jack was always described as moody. . . . Jack was, to a large extent, misunderstood. Jack felt as long as he was here he was doomed to play on a club that was never going to win. And that bothered him. And he'd make comments about it. He really wanted to win. He'd get discouraged."[20] Glenn Dickey, the longtime *San Francisco Chronicle* writer, added that Clark was "a very interesting guy" whom Dickey appreciated because Clark would make his criticisms of Giants management, views that

Dickey shared, on the record. Dickey also added with a tone of understatement, "He was a good hitter."[21]

Questions about Clark's attitude arose early in his career as well. Some even attributed his excellent 1978 season to improvement in this regard. In a 1978 article with the straightforward title "Better Attitude Boosts Clark's Play as Giant," Nick Peters of the *Sporting News* wrote about Clark's 1977 season: "Not evident in the statistics were the grounders he would not run out and some languid play afield. He gave the impression of squandering his great potential and of not being mentally alert."[22] Another, more charitable interpretation of Clark's 1977 season was that at twenty-one years old he demonstrated that he could handle big league pitching by hitting .252/.322/.407 on a bad team in a pitcher's park, but many in the media, and indeed many Giants fans, never gave Clark that kind of benefit of the doubt.

Clark made his big league debut on September 12, 1975, when he was only nineteen. He pinch hit for catcher Mike Sadek in the eighth inning. Fittingly, Clark drew a walk and later came around to score on a single by Bobby Murcer. The Giants' shortstop that Friday night at the 'Stick, when they lost to the Reds 6–3, was Johnnie LeMaster, who was one for three with a single in his eleventh big league game. LeMaster and Clark remained teammates through the 1984 season. LeMaster did not become the regular shortstop until 1978, a year after Clark had become the everyday right fielder, but for seven years the two were teammates and starting players for some pretty bad Giants teams, as well as one or two good ones. The best team they ever played on was in 1978, while in 1984, their last year as teammates, the Giants finished in last place.

By the time the Giants traded Clark just as spring training of 1985 was beginning, rumors of Clark's departure had been growing more intense. The Giants shipped him to the Cardinals for a package of players that included David Green, Dave LaPoint, Gary Rajsich, and Jose Gonzalez. Gonzalez later changed his last name to Uribe. This was an excellent deal for the Cardinals, who got a middle-of-the-order slugger for several players who at best were useful but not standouts. For the Giants, it was a trade that seemed to be made more out of exasperation than anything else.

Green, LaPoint, and Rajsich never amounted to much with the Giants. Rajsich played terribly as a part-time outfielder in 1985 and never played for the Giants or any other big league team after that. LaPoint went 7–17 in 1985 for the Giants and stayed in the majors as a pretty unremarkable pitcher through 1991. Green didn't hit much in 1985 and was sent to the Brewers in a minor trade after the season. The best player the Giants got in the Jack Clark trade was Jose Uribe, who was their starting shortstop, more or less, from 1985 to 1991. Uribe never hit much, but he was a reliable, and sometimes excellent, fielder.

Uribe also made LeMaster expendable, so on May 7, 1985 after appearing in only twelve games for the Giants in the relatively young season, the longtime Giants shortstop was sent to the Indians for Mike Jeffcoat and Luis Quinones, who were fringe Giants players for one season each. Perhaps because at the time LeMaster was traded I was a high school senior a month or so away from graduation, it felt very much like the end of an era. The two players who captured the vibe of the Giants of my adolescence, essentially the years from 1978 to 1984 were Jack Clark and Johnnie LeMaster. The former was a very good player who somehow always seemed to disappoint, while the latter was an excellent reflection of the inept Giant teams of the era. In 1978, they had been symbols of what the future might hold for the Giants. It seemed fitting that they would be traded within a few months of each other and that they were the last significant players from that 1978 team to leave the Giants.

PLATE 1 Downtown San Francisco in 1978. (San Francisco History Center, San Francisco Public Library)

PLATE 2 George and Gina Moscone celebrating Moscone's 1975 election as mayor of San Francisco. (San Francisco History Center, San Francisco Public Library)

PLATE 3 A George Moscone for Mayor rally in 1975. (San Francisco History Center, San Francisco Public Library)

PLATE 4 George Moscone campaigning for mayor in 1975. (San Francisco History Center, San Francisco Public Library)

PLATE 5 Supervisor Harvey Milk with Muni general manager Curtis Green. Milk was an advocate for public transportation. (SFMTA Photo Archive | sfmta.com/photo)

PLATE 6   The San Francisco Board of Supervisors in 1978. Dianne Feinstein is in the center. Harvey Milk is first from the left in the back row. Next to Milk is Carol Ruth Silver. Next to Silver is Dan White. On the back of this photo are the words "San Francisco's 11 Supervisors don't often agree. But they all are united in urging you to vote NO ON PROPOSITION 6. 'Proposition 6 is so vaguely worded as to include not only homosexuals, but also all other school employees and include conduct which is private, legal or nothing more than a statement of opinion. It poses substantial constitutional questions and would result in severe restrictions on the right to privacy and free speech.' Board of Supervisors Resolution, June 19, 1978." (San Francisco History Center, San Francisco Public Library)

PLATE 7   Flowers left on the steps of City Hall in the days following the assassinations. (San Francisco History Center, San Francisco Public Library)

PLATE 8 Pier 39 in 1975 (left) and in 1978 (right). Pier 39 was an early part of the redevelopment of San Francisco's waterfront. (San Francisco History Center, San Francisco Public Library)

PLATE 9 Huge crowds turned out to Candlestick Park in 1978 whenever the Dodgers came to town. However, once the shade fell over a section, the temperature would drop very quickly. (© 2018 San Francisco Giants)

PLATE 10 The Giants traded for Vida Blue in spring training of 1978. Blue instantly became a fan favorite and was one of the best pitchers in the National League in 1978. (© 2018 San Francisco Giants)

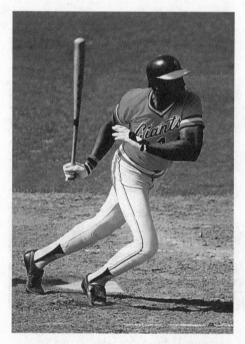

PLATE 11 Willie McCovey turned forty in January 1978. The great power-hitting first baseman is still one of the most beloved San Francisco Giants ever. (© 2018 San Francisco Giants)

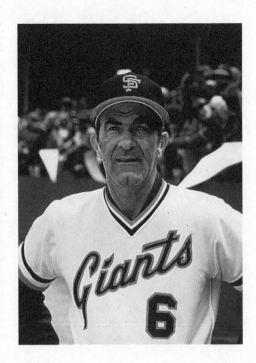

PLATE 12 Manager Joe Altobelli seemed to have the magic touch during the spring and summer of 1978 as he kept the team in first place until August. (© 2018 San Francisco Giants)

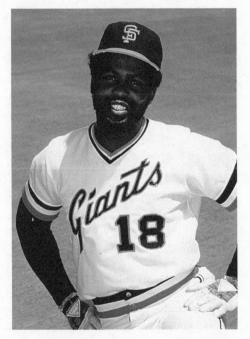

PLATE 13 Bill Madlock's moves to second base and the leadoff spot were instrumental in the Giants' strong 1978 season. (© 2018 San Francisco Giants)

PLATE 14 John "The Count" Montefusco was the Giants Opening Day starting pitcher in 1978. (© 2018 San Francisco Giants)

PLATE 15 In 1978 Jack Clark was the Giants best hitter and had a twenty-six-game hitting streak, a post-1900 franchise record that still stands. (© 2018 San Francisco Giants)

PLATE 16 Darrell Evans was a valuable and under-rated member of the 1978 Giants. (© 2018 San Francisco Giants)

PLATE 17 Mike Ivie provided Giants fans with one of the most exciting moments of 1978. Despite his talent, he never became a big league star. (© 2018 San Francisco Giants)

PLATE 18 Johnnie LeMaster was the Giants primary shortstop in 1978 but became a symbol of the team's struggles into the 1980s. (© 2018 San Francisco Giants)

PLATE 19 Terry Whitfield had a career year as the Giants left fielder in 1978. (© 2018 San Francisco Giants)

PLATE 20 Peoples Temple members in San Francisco packing crates of supplies to be sent to Jonestown. (Courtesy, California Historical Society CHS_052)

PLATE 21 Peoples Temple members working to build Jonestown. (Courtesy, California Historical Society CHS_066)

PLATE 22 Jim Jones with Peoples Temple members in Jonestown. The boy to the right of Jones is wearing a San Francisco Giants cap. (Courtesy, California Historical Society CHS_101)

PLATE 23 Jim Jones, second from right, hosting visitors in Jonestown. (Courtesy, California Historical Society CHS_167)

PLATE 24 Dead Kennedys, shown here performing in the early 1980s, are the band that is most remembered from San Francisco's 1970s punk scene. (San Francisco History Center, San Francisco Public Library. Photo: Greg Gaar)

PLATE 25 The Dils were among the most political bands in San Francisco's punk scene. (Special Collections and Archives, Merrill-Cazier Library, Utah State University)

PLATE 26 The Nuns and the Mutants were among several bands playing at the Mabuhay on October 21, 1978. (Special Collections and Archives, Merrill-Cazier Library, Utah State University)

PLATE 27 Crime was one of San Francisco's first punk bands. (Special Collections and Archives, Merrill-Cazier Library, Utah State University)

A DIRKSEN-MILLER PRODUCTION

Leila and the Snakes

MUTANTS plus LUCKY STIFFS

Thursday July 20TH 11PM

443 BROADWAY
SAN FRANCISCO **MABUHAY GARDENS**
TELEPHONE:
(415) 956-3315

TICKETS AND LATEST RECORD RELEASES AT AQUARIUS RECORDS (S F.)

PLATE 28 Leila and the Snakes headlined at the Mabuhay on July 20, 1978. (Special Collections and Archives, Merrill-Cazier Library, Utah State University)

BILL GRAHAM PRESENTS
THE CLOSING OF WINTERLAND

MASQUERADE BALL

THE **GRATEFUL DEAD**

THE **BLUES BROTHERS**

FEATURING JOLIET JAKE AND ELLWOOD BLUES

NEW RIDERS OF THE PURPLE SAGE

BREAKFAST AT DAWN

NEW YEAR'S EVE SUNDAY DECEMBER 31 · 8 PM

TICKETS: $30 PLUS SERVICE CHARGE. THERE WILL BE NO PHONE ORDER FOR THIS SHOW.

THE GRATEFUL DEAD ARE ALSO PLAYING AT THE PAULEY PAVILION UCLA ON DECEMBER 30TH
TICKETS AVAILABLE AT BASS

PLATE 29 On December 31, 1978, the Grateful Dead played the last concert ever at Winterland. (Design by Randy Tuten, Courtesy Special Collections, University Library, University of California Santa Cruz, Grateful Dead Records)

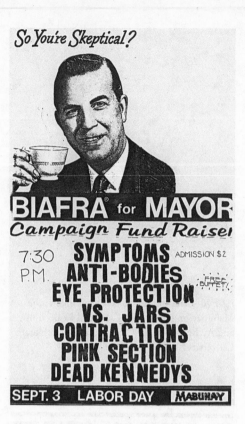

So You're Skeptical?

BIAFRA® for MAYOR

Campaign Fund Raiser

7:30 P.M.   ADMISSION $2

SYMPTOMS
ANTI-BODIES
EYE PROTECTION
VS. JARS
CONTRACTIONS
PINK SECTION
DEAD KENNEDYS

FREE BUFFET!

SEPT. 3   LABOR DAY   MABUHAY

PLATE 30 Dead Kennedys headlined an event at the Mabuhay to raise money for Jello Biafra's 1979 mayoral campaign. (Special Collections and Archives, Merrill-Cazier Library, Utah State University)

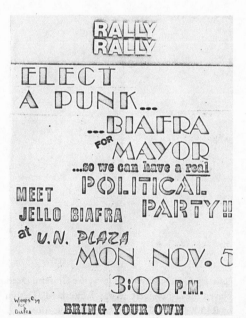

RALLY
RALLY

ELECT
A PUNK...
...BIAFRA
FOR MAYOR
...so we can have a real
POLITICAL
MEET PARTY!!
JELLO BIAFRA
at U.N. PLAZA
MON NOV. 5
3:00 P.M.
WIMPS 79
BIAFRA
BRING YOUR OWN

PLATE 31 A flyer for an election-eve rally for Jello Biafra's 1979 mayoral campaign. (Special Collections and Archives, Merrill-Cazier Library, Utah State University)

6

The Band Is Called What?

● ●

When the Sex Pistols, the signature band of the British punk scene, broke up following their San Francisco concert in January 1978, punk rock entered a new era. The Clash, who went on to become the best of all punk rock bands, had not yet released an album in the United States, so there was no natural successor to the Sex Pistols. It was the moment for U.S. punk, the rumblings of which had become hard to ignore by 1978. Already bands like the Avengers were gaining some fame and followings in the Bay Area, but in early 1978 American punk rock was still primarily based in New York. Early New York punk bands like Richard Hell and the Voidoids, Television, and the Dictators were reasonably well known in that scene, but the best known of all the American punk rock bands at that time was the Ramones. While the Ramones were a great band that played fast-tempo catchy tunes and helped create the American punk rock gestalt and aesthetic, they were also very much a New York band. The Ramones had their roots in Queens, made their mark at CBGB's, and had a distinctively New York feel and sound. This left an opening for San Francisco's punk rock movement, with its more political feel and West Coast vibe, to become more visible and significant in the broader American context.

The Sex Pistols, who until they broke up were by far the most recognized punk band, had often been as much about marketing as about music, beginning with the name itself. The Sex Pistols always sounded like a name that had come from a Malcolm McLaren–sponsored focus group or company meeting. You can almost picture McLaren throwing names around that combined sex and guns, two ideas that always sell. Other ideas might have been "Whoopie Guns," "Shag Muskets," "Shtup Uzis," or "Screw Rifles."[1] On balance, "Sex Pistols" was a great name for a punk rock band. It got people's attention, sounded just intimidating enough, was memorable, and, because of the word "sex," had some real shock value.

But it did not have the power or shock value of Dead Kennedys, the San Francisco band that was coming together around the time the Pistols played Winterland for the last time. It is difficult to imagine the effect the Dead Kennedys' name had in 1978. People who knew nothing about punk rock, or even popular music at all, were outraged and offended at the name Dead Kennedys. It was the kind of thing conservative San Franciscans in their thirties and older talked about as a sign of the youth apocalypse. Joel Selvin, the longtime *San Francisco Chronicle* music critic, told me Dead Kennedys had "absolutely the most offensive possible name."[2] What made the name so uniquely distasteful was that rather than simply use profanities or sexual or violent images, Dead Kennedys went right to the heart of something so many good liberals, as well as Catholics, held sacred. Dead Kennedys started their musical journey fewer than fifteen years after the assassination of President Kennedy and only a decade after the murder of his brother Robert. Those memories were fresh, particularly among liberal Democrats and, in the case of Bobby Kennedy, the hippies that were about half a generation older than Dead Kennedys and their punk rock fans.[3]

When I spoke with Dead Kennedys guitarist East Bay Ray in 2017, he conceded that the band's name was in poor taste, but he also said that "the assassinations were in much more poor taste than our band." He explained further: "We actually respect the Kennedy family. . . . When JFK was assassinated, when Martin Luther King was assassinated, when RFK was assassinated, the American Dream was assassinated. . . . Our name is actually homage to the American Dream."[4]

Dead Kennedys were distinctly Northern California and helped put a Bay Area imprint on punk rock. They played San Francisco all the time, frequently appearing at free concerts, particularly those with a political agenda, such as the Rock against Reagan concerts in the 1980s. Their guitarist was Raymond Pepperell. He was from Oakland and had attended UC Berkeley, so naturally he was known as East Bay Ray. To fans in other parts of the country, this probably just sounded cool, but every kid in San Francisco knew what this meant. Most of us had a friend or two who lived in Oakland, Berkeley, or somewhere else in the East Bay and who had to confront the ongoing hassle of getting to the city for shows, borrowing BART fare back, needing a place to crash many nights, and the like.

Dead Kennedys were not the only San Francisco punk rock band around in 1978, but they are the one most remembered today. Dead Kennedys played their first concert at the Mabuhay Gardens in July 1978. By that time, the Mab had already been the hub for San Francisco's nascent punk rock movement for over a year. Dead Kennedys went on to play the Mabuhay frequently in 1978 and in later years as well. On November 22, 1978, in the middle of a month that would turn out to be one of the most important in modern San Francisco history, Dead Kennedys observed the fifteenth anniversary of President John Kennedy's assassination by playing the Mab. This prompted outrage, which was summed up best by the longtime *San Francisco Chronicle* columnist Herb Caen, who understood the cultural complexity of the city better than most. Caen's comments reflected the consensus in San Francisco, and probably nationally, of everybody over about the age of forty: "Just when you think tastelessness has reached its nadir, along comes a punk rock group called the Dead Kennedys which will play at Mabuhay Gardens on Nov. 22, the 15th anniversary of John F. Kennedy's assassination. Despite mounting protests, the owner of Mabuhay Gardens says 'I can't cancel them NOW—there's a contract.' Not, apparently, the kind of contract some people have in mind."[5]

For years now, nose rings, unnaturally colored hair, torn clothes, and other remnants of the early days of punk rock fashion have been mainstream. In most major cities, nobody looks twice at a sixty-something professional with a few piercings and an interesting haircut and hair color, but at the beginning of the punk rock era things were very different. When I spoke with Penelope Houston, who had been the lead singer of the Avengers, she described the reaction to unnaturally dyed hair in San Francisco in the early years of punk: "I dyed my hair peacock blue [in 1977], and people would just stop in the streets and their mouths would fall open."[6] Jello Biafra, the lead singer of Dead Kennedys, expressed a similar sentiment about that period during a 2018 interview: "Punk was just exploding . . . [and] scaring the shit out of all the right people."[7] Punk reveled in its newness and ability to shock and was always more oriented toward becoming an all-encompassing movement for a few, rather than a broad trend for the many. Central to being a punk in San Francisco in 1978 was the idea of doing something dramatic to your appearance that made you stand out, and frequently draw hostile attention, in other communities. This forced punks to look to each other for support and to be careful about their interactions with the larger city.

The generational appeal of punk was also very important. The kids that embraced punk rock were half a generation younger than the hippies and about half a generation older than the young people who, in the twenty-first century, helped turn San Francisco into a global center of tech and innovation. In a baseball parallel, our generation was also too young to have seen Mays and McCovey slugging in their prime, but we were well into adulthood by the time our Giants won three World Series between 2010 and 2014. Even in 1978, part of our anger was because the generation before us still dominated the culture with boring stories of the Summer of Love and even of Willie Mays.

Additionally, while hippies may have been freaks in 1967, and remained outside the establishment in some parts of the country as late as 1978, in San Francisco it was different. If you were an adolescent in San Francisco in 1978 or a few years later, hippies were the authority figures. The bus driver who looked at you with disdain because of your haircut or clothes often had a ponytail and a beard. The schoolteacher who told you to sit down and sit still wore a peasant blouse and ate sprouts for lunch. The couple walking behind you in Golden Gate Park that looked at you with a little fear because of your black leather jacket smelled of patchouli and reminisced about the Summer of Love. This meant that to rebel against authority and the failures of the system also meant to rebel against the newly formed hippie establishment.

Moreover, for many San Franciscans, even those with progressive political ideas who had no problem with long hair and hippie culture generally, punk rock was perceived as genuinely menacing. Concerts were covered in the media as violent events. The leather, chains, and studs that punks wore looked dangerous, and punks were viewed as capable of erratic, even violent, behavior. Joseph Torchia captured, and in fact fed, this fear of punk rock in an article in January 1978:

> Swearing and spitting, bleeding and hitting the audience with violence as well as vibrations, masochism as well as music—it's all part of a new wave of rock 'n' roll that one man has called rock 'n' raunch. They call themselves the Sex Pistols or the Nuns or the Mutants or the Weirdos or any name that will

conjure up the decadent, the perverse, the violent, the grotesque yet carefully groomed image they thrive on. . . . "Punk" said one black-eyed teenager at the recent Sex Pistols Concert. "If you don't get the f—out of my way, I'll show you what Punk is."[8]

Interestingly, despite writing a piece that sounds like it could have been written by Archie Bunker after taking the wrong subway from Queens and ending up at CBGB's, Torchia gives the last line of the article to a punk woman he interviewed at the Sex Pistols concert on January 14. The woman offers a definition of punk that is a great summary of the vibe of early punk rock in San Francisco and punk rock in general: "'You want to know what punk is?' she yelled. 'I'll tell you what punk is—it's something you'll never understand! It's something the media will never be able to explain! It's loud and it's rough and it's hot and it's violent and sexual and it's me,' she said. 'It's goddamn ME.'"[9]

Torchia was not the only person in the media who presented punk to readers and viewers as something menacing that threatened to draw their children into a maelstrom of violence, drugs, and danger. Michael Fox, a mainstay in the punk rock scene in the late 1970s and beyond, remembered how the media portrayed punks as "a bunch of people who just want to beat up each other, and it's just horrific."[10] Ginger Coyote, whose work in punk rock includes being part of the band White Trash Debutantes beginning in the late 1980s and being the longtime editor of the punk publication *Punk Globe*, shared a similar recollection: "Television was making it [punk] shock . . . sensationalism." Coyote also pointed out that this coverage had the unanticipated effect of "creating a buzz, which made people want to go and see it."[11] Coyote's recollection captures something vital about those early days of punk. The media efforts to portray it as something shocking, ugly, and threatening worked with parents and even with many kids, but many other young people were drawn to punk precisely because it felt shocking, ugly, and threatening. By 1978, much of the music scene could not be described that way. Crosby, Stills, and Nash may have been fine singers, but there was nothing threatening or empowering about going to one of their shows and running into your parents' friends, or singing a Grateful Dead tune to yourself and hearing your moderately cool English teacher sing along for a few beats. Those bands may have been youthful and rebellious in the 1960s, but by 1978, and into the 1980s, they were part of the establishment, musical and otherwise.

One of those kids drawn to punk was Jennifer Blowdryer, who was a high school student in Berkeley when she first encountered punk rock sometime around 1976 or 1977. In her 1997 memoir, *White Trash Debutante*, Blowdryer, whose name is taken from her first band, Jennifer and the Blowdryers, described the pull that punk had for her and many like her and how attending shows as a teenager made her feel: "The important thing was that I was not at high school. Instead of trying to fit in with a disdainful and far more attractive peer group, I was in a huge room full of oddly dressed people who were focusing not on me or something I didn't understand, but on a ridiculous and malicious stage act I adored. I was hooked."[12] When I met with Blowdryer in a café in New York's East Village, she recalled her first experience with punk forty years earlier: "I think I saw an article. My big sister had *Creem* magazine, and I just knew that I had to get there. I was underage. I didn't have any money. I'd have to take a bus to get in. It was like a magnet to me, punk rock. Wherever it was, I had to go there."[13] Jello Biafra's reflection that "99 percent of the punk rockers back then, we were kinda outcasts even from other outcasts back then ... [and] we had a passion for this fresh, new, and super-high-energy primal kind of music,"[14] also demonstrates that punk wasn't for everybody but that some young people got it right away and found themselves becoming increasingly drawn to a movement that was much bigger than just the music.

Disco was also an important part of the music of the time, particularly among African American and gay San Franciscans, but despite its important role in the culture, many thought it lacked the edginess and anger of punk. Ginger Coyote described her own views on disco and punk: "After a while, you get sick of hearing 'Love to Love You Baby' and all that crap on the radio, so you're really happy that there's something that's coming in that's driving, that's got some energy, that's got some force."[15] Disco fit into San Francisco differently than the rock of the period because of its appeal to gays and African Americans, and it was a much more radical and groundbreaking genre than was recognized at the time, although its radical attributes fueled much of the "Disco sucks" backlash throughout a large segment of white straight youth culture at the time. Nonetheless, most of those who found their way to punk understood disco as Coyote described it and did not see it as a significant enough break from the arena rock, glam rock, and stadium rock that was dominating the airwaves.

When Penelope Houston and I spoke in an East Bay café in 2017, she described the incident that drove her to become a punk singer: "My friends were putting a band together, and they had a warehouse South of Market. They had a PA set up. . . . I put some records on, and I started singing along. And I was like, 'Ahhh, I'm so f**king loud. This is incredible.' They came back. I said, 'I'm your singer.' . . . They let me join."[16] In the rock and roll version of this story, the other band members or somebody from the industry hears the singer and recognizes her great voice, but in punk rock things were different. Houston was not excited about how good she sounded, but by how loud she was. The band members did not invite her to join; she announced her intention and they agreed. However, Houston was not merely a loud singer; she was a very good one too, bringing irreverence, anger, and energy to her music. John Gullak echoed the antimusicianship feel of the early punk rock days. His remark that "I'm not a musician, but I play one in the Mutants" sounded self-deprecating when he said it to me in a 2018 interview, but his admission that when the band started in 1977 he "couldn't play an instrument" was an accurate reflection of his musical background at the time.[17]

One of the major ways in which Bay Area punk rock was different from punk in New York, London, or even other American cities like Chicago and Los Angeles was that it was more explicitly political. Bands such as Dead Kennedys, the Avengers, the Dils, Verbal Abuse, and Code of Honor sung more about radical politics and criticism of the conservative movements that grew into Reaganism in the 1980s than did their East Coast, Southern California, or London cohorts, who frequently had more of an angry, nihilistic feel. This was particularly true in the late 1970s.

One of the reasons that San Francisco punk was more political was because of its distance from New York or Los Angeles. As Howie Klein described it to me in 2018, "No matter how cool you were, you're in f**kin' New York, you're in f**kin' LA, and you're looking to the industry. San Francisco didn't have that. There was something about San Francisco that was devoid of the industry. People weren't trying to kiss up to record executives."[18] Henry S. Rosenthal, the Crime drummer made a similar point, describing Los Angeles punk as "very different from here [San Francisco]." He continued: "The bands that came out of LA we perceived as being more commercial, poppy, less politically engaged, less authentic."[19]

The political ethos of San Francisco's punk rock movement was not just expressed through the lyrics of the Dils, Dead Kennedys, the Avengers, or myriad other local bands. Even in 1978, punks got involved in progressive political causes. This included the rare foray into electoral politics, such as the "Nix on Six: Save the Homos" event at the Mabuhay Gardens to oppose Proposition 6, at which the emcee was Harvey Milk, or Dead Kennedys singer Jello Biafra's 1979 mayoral campaign, as well as direct action and providing support for other progressive activists. San Francisco punks also raised money for striking coal miners and took positions on local issues—for example, standing with the elderly Asian American residents of the International Hotel who were being evicted so that the hotel could be torn down. Rosenthal explained to me how "it was different here, because these bands who took on a political bent and decided to get involved in things like the coal miners' strike and 'No on Six' and all that stuff. There were these local issues . . . that the bands latched onto [and] drove that process."[20]

In mentioning the punk involvement in the coal miners' strike, Rosenthal was referring specifically to a big benefit concert to raise money for striking miners in states such as Kentucky, Ohio, and West Virginia, so it was not so much a local issue. The concert was held at the Mab on March 20, 1978, during the same period that the board of supervisors was voting on Harvey Milk's gay rights ordinance. The concert at the Mab featured an extraordinary lineup of some of the best bands in San Francisco's punk scene at the time, including the Avengers, the Dils, the Mutants, Negative Trend, the Nuns, and Tuxedomoon. Tickets were cheap, $4.00 in advance and $4.50 at the door, so it is not likely the benefit raised much money, but it demonstrated a commitment on the part of the punks that went well beyond their own interests or political battles. Alejandro Escovedo, the guitar player for the Nuns, made the connection for the benefit of a reporter from the *San Francisco Bay Guardian*: "When you read about the coal miners' strike, you start to think it's the miners' fault, not the owners'. We're combating the same thing in the media problem. The whole punk thing has been totally warped by the media."[21]

Michael Stewart Foley argues that the San Francisco punk scene was uniquely political: "By the time Dead Kennedys started playing the Mabuhay in the summer of 1978, San Francisco had established itself as the most political punk scene in the country. . . . No other scene saw punks joining with other activist groups to fight evictions of people who were decidedly not punks. No other scene saw punks holding benefits for striking Kentucky miners, striking railroad workers, falsely convicted Black Panther Geronimo Pratt, the 'No on 6' campaign, the city's Gay Day Parade."[22] This is one of the major ways in which the punk scenes in San Francisco and New York differed. San Francisco punk rock veered more toward the politically radical and away from the more generalized nihilism of the New York scene. Scott Stalcup's assertion is accurate regarding the scene on the East Coast, but much less so regarding San Francisco: "Another difference between British and American punks was the American bands' disdain for taking any political stance. . . . Those on the East Coast looked inside and saw nothing. Their message was not of peace and love, but of boredom and frustration."[23]

The miners' benefit was both a major way that San Francisco punk distinguished itself from punk in other cities and a significant event in San Francisco's punk rock community. Many of the best Bay Area punk bands played at the event. Dead Kennedys were not on the bill, but that is presumably because they had not played anywhere yet. Because so many good bands were part of the benefit, more bands wanted to be part of it, and naturally everybody who was a punk wanted to go to the concert. To a great extent, punk in San Francisco became and remained politicized because the top bands were political. As Klein observed, "If you wanted to be one of the cool kids and you wanted to be part of it, you had to be on that miners' benefit thing. . . . That seems like a San Francisco kind of thing where politics are very cool."[24]

While punk in San Francisco was more political than in other places, it still had elements of the anger and frustration with the larger culture that characterized the movement elsewhere as well. Punk rockers of that era were far from being earnest progressives working dutifully for social change. Most would have chafed violently at being described that way. Their politics were a kind of high-energy, left-of-center anarchism not overly burdened by a deep understanding of political history or theory. Alex Ogg described punk politics as "restrained hysteria reminiscent of Jonathan Swift."[25] In a 1978 interview with Howie Klein in *BAM (Bay Area Music)*, Tony Nineteen of the Dils, a band that was originally from Southern California but nonetheless an important part of the San Francisco scene in the late 1970s, captured the radicalism, grandiosity, and anger that drove punk politics: "What we see as the over-riding political characteristic of punk is a means to threaten every existing form of order—musically, socially, politically. Punk has to move from a stance of mindless, stupid outrage to a threat. . . . It's not good if it doesn't challenge anything and change anything."[26]

Forty years later, Michael Fox summarized the politics of punk to me in a somewhat similar manner, describing his goals as the primary songwriter for Code of Honor: "I was interested in bringing up some important questions. I didn't know how to fix things, but I believed if people got together and participated, to change things . . . without the fascist system smashing us or ending us . . . that was a big deal. I never had an answer really, but we were exploring the questions. . . . The punks didn't really have an answer other than "Pull your f**king big boy pants on and participate, and maybe we can change this ridiculous fascist country that's bombing three different countries and women and children every day that I've been alive."[27]

Biafra described how the approach not just to punk politics but to punk sensibilities merged in a way that differed sharply from that of the 1960s: "If I'm gonna do an antinukes song, the last thing we need is another 'Boohoo, nuclear war is bad' song. . . . What about doing a song from the villain's point of view? So from the military-industrial complex there was [Dead Kennedys' song] 'Kill the Poor.'"[28] Fox, Nineteen, and Dead Kennedys shared a punk rock politics that was part left-wing, part political paranoia, part anger at hippies, always stream of consciousness, and, while usually weird, frequently compelling. This led to many young people in San Francisco, and later elsewhere, being radicalized by the Dils, the Avengers, MDC (Millions of Dead Cops), and most frequently, Dead Kennedys.

Chris Carlsson, who moved to San Francisco from Sonoma County at the end of 1977 as a young adult, describes how punk in those years was "part of a much longer and strongly politicized culture that flourished in San Francisco during the mostly forgotten interregnum between what we might call the 'the long sixties' and the Reagan restoration." Carlsson adds, "Dozens of songs left little doubt about the repudiation and refusal at the heart of the radical subculture during the time."[29]

In one of the first interviews Dead Kennedys ever gave, with the influential San Francisco punk rock magazine *Search and Destroy*, even forty years later you can almost hear the manic tone in Biafra's voice as he skips from topic to topic while never being boring. In response to the first question about the song "Kepone Kids," Biafra explains that Kepone is "a chemical poison that was manufactured in this plant in Virginia that took no safety precautions, so it got dumped all over Chesapeake Bay so they can't fish there now and the people that worked there breathed it into their lungs and it spread over their bodies and they all have double vision & gnarled arms."[30]

Biafra then follows with an extraordinary riff connecting Lenin's Tomb in Moscow with efforts to profit from the death of Elvis Presley: "Of course, it's always easier to sell a dead horse than a living one. Slowly becoming Leninized, like in Russia, they have the government's favorite hero preserved so you can go look at the corpse.... Now we have things in the *National Enquirer* like Win Elvis' Ring. Enter Now. No obligation!!!"[31]

From there Biafra spends the rest of the interview talking about hippies and the failures of the 1960s, and he notes, "Nixon almost became dictator of America, but he wasn't quite clever enough—too flaky. [Jerry] Brown seems to have more control. You'll never see him pull a Checkers speech-type con!"[32] Most of those claims are either unsubstantiated, wacky, or just don't make much sense, but if you were a sixteen-year-old in San Francisco in the waning years of the 1970s or the early Reagan era, they were exciting and could easily leave you questioning everything, particularly all the things your conservative family or hippie teachers had told you.

Dead Kennedys were not the only punk band to sing about politics or wrestle with the legacy of the Kennedys. The Avengers, a stalwart of the punk rock scene in San Francisco for years, opened for the Sex Pistols at the latter's last show at Winterland. Perhaps the most well-known Avengers song was "The American in Me":

> It's the American in me that makes me watch the blood running out of the
> bullet hole in his head.
> It's the American in me that makes me watch TV see on the news, listen what
> the man said.
> He said, "Ask not what you can do for your country what's your country been
> doing to you?
> Ask not what you can do for your country what's your country been doing to
> your mind?"[33]

This song alludes to President Kennedy's famous challenge to young Americans in his 1961 inaugural address. The "blood" and the "bullet hole" refer to the images of the president's assassination that almost every American adult in 1978 would have seen at some point. Additionally, in the song's last verse, Houston sings, "It's the American in me that never wonders why Kennedy was murdered by the FBI."[34] Thus, one of the leading San Francisco punk bands was named, in large part, after the late president, and another's most famous song was about him. It is not hard to see why for a generation with no appetite left for the idealism of their parents or older siblings but who still held left-of-center political views, John Kennedy would have been a complex and intriguing figure.

Old Hippies, New Punks, and the City

Punk rock in San Francisco, as in many cities in the United States, the United Kingdom, and elsewhere, arose from the ashes of the failures of the midcentury growth model of urban politics and of the failure of what was generally characterized as the softer, peace-and-love, back-to-nature movements of the hippies. It is also no coincidence that punk rock grew out of a San Francisco from which manufacturing had left and where the population was at its postwar nadir. While a handful of venues such as the On Broadway, the Tool and Die, and the Mab are now frequently celebrated as the most important punk rock clubs of the time, it was the many empty or abandoned spaces in different parts of the city where punk rock really occurred. Squats in South of Market; a social club for deaf people in the Mission district; low-rent shared houses in Potrero Hill; an abandoned synagogue known as the Temple Beautiful that was on Geary Street next door to the Peoples Temple; empty warehouses; and other cheap spaces that had once been central to the hippie movement were all home to shows, shared living spaces, and even record release parties during the early days of punk rock.

In this respect, the San Francisco of the mid-1970s was like much of urban America. The Lower East Side of Manhattan, where the first U.S. punk scene appeared, economically depressed areas of Chicago, and similar cheap and sparsely populated neighborhoods in other big cities were where punk rock was happening. In the mid-1970s, punk was beginning to take root in many American cities because they all shared these traits. San Francisco back then looked a lot like many other cities suffering the effects of a declining industrial economy. Many cities saw the beginnings of punk rock during this period, but in San Francisco punk turned out a little differently.

Joe Dirt, formerly of Society Dog and the F**kups, recounted a story to me about rehearsing in "a great warehouse on Powell Street right near Fisherman's Wharf." He continued: "A sandwich shop moved in upstairs, and they had the circuit breakers. There was this one song in our set that had the word "f**k" in it, and every time . . . when we got to that one word, they turned the electricity off and then we couldn't play anymore. You would think that we would figure it out and skip the word, but we never did that." Dirt also recounted how punks "were the outsiders" in the San Francisco of that time: "They wouldn't let us play. . . . We started playing in some of these underground places like the Hellhole in the Tenderloin. . . . The Hellhole was a basement of a grocery store. . . . Some Asian dude owned it, and he was cool with the young people."[35]

In his book on Dead Kennedys, Alex Ogg argues, "San Francisco was a natural crucible for punk. For years it had been synonymous with liberal thought . . . and in the 60s became a magnet to the beats and base camp for the Summer of Love. It also had working class districts. . . . [It was] a haven, then, for weirdos, hippies and eccentrics as well as more rational left-leaning thinkers."[36] This description is not inaccurate, but an equally important part of punk's origins in San Francisco was that the late 1970s was a moment when San Francisco's weak economy, and corresponding low cost of living, could nurture a movement like punk.

The punk rock politics of the San Francisco scene in general, and Dead Kennedys in particular, were not simply opposition to racism, sexism and, in the language of the time, fascism; they were also in opposition to the hippies and their politics. From the outside it may have seemed strange for a band to sing about fighting racism in one song and hating hippies in the next, but from the floor of the Mab, or the On Broadway one floor up, it made pretty good sense.

Jeff Goldthorpe, who was an early adherent of punk rock in San Francisco in the late 1970s, describes this tension between punk rockers and the hippies that were half a generation older:

> Like most of their peers, first wave California punks grew up with rock and roll and sixties counter-culture. Punk style was both an ironic-celebratory funeral anthem for white youth's particular effort to change the world and an attempt to clear new symbolic space for an oppositional cultural stance. This space was impossible to create as long as the decaying, media-packaged sixties experience set the parameters of activity. Thus, American punk can best be understood as an energetic annihilation of the leftover hippie-new age-liberal-stadium rock symbolism.[37]

Rosenthal captured the relationship between punk and the hippies that preceded them similarly, in an interview in his South of Market home in 2017: "The feeling was that the hippie movement had somehow failed, and that judging by Haight Street it had just fallen into decay. While the utopian vision maybe was shared by the punk community, it was a different one. The punk community . . . was about taking a more aggressive stance towards everything. The vestiges of the hippie movement were laying on the sidewalks around town and didn't make much of a case."[38] The sad end of much of the 1960s that Rosenthal identified, particularly in San Francisco, contributed to the punk ethos as well. Jello Biafra alluded to this as well in a 2018 interview, stating that "because of the cynicism of the burning out of some of the good stuff of the 60s, punks were way cynical and way angry."[39]

John Gullak, the guitar player for the Mutants, another punk rock band of that era, expressed a similar view to Rosenthal's, albeit somewhat more charitably: "By the '70s, the hippie movement . . . wasn't really relevant anymore. It wasn't pushing any boundaries. It had become very comfortable with itself and completely taken over by commercialism, so the punk mood was, in a sense, a reaction to that to kind of shake things up again."[40] Jack Boulware, co-author of *Gimme Something Better*, offered the perspective of a younger person growing up in the shadow of the hippies: "If you were younger and tired of the hippie generation telling you what to do and constantly dispensing advice, this is what you get. You get punk rock. It [the hippie movement] is the antithesis of punk rock."[41]

For Jennifer Blowdryer, who is a little younger than Rosenthal or Gullak, this sentiment was part generational and part aesthetic. She recounted to me an anecdote about a therapist to whom her mother had sent her that led her to write a song called "Berkeley Farms," which mocked hippie sensibilities:

Eat lots of granola and brown rice.
Never be mean. Always be nice.
I cried about Wounded Knee.
If I was there, they could've shot me.
My Birkenstocks are the tops.
They're the only shoes I wear.
To be tasteful, I wouldn't dare.
Then I couldn't go to Berkeley.
They wouldn't take me there.

Blowdryer also told me that her disdain for hippies in the late 1970s was partly aesthetic: "[They had] that kind of grubby look. I just didn't care for it. . . . I remember Alvin [Orloff] took me to see a Grateful Dead documentary, and I said, 'Don't you know, this is just not it,' and I played him some

Blondie and Ramones."[42] A Los Angeles band, the Deadbeats, expressed this sentiment most directly in a song with the not very subtle title "Kill the Hippies." The song itself was more sophisticated than the title suggests and also offered a critique of punk intolerance.

A similar anti-hippie sentiment was summarized in one of Dead Kennedys' most famous songs, "California Über Alles." As the title suggests, the song warns of a coming fascist, Nazi-style takeover of California. However, the leader of the fascist takeover will be a dictator whose "aura smiles and never frowns" and who plans to send the "suede denim secret police" for "your uncool niece."[43] The person alluded to was not former California governor Ronald Reagan or any other prominent conservative, but Jerry Brown, who at the time was one of the most progressive governors in the country (a claim that, amazingly, he could also make in 2018). Only in San Francisco, his hometown, could Jerry Brown—who in the rest of the country was frequently a punch line about how weird California was becoming—be seen as a harbinger, even ironically, of hippie fascism.

According to Dead Kennedys historian Alex Ogg, while most of America, and California, saw Brown as a liberal politician, Dead Kennedys saw Brown as "an ambitious politician with an ostensibly left-leaning agenda." Ogg also argued, "Other references to 'Zen fascists' in the song recall Biafra's adolescence in Boulder where the ideals of the 60s retreated to the greed of the 70s, garbled in fake hippie mysticism."[44] Biafra confirmed for me in a 2018 interview that the idea for the song indeed drew on his youth in Colorado: "I come from Boulder, Colorado, where every other person I ran into was looking for a guru to do their thinking for them, and I thought that was a one-way ticket to fascism and only one politician in America was tapped into that."[45] This speaks to both the frustration of punks with the hippie hegemony in popular culture as well as their deep discontent with center-left politicians like Brown.

Biafra also conceded that his view that Jerry Brown was poised to lead the country into fascism was "my own little pet conspiracy theory that turned out to be wrong."[46] Ultimately, the absurdity of seeing Jerry Brown as the agent of a Nazi-like takeover of the United States was not lost on Dead Kennedys, who later updated the song, using the title "We've Got a Bigger Problem Now," which spoke of "Emperor Ronald Reagan, born again with fascist cravings" and included the line "Welcome to 1984. Are you ready for the Third World War?!?"[47] Biafra said in a 2010 interview, "I realized I was off-base with Jerry Brown when the Reaganoids stormed in in 1980."[48] East Bay Ray explained to me the song's ongoing relevance in the era of huge tech wealth: "California Über Alles is specifically about decadent hippieism. . . . It's a really good song. . . . The lyrics are a little outdated, but it's actually kind of coming back because all the tech billionaires go to Burning Man."[49]

While Dead Kennedys and other punks may have claimed to hate the hippies, the punk rock movement of which, in the Bay Area at least, they were perhaps the most visible symbol, had some similarities with those very hippies. In addition to sharing vaguely left-wing politics, hippies and punk rockers were both living expressions of the generation gap, specifically by 1978, between the generation of Americans born before World War II and those born after. Punk rockers, like the hippies before them, were a source of concern, fear, and fascination to older San Franciscans.

The relationship between punks and hippies in 1978 was quite complex and went well beyond simple animus. There was much more overlap between the two communities than punk orthodoxy would suggest. Many punks, including Joe Strummer of the Clash and Jello Biafra himself, had been hippies. Most of the early punk musicians were of the generation that came of age during the hippie era. Strummer was born in 1952, and Penelope Houston, Biafra, and East Bay Ray were born in 1958. V. Vale, the publisher of the San Francisco punk zine *Search and Destroy,* was born in 1944, making him among the older members of the hippie generation. Influential writer and punk promoter Howie Klein was born in 1950 and spent his college years at Stony Brook on Long Island promoting bands such as the Doors and the Jimi Hendrix Experience. Thus, while many of the kids who came to the shows were high school students in the late 1970s and early 1980s, others, including many of the performers, were frequently a half generation or more older and, in many cases, had been hippies before landing in punk.

Selvin was more direct about this: "These guys were all old hippies. . . . There's high school pictures of those guys with long hair."[50] Henry S. Rosenthal concurred: "I personally was never anti-hippie. . . . Growing up I aspired to be a hippie."[51] Michael Lucas, a devotee of San Francisco punk rock as a high school student at the time, believed that this anti-hippie sentiment was "always expressing complete disdain for them [hippies] . . . but [it was] theatrical and tongue in cheek." He continued: "Some of the punk bands, especially if they were from outlying areas, had, it seemed like, the token hippie."[52] The vitriol toward hippies and the 1960s was tempered by a sense of poignancy as well and a realization that the era also represented failed hopes. Jello Biafra told me that the song "California Über Alles," a critique of hippie excesses, also "came, in my case, not just from cynicism, but from a sense of heartbreak too."[53]

Resentment of hippies and the styles and music associated with them, more than the politics, were part of punk rock everywhere but were particularly acute in San Francisco, as no city in the world was more associated with hippies and 1960s counterculture. The 1960s were still very present in the political, cultural, and everyday life of San Francisco in 1978. This remained true well into the 1980s. Harvey Milk, for example, may have been many things—an urban visionary, the martyred leader of what became a global civil rights movement, and a hard-nosed big city politician. However, he was also one of thousands, probably tens of thousands, of people who came from somewhere else to San Francisco sometime between 1966 and 1974 with long hair, not much money, and the hope of a new life. In that regard, Milk was similar to many San Franciscans, gay and straight, in 1978.

Throughout the first wave of punk rock, from roughly 1977 to 1985, punk rock coexisted with much of the 1960s music and musicians. There were many nights when Dead Kennedys or Crime were playing a few blocks away from the Grateful Dead, Country Joe McDonald, or other old hippie bands. I was a strange kid in the early 1980s because I enjoyed both genres equally. Today, many of my friends from back then share that view, but at the time my punk friends ridiculed me for attending the occasional, or not so occasional, Grateful Dead show, while my Deadhead friends were puzzled by my affinity for punk rock. This tension could be found in most Bay Area high schools and other places where young people gathered.

San Francisco punk was therefore very much a reaction to the hippie hegemony in youth culture as well as the growing influence that generation had on music, culture, and politics at the time. Jeff Olener of the Nuns summarized this sentiment: "What I saw happening [in San Francisco circa 1976] was just the tail end of an old era. . . . There was basically no real scene."[54] Jack Boulware and Silke Tudor begin their oral history of Bay Area punk with comments from seven people who were central players in late 1970s San Francisco punk rock. The section is long, but quoting it at some length captures an important angle of punk as a reaction to the mid-1970s music and cultural scene in San Francisco.

HOWIE KLEIN: There was this hideous interlude of corporate rock where the Yardbirds turned into Led Zeppelin, and suddenly there was Journey and Kansas and REO Speedwagon, just all this pure garbage.

JELLO BIAFRA: 99.9 percent of the population listened to Elton John and *Saturday Night Fever*. In a way, that music was a major influence on us because we hated it so much.

DAVE DICTOR: I couldn't go see Marshall Tucker one more time. Allman Brothers, Grateful Dead, the Who, Yes. That arena rock, it was just numbing. You were like an ant, with 40,000 other people, and you really felt disconnected from what was going on.

MAX VOLUME: Journey. They were one of the worst.

JAMES STARK: Jefferson Starship, all that kind of shit. Genesis.

ROZZ REZABEK: Boston, Toto, REO Speedwagon, Air Supply, Michael Murphey's "Wildfire."

JENNIFER MIRO: I was in this horrible band in Mill Valley, and we did Doobie Brothers songs. I had to sing "China Grove." It was the lowest point of my life.[55]

Although this passage reads like a conversation, it is really a collection of separate quotations by these people on a similar topic. Nonetheless, it is a telling way to begin a book about punk rock because it demonstrates just how central rebellion against the established, increasingly corporate—and in the eyes of many, boring—youth culture was to the punk rock movement.

Houston's description of the pre-punk music scene in San Francisco shares this contemptuous tone. Referring to the entertainment section of the Sunday paper in San Francisco in those years by its color, and more frequently used name, she told me, "If you pull out a pink section from the first half of 1977 and you look at all the bands that are playing small clubs[,] . . . there's probably a large percentage of cover bands and then there are bands that sound just like bands from the 1960s."[56] John Gullak echoed this notion: "The rock and roll was really horrible at that point—in the mid-'70s. All the bands were getting really self-referential, talking more about being rock stars—something you couldn't relate to."[57] Joe Dirt succinctly expressed a similar view to me: "Music was pretty much dead. . . . Everything kind of got overplayed. There was a lot of music, but nothing new stood out."[58] Michael Fox, who played in punk bands including the Tools, Code of Honor, and Sick Pleasure and who also was one of the founders of the punk record label Subterranean Records, framed this critique of the music in those years in a vaguely political context as well: "I didn't really like middle of the road and all that crap. . . . Nobody was interested in doing anything but Stevie Wonder, Bread, or whatever. I was just pulling my hair out." Calling the music "pablum, exploitism," he added, "It had nothing to do with anything but the typical exploitative bullshit."[59]

The comments about arena and corporate rock are spot on. Although the Grateful Dead, the Allman Brothers, Stevie Wonder, and Elton John have been enduring and influential artists, the same cannot be said about most of the other bands mentioned. Few people would defend Air Supply, REO Speedwagon, Boston, Bread, or Toto on the grounds that they were good or important bands. Today, most of these bands are relegated to the category of yacht rock—the music that rich but not very hip white folks over fifty listen to when they want to relax or feel like they are cool. However, in the mid-1970s, that was more or less the state of rock and roll.

The comments about Led Zeppelin and Jefferson Starship also provide some insight. Although Led Zeppelin is better regarded today than some of the other bands mentioned, Klein's argument is that they had become a boring corporate version of the Yardbirds. Similarly, Jefferson Starship was a pretty mediocre band in the mid-1970s and early 1980s, but their antecedent, the Jefferson Airplane, had been one of the best bands of the psychedelic era. The point in these comments is that the corporate and toned-down approach of the mid-1970s was destroying what had once been good bands and an exciting music scene. Klein elaborated on this point to me in a 2018 interview: "This whole horrible corporate rock thing that came up in San Francisco—we had Journey, for example, then bands like REO Speedwagon, just this kind of thing that I thought of as garbage and had no interest in at all. I felt that the motivation for . . . this corporate rock was just about paying your mortgage or something like that."[60] Klein was careful to distinguish between what he viewed as corporate rock and the more meaningful hippie music of the late 1960s and early 1970s.

According to the punks, at least the more thoughtful ones, these arena rock bands and the music culture around them were deeply inauthentic. Houston contrasts this with the early days of punk: "I used to tell people, 'We make folk music. We make front-porch music, except it's in the garage.'"[61] Punk everywhere brought a rawer sound that was, in Joel Selvin's words, "a reaction to the overproduced pop music of the day."[62]

The collection of comments from *Gimme Something Better* will also res-onate with anybody who was even remotely interested in punk rock in the late 1970s and early 1980s. We either participated in or listened to conver-sations like this all the time. Those comments by people at the center of the punk rock movement in San Francisco could have been made by me and some of my punk rock friends hanging out at Baker Beach, sitting around somebody's flat in high school, or waiting for the 41 Union to take us home from a show.

At the time, these distinctions felt very important. Young people built their identities around their taste in music. For kids exploring punk rock, the rejection of the music the mainstream youth culture was offering, which in San Francisco was still very heavily influenced by the Summer of Love era, was as important as listening to the newest punk band. I have an old friend I met in 1983 or 1984 who, at that time, was a punk rocker. He recently told me that his first memory of me was arguing with me at a party because I wanted to listen to the Grateful Dead.

Biafra's comment about the musical tastes of 99.9 percent of the Ameri-can people is also instructive. Biafra was clearly using hyperbole, but by defin-ing punk rockers as less than one-tenth of 1 percent of the American people, Biafra was making an important point. Part of the punk rock ethos was that punks were always a small minority, even within youth culture. This was not true of the hippies, who by the early 1970s represented a large part of youth culture. No punk rock band, not even the Clash or the Ramones, ever became as popular as even midlevel 1960s and 1970s hippie or arena rock bands. Rosenthal told me, "In the minds of the bands, we were what was happening at that time, but it was an illusion. The Mabuhay on its best day was not the Winterland or the Fillmore or the Warfield or any of the other Bill Graham venues. It was always a tiny little thing."[63] Joe Dirt similarly observed, "Punk wasn't a big commercial thing. . . . Punk rock never got to that level."[64] Michael Lucas, who was in high school in 1978, added more plainly that even among the people at those early punk shows, there were "not a lot of youngsters."[65] This sense of being a small group gave punks a sense of constantly being threatened and of fighting a two-front battle—against both the dominant youth culture and, more broadly and more political, against American consumerism and imperialism.

In San Francisco, the outsized impact of the 1960s had meant that by the late 1970s the music scene had become quite moribund and resistant to change. The music press, whether in the *San Francisco Chronicle*, the *San*

Francisco Bay Guardian, or *BAM (Bay Area Music)*, covered the leftover scene from the 1960s in great detail. In reading those papers now, it feels like every new reconfiguration of the Jefferson Airplane/Starship, every guitar solo by Carlos Santana, or every concert by Boz Scaggs was analyzed in depth, while everything outside of that relatively narrow bandwidth was almost entirely ignored. Howie Klein, one of the few advocates for punk who contributed to *BAM*, captured the contrast between punk and much of the rest of the music scene in a December 1977 article about the Avengers: "To people used to listening to Pablo Cruise and Fleetwood Mac, the harsh Avengers sound was jarringly abrasive—an impenetrable wall, a solid barrage of loud, raucous, same-sounding tirades, revolving around simple, breakneck-speed playing and cacophonous screeching. And for people fed up with the pablum and muck (of bands like Pablo Cruise and Fleetwood Mac), it was godhead—San Francisco's very own Sex Pistols."[66]

As 1977 wound down, the Summer of Hate that had represented the first major rumblings of the punk movement in San Francisco was not exactly recognized as a major musical development. *BAM*, which was a pretty fair measure of the white musical establishment in San Francisco, had its annual award ceremony in early 1978, for which it had made nominations in late 1977. The nominees for best group were Jefferson Starship, Santana, the David Grisman Quintet, the Steve Miller Band, and the Hoodoo Rhythm Devils. The nominees for best female singer included Grace Slick and Joan Baez, but also mostly forgotten names such as Terry Garthwaite and Mimi Farina, with no room for Penelope Houston among the five nominees. The only somewhat punk band that got any recognition was Mink DeVille, whose eponymous album was nominated for best album and whose singer, Willy DeVille, was nominated for best male vocalist. That was a pretty good reflection of the gap between punk and the rest of the music scene in San Francisco as 1978 began.

In 1978, the Mab began to advertise in most issues of *BAM*, so readers could have some sense of the burgeoning punk scene. Nonetheless, at the end of 1978 when voting began for the Bay Area Music Awards, the nominees for best debut album included efforts by such less than seminal artists as Snail, Ed Kelly, Jesse Barish, Cockrell and Santos, and Any Old Time. The best album nominees read like a list of mid-'70s schlock rock, including Van Morrison, Eddie Money, the Greg Kihn Band, Neil Young, and Jefferson Starship. The nominees for best group were similar: the Greg Kihn Band, Jefferson Starship, the Grateful Dead, Pablo Cruise, and Santana. The only

punk performer nominated for anything was the Readymades, whose eponymous debut album was in the running for best independently produced
record. Given how little traction punks were getting outside of their
extremely small scene, their rancor toward the music and musical scene
from the 1960s, which still defined the San Francisco sound, is pretty
understandable.

Despite the contempt many of the punks felt toward the music of the hippies, the musical antecedents of punk are deeply rooted in the 1960s. Punk
did not emerge fully formed out of the economic chaos of the United Kingdom in the mid-1970s or on the stage of CBGB's. Nor were punks in New
York or San Francisco entirely disconnected from the music of the 1960s.
As Houston told me, "So many people we had coming to us had experienced
the whole hippie thing."[67]

The history of punk is complex, but many of the protopunk bands and
performers such as Lou Reed, the MC5, the Fugs, or David Peel and the
Lower East Side have strong connections to the 1960s. David Peel was
friendly with John Lennon and wrote "The Hippie from New York City,"
but also "Up Against the Wall Motherf**kers," a song that would not have
sounded out of place being performed at the Mab in 1978. Lou Reed hung
out with Andy Warhol and other legendary 1960s figures. The MC5 and the
Fugs were favorites of the Yippie movement.

There was another similarity as well, one that does not go quite so
smoothly with the politics of either group. Despite some of their views on
civil rights and racial equality, both hippies and punks were overwhelmingly
white. Stephen Duncombe, who was briefly in a punk band in the early 1980s
called White Noise, describes the interaction between punk and being white,
arguing that some elements were racist while others were not:

> The lead singer of White Noise was my best friend.... We also came from
> different worlds.... He was a great guy, but could easily talk about "n***ers"
> and "sp*cs." He was obsessed with the Vietnam War and killing "g**ks."... He
> shaved his head and wore combat boots. White Noise, a simple acknowledge-
> ment of our obvious whiteness to me, may have meant something different to
> him: White Power.
>
> I ended up moving in another direction. Listening to bands like the Clash,
> Stiff Little Fingers and the Dead Kennedys, a new definition of whiteness
> began to make sense for me.... In recognizing that my whiteness was not
> universal, and in understanding that it was merely one race among many, each

with its own struggles and histories, I discovered the possibility of cross racial solidarity. Through punk I attempted to embody what rock critic Jeff Chang, writing about the Clash, called a radical whiteness.[68]

As Duncombe indicates, the punk rock moment had an ugly racist underside from an overlap in some places with the racist skinhead movement, but this was less frequently the case in San Francisco, where bands such as the Avengers and Dead Kennedys had a decidedly antiracist bent. When Dead Kennedys weren't warning about the dangers of a fascist takeover led by Jerry Brown, they made it clear that their vision of punk rock was in opposition to the growing white supremacist element that was poisoning the movement. The band addressed this issue directly, although not with much subtlety, in their 1981 tune "Nazi Punks F**k Off":

You still think swastikas look cool
The real Nazis run your schools
They're coaches, businessmen and cops
In a real fourth reich you'll be the first to go
Nazi punks, Nazi punks, Nazi punks—f**k off![69]

Despite these sentiments, and despite a few relatively well-known African American punk bands such as the Bad Brains out of Washington, D.C., punk rock was a largely white phenomenon, and the scene in San Francisco was not an exception.

While the bands that were popular at the time frequently took principled antiracist positions, the same was not true of all their fans. For example, at more than a few Dead Kennedys shows, the band was booed when they played "Nazi Punks F**k Off." The reason for this was that there were some skinheads in the audience who held white supremacist views and did not appreciate being told to "f**k off," even by punk rock royalty like Jello Biafra.

Although most punks in San Francisco were white, there were exceptions. Given the great diversity of San Francisco even in the late 1970s, this meant there were some Asian American, Latino, and African American punks. Additionally, most punks in San Francisco were not white supremacists and, on the contrary, saw fighting racism as part of their broader political agenda. However, in most African American communities, punks were very rare, and many of them, like their white working-class cohort, confronted problems in their own neighborhoods for choosing to be punks. Coyote recalled, "Black people who had crazy colored hair and stuff—they got harassed more than anybody did, and that was from other black people."[70]

Jews, Swastikas, and Punks in New York and San Francisco

Bay Area punk was also a largely gentile phenomenon, although there were some Jewish punk musicians in San Francisco. Jeff Olener of the Nuns, who wrote the song "Decadent Jew," was the most well known of these musicians. Crime's drummer Hank Rank was also Jewish. I knew a small handful of Jews who went to punk rock shows and am certain there were others, but the scene in San Francisco never had a particularly Jewish feel.

The Jewish influence on punk rock more generally, however, is stronger than might be initially thought. Lou Reed, David Peel, and Tuli Kupferberg of the Fugs, all of whom were influential in the creation of punk, were Jewish. Two of the Ramones (Joey and Tommy) and all of the members of the Dictators were Jewish. Danny Fields, the seminal punk rock promoter most known for his work with the Ramones, and Hilly Kristal, the owner of CBGB's during punk's heyday, were also Jewish. Veterans of the New York scene have described heavily Jewish crowds, many of whose members were one generation removed from the Holocaust, at clubs like CBGB's as well. All of these people had something in common besides their musical tastes and religion. They were all New Yorkers. A similar collection of Jewish San Franciscans who were influential in the punk rock scene there cannot quite be assembled.

While New York punk was never as political as it was in San Francisco, when New York's most well-known punk band, the Ramones, became interested in politics, it was from a Jewish angle. Probably their most political song, "Bonzo Goes to Bitburg," was a critique of President Reagan's decision to lay a wreath in a cemetery in Germany where SS men lay buried. Joey Ramone's comments about the visit to Bitburg—"What Reagan did was f**ked up. . . . How can you f**kin' forgive the Holocaust?"[71]—were consistent with the opinions of many American Jews at the time. While almost nobody in the punk scene in San Francisco liked Reagan, this particular incident was not as important or galvanizing because Joey Ramone's response to Reagan's Bitburg visit was not so much a punk sentiment as a Jewish one.

The comparative sizes of the Jewish communities explain this difference somewhat. According to the *American Jewish Year Book* of 1979, there were 75,000 Jews living in San Francisco in 1978, but 1.28 million in New York City. There were 2 million Jews living in greater New York, but only about 110,000 in the five counties (San Francisco, San Mateo, Alameda, Contra Costa, and Marin) that constitute the core of the Bay Area.[72] These numbers would have skewed even more toward New York a decade earlier when the punk musicians of 1978 were growing up. However, some of the other differences between New York and San Francisco, which are in part attributable to the relative size of the Jewish populations, are also part of the explanation.

Steven Lee Beeber's excellent book on Jews in punk, *The Heebie Jeebies at CBGB's: A Secret History of Jewish Punk*, is a Jewish story but also a New York one. Beeber recognizes this as well:

> Only in New York, the city where as Lenny Bruce said, "It doesn't matter if you're Catholic . . . you're Jewish" could a popular art form like punk have found a birthplace. There, on that island of immigrants, where Jews formed such a sizable portion of the population, they could take their Jewishness and all its intellectual, nonviolent, comic-driven aspects for granted. Joey Ramone, a figure straight out of Kafka's *The Metamorphosis*, Richard Hell, a Jewish mother's worst nightmare, and Lenny Kaye, a kind of post-1960s Jewish mystic, rose up ready to take over the world. . . . For a few years, at least, they reigned as gods on that island where they had been born, raised and nurtured, that city that had formed them, Hymietown. . . . In other words, it didn't matter if it was known as punk. If it had those components of New York culture that Lenny Bruce epitomized, it was Jewish.[73]

Punk in general may not have been particularly Jewish, but New York punk was. The hegemony of New York in the historiography of many cultural phenomena means that the New York story often gets mistaken for the larger American one. This has occurred with punk rock, as the early days of the New York scene are frequently presented as the early days of American punk, but that was not quite the case.

The people making the punk scene in San Francisco tended to come from California or elsewhere in the West. These people came not from first- or second-generation Jewish homes in the outer boroughs or Long Island only a few decades, and in some cases years, removed from pogroms and genocide. Instead, their roots were in large part grounded in the huge post-war western middle class that was not very Jewish. These people were much more likely to be a few decades removed from the Dust Bowl or the pioneers than from the New York Jewish world from which Joey Ramone or Lou Reed emerged. Jello Biafra grew up in Colorado, Penelope Houston in Seattle and Palo Alto, and Ray Pepperell in the East Bay. The bands that came to California tended to be from other parts of the West, such as MDC, who were originally from Texas. These were distinctively, to use Lenny Bruce's parlance, goyishe places.

Although there were relatively few Jews involved in punk rock in San Francisco, the sensibility was still somewhat Jewish. The San Francisco punk rock scene, while three thousand miles away from New York, drew on what punks saw from New York for ideas and inspiration. By 1978, there was a fair amount of cross-fertilization, as Jewish punk rockers such as the Ramones and the Dictators had played San Francisco a few times and other Jewish performers such as Jonathan Richman and Lou Reed were well known in San Francisco.

Jello Biafra's blend of humor, outrage, and radical politics, deliberately or not, drew heavily on left-wing Jewish (counter)culture. Songs such as "Kill the Poor" or "Holiday in Cambodia" had clear antecedents in the man Beeber refers to as the "patron saint" of punk, Lenny Bruce.[74] Biafra's 1979 campaign for mayor is precisely the kind of synergy between clownishness and progressive politics that Jewish Yippie pranksters Jerry Rubin or Abbie Hoffman might have done a decade earlier. Rubin had, in fact, run for mayor of Berkeley in 1967.

While there may have been an indirect Jewish influence on punk in San Francisco, Jews who went to shows, played in bands, or otherwise were part of San Francisco punk rock had a complex experience, one that was not always easy. Beeber quotes Steven Blush, a chronicler of music whose book *American Hardcore* is an oral history of punk, describing his experience in the San Francisco punk scene: "I was shocked out of the rock scene there. . . . At one point I was going to move to San Francisco. . . . But I heard 'k∗ke' and those words coming out from hipsters so many times after a few drinks. I heard it so many f∗∗king times."[75]

Others assert that San Francisco punk was very welcoming to Jews and that there was little anti-Semitism. This is the view of Howie Klein, one of the most influential people in the punk scene in the late 1970s: "There were swastikas, but it was a very anti-Nazi movement, and . . . many of the people who were doing that were Jewish themselves."[76] The use of swastikas and other Nazi imagery in San Francisco punk cannot be dismissed quite this easily, however. At the time, the claim was made frequently that those symbols were used ironically or as an implicit critique of Nazi ideologies, but that argument was often unconvincing. After all, there are many other ways to demonstrate one's contempt for Nazism, as well as for anti-Semitism, than embracing the swastika as a symbol. However, Klein is not entirely wrong either. While the punk scene was not altogether free of anti-Semitism, it was also, at least in San Francisco, not exactly a hotbed of anti-Jewish violence. When I saw swastikas at shows I felt angry, but not frightened. In our interview, Klein also related a discussion he'd had with Bill Graham in which the legendary promoter, and Holocaust survivor, made it clear that he was not comfortable with the Nazi imagery either: "Bill Graham came to me one time and said 'Howie, if they [the Nuns] will stop doing "Decadent Jew" and will get rid of the swastika-type artwork, I will sign them to management and they will become a gigantic band.'" The Nuns and Graham never agreed to these terms, so Graham never managed them.[77]

Punk Rock Kids in San Francisco

Punk was not just a musical movement. It was a cultural phenomenon that included music, but also film, graphic art, and fashion. Penelope Houston's description of how late-1970s San Francisco punks viewed themselves and their movement reflects this: "We also didn't think of ourselves as musicians, as the music scene. We thought of ourselves as this cultural scene called punk that included music, art, photography, films, dressing in a f**ked-up manner. It was a whole movement."[78]

Punk was indeed more than the music. In North Beach, and later the Haight as well as other areas of San Francisco where punk eventually got a foothold, one could frequently see the punk graphics on display. Posters advertising concerts that looked to be made of letters cut out from different newspapers and magazines, similar to ransom notes, were the most recognizable example of this. By the late 1970s in art schools around the country, including the one Houston attended in San Francisco, photography and film students were experimenting with ways to bring punk to their medium. These art schools were a major way for smart, rebellious, middle-class kids to find their way to punk rock. Houston was not the only punk who followed that course. In the early days of punk, the sound itself was also varied. Bands such as Dead Kennedys or MDC had a distinct hardcore sound, but other bands, such as Tuxedomoon, were also part of that early punk scene and had a much more arty sound.

For kids with limited artistic talent or access, appearance was a central aspect of being punk. In San Francisco high schools in this period, every year a few, but only a few, kids would make the transition from being preppy rich kids or working class WPODs to being punks. Pegged jeans or miniskirts with torn fishnet stockings would be phased in, followed by T-shirts bearing the right punk logo, usually Dead Kennedys, then came the spiked or dyed hair, and a few weeks later the punk haircut.

Selvin, the music critic, echoed Houston's sentiment that punk was "more of a cultural movement than a political movement" when I interviewed him, adding, "It spoke very directly to the hardcore alienated youth, people who felt uncomfortable in their skins, in their social and family situation. . . . What motivated these people? Personal unhappiness, conflict with the culture, a sense of not fitting in anywhere. In many regards, this is the exact sort of thing that motivated people in the hippie movement ten years before. But, oddly enough, the hippie movement had come to represent this kind of conservative social movement that had been."[79]

Selvin was born in 1950 and has always identified more with, and written more about, the hippie culture than punk. But he has been a keen observer of youth cultures and music in San Francisco since the early 1970s. The points he makes here, while sounding a bit like those of a sociology professor asking to comment about punks on a television show in 1980, are not inaccurate. In the early days of punk, it was that alienation and sense that the rest of the culture did not offer anything that drew people to punk. Few of those people were drawn into the scene by the politics, but most picked some up along the way. More than a few got radicalized by punk.

Both Houston's and Selvin's comments are also revealing because of something that is left out. Neither of them addresses the economic conditions in the United States or San Francisco at the time. This is because while the late 1970s were famously a period of economic stagnation, they had not reached the level of crisis that existed in the United Kingdom. That economic crisis and the sense that, in the words of the Sex Pistols, there was "no future," is what drove people in the United Kingdom to punk. By contrast, in the Bay Area, at least at first, punk drew at least in part from the middle class. Houston was the child of professors; East Bay Ray had been raised by progressive activists and had studied mathematics at UC Berkeley. Many other San Francisco punk musicians came from similar backgrounds. Some of the first generation of punk kids often had family stories that were no different. One of these kids, Jennifer Moscone, was the mayor's daughter. Perhaps because of that, Mayor Moscone was never hostile to the nascent punk scene in North Beach. Ginger Coyote speculated of Jennifer, "It was her that came to the clubs. It was her that liked the clubs, and it was her that probably told her dad that the clubs are not what a lot of people were saying it was."[80]

Perhaps the lyric that best summed up the political perspective of the San Francisco punk rock scene in those years was by Code of Honor, a band that was very well liked in the Bay Area but never developed a national following: "Here we are a small group of kids who realize our government's f**ked, but what are we gonna do?"[81] This line from a 1982 single, "What Are We Gonna Do?" reflects both the politics and the anger of the period. It also speaks to the way the punk rock generation believed they saw something that the rest of the country was missing. It turns out they were probably right.

The word "small" in the Code of Honor lyric is significant because punk was never a mass phenomenon. Few punk rock bands became popular with a larger audience. Some that did, like Blondie, stopped being punk in any meaningful sense as they became popular. Bands such as the Sex Pistols and Dead Kennedys that were hugely important within punk were never very popular in the broader culture. The Ramones were briefly popular beyond the punk rock world, not least because of their role in the 1979 film *Rock and Roll High School*, but even then they were never among the top-selling bands in America. The best band to come out of the early years of punk was the Clash, who with the release of their 1982 album *Combat Rock* transitioned from being a punk band to reaching a broader audience while maintaining a somewhat punk feel, at least for a while.

Despite a few bands like the Clash or Ramones becoming a little bit better known beyond the punk world, punk rockers in San Francisco were always "a small group of kids" drawn from a small subset of teenagers and young adults. Moreover, those kids were almost entirely white in an increasingly diverse San Francisco. Selvin described punk in those days as not being "for everybody . . . it was only the severe extreme side . . . real small."[82] To be a punk rocker in San Francisco in 1978, or even through the mid-1980s, was to be one of a handful at your school. It meant drawing stares almost everywhere in the city. If you came from one of the white working-class areas of town, it meant regularly running the risk of being beaten up or otherwise harassed by the sons of families who had either voted for Dan White or supported his political views.

There were certainly neighborhoods with more punk rockers. North Beach, once an Italian American community where, among others, the DiMaggio brothers had grown up, had become the center of beatnik culture twenty years earlier. According to Boulware, whom I interviewed in San Francisco in 2017, in the early years, "Punk was a North Beach thing."[83] By 1978, because of the location of clubs such as the On Broadway and the Mab, the numerous affordable cafes and bars and cultural institutions such as Lawrence Ferlinghetti's City Lights Bookstore, North Beach was a punk rock hub. Similarly, the Haight-Ashbury, with its counterculture history, widespread drug culture, rundown feeling, cheap restaurants, affordable rent, and used clothing stores, was another center of the city's nascent punk rock scene.

In the rest of the city, including wealthy neighborhoods such as Pacific Heights, Presidio Heights, and Sea Cliff, as well as working class areas such as Bernal Heights, the Excelsior, or the Outer Sunset, punk rockers were rare. In most neighborhoods there were a few, but they were treated with a mixture of scorn and shock. Most tried to get to the Haight or North Beach as early as they could on the weekends and did not look forward to the long ride home on the 38 Geary, the N Judah, or the 43 Masonic at the end of a Saturday night.

The Little Orange Skateboard

During the early part of the summer of 1978, Dead Kennedys played their first show at the Mab, a few more kids every week were swapping their Santana jerseys for torn Sex Pistols or Ramones T-shirts, and the Giants were finding a way to stay in first place. The first half of the baseball season wrapped up on July 9. The Giants and their fans could not have been more pleased with how the Giants had played. It was the kind of year where, as W. A. Van Winkle had written in June, "someone will appear from the bench or out of the bullpen and drive in the winning run—despite a low batting average, a hitting slump or near-blindedness. Someone will walk in from the bullpen and retire each of the last nine batters to preserve a win. Someone will steal a base and put a run in scoring position—last year he would have been thrown out. And someone will hurtle the baseball from the left-field corner all 335 feet to home plate to force the final out of the game."[84]

As the All-Star break brought a brief pause to the season, the Giants had a record of 52–34, the best in the National League. Only the Red Sox, who appeared to be making a mockery of the American League East, had a better record. Many fans were hoping for a Giants–Red Sox World Series, which would pit two storied and hard-luck franchises against each other. However, while the Red Sox, nine games ahead of the second-place Brewers and eleven and a half games up on the Yankees, appeared to have the AL East already won, the Giants could not put much daylight between themselves and the second-place Reds or the third-place Dodgers. At the break, the Dodgers were only two games back, with the Reds only one game behind the Dodgers.

Although they had the best record in the National League, only two Giants, Vida Blue and Jack Clark, were chosen for the All-Star team. None of the Giants regulars were voted by the fans into the starting lineup. Jack Clark, Darrell Evans, and even Willie McCovey had not made it onto the ballot, prompting Mayor Moscone to pledge, "We're going to be circulating over half a million extra All-Star ballots throughout the Bay Area, and we're asking Giants fans everywhere to write-in McCovey's name and send the ballots to the office of the National League."[85]

Many of us felt that Dodger manager Tommy Lasorda, who was managing the NL All-Star team that year, might have picked a few more Giants in addition to Clark, who was hitting .309/.362/.554, playing solid defense, and carrying the Giants offense. For example, Bill Madlock was hitting .314/.388/.491 at the break and could have made the team as a backup infielder. At 10–5 with a 2.57 ERA, Bob Knepper's numbers were almost as good as Blue's. Better news for Giants fans came when Lasorda announced that he was going to have Vida Blue be the National League starter.

By June it was clear that the Giants had fleeced the A's in the big spring training trade. Blue came into the All-Star break with a record of 12–4 and an ERA of 2.42 and had been instrumental to the Giants success in the first half of the season. Blue had also become a symbol of the excitement the Giants were generating for the first time in years. He wore his first name on the back of his uniform, often led the fans in cheers when he wasn't pitching, and provided veteran leadership to a young and inexperienced pitching staff. Blue's pitching success, affable outgoing personality, and the Giants' winning record endeared him to Giants fans in 1978. Additionally, both big league baseball and San Francisco itself were much more heavily African American in the late 1970s than today, and Blue was a particular favorite among African American fans. Blue would turn twenty-nine a few weeks after the All-Star break, so he was not exactly old, even by baseball standards, but unlike anybody else on the Giants, he was a three-time World Series champion.

Being named as the starter for that All-Star Game was a vindication for Vida Blue, who seemed to be enjoying a career renaissance. It also meant that Blue would be the first pitcher in baseball history to start the All-Star Game in both leagues. In 1971, in the middle of his fantastic rookie season with the A's, Blue had started for the American League. That year had also been the first, and so far only, All-Star Game in which both starting pitchers were African American, as Dock Ellis of the Pirates had started for the National League. Blue was also the American League starter in 1975.

By midseason, earlier in some cases, the national press had begun to understand Blue's value to the first-place Giants, as exemplified by report in *Sports Illustrated*: "Meanwhile, attendance back in San Francisco was up 68% from a year ago, and expectations soared even higher than that. An important reason for this turnaround is Vida Blue, the sassy newcomer who is 6–1 with a 2.90 ERA since crossing the Bay Bridge from Oakland." The author of that piece, Larry Keith, also stressed Blue's value to the team while not on the mound: "Not only has he won but he has also proven himself to be a regular guy, working hard, leading cheers, boosting morale. . . . The closest thing to a complaint comes from Catcher [*sic*] Marc Hill. He is amazed that even with the thick mitt his calloused left hand can feel the sting of the Blue blazer."[86] Blue had also come up with a nickname for the resurgent Giants, riffing on the Cincinnati Reds' intimidating sounding nickname "the Big Red Machine." Blue suggested calling the Giants "the Little Orange Skateboard."

Vida Blue's career path had been an unusual one. Few players have burst onto the baseball scene the way Vida Blue did. During his first full year in the big leagues, he was one of the biggest stories in the game, as he captured his league's MVP and Cy Young Awards while helping the A's win a postseason berth for the first time since 1931 when they were still in Philadelphia. It is not easy to follow up on a year like that, and Blue struggled in 1972. He held out for more money in spring training, causing him to get a late start and end up with a 6–10 record. However, Blue's ERA was a very respectable 2.80, while his strikeout-to-walk ratio was 2.31 to 1, strong for those days. The A's won the World Series that year, but Blue was not a major contributor. That changed the following two years when Blue reestablished himself as one of the top pitchers in the league, going 20–9 and 17–15 with ERAs of 3.28 and 3.25 in 1973 and 1974 for World Series–winning A's squads. He also finished seventh in the Cy Young balloting in 1973. From 1975 to 1977, Blue continued to be a very valuable pitcher, but the A's were being dismantled. By 1977, Blue and centerfielder Bill North were the only impact players left from the 1972–1974 champions.

Blue had always been more than just a great pitcher. He was part of a cadre of African American stars who made it to the big leagues in the mid-1960s and early 1970s. These players were no longer breaking new ground the way Jackie Robinson, Larry Doby, Willie Mays, Monte Irvin, Elston Howard, Henry Aaron, and others had done ten to twenty years earlier, but they were acutely aware of the racism that was still widespread in baseball and American society more broadly. Some of the more notable players of this group included slugging infielder Dick Allen, slugging and speedy outfielder Bobby Bonds, pitcher Dock Ellis, Blue, and Reggie Jackson, a teammate of Blue's on the A's. These stars were frequently described in the media as "disgruntled," "controversial," "troublemakers," or with other racial code words. Many of them, notably Allen and Bonds, found themselves traded a lot. This was a reflection of the double standards regarding race and baseball players and the resistance from the baseball establishment when confronted with the ongoing problems of racism. Blue, like many of these players, spoke his mind, demanded to be treated with respect, and, appropriately, thought very highly of his abilities.

In 1976, Blue gave an interview for poet and essayist Tom Clark's book *Baseball*. In his final words of the interview Blue stated, "I'm just as proud of my 24 wins in 1971 as Hunter was of his 25 in 1974. I think he won his 25 with a better team. I'm not pitching for Charlie Finley, the Oakland A's or all of baseball. I'm pitching for Vida Blue."[87] In reading these comments, one gets a sense of Blue's exhaustion with the A's, Charlie Finley, and baseball in general. Blue's frank and honest remark that he was pitching for himself is not the kind of thing ballplayers said then, or even now. According to the media and much of the public, players are supposed to play for the team, or at least to make that claim when speaking to the media. After seeing Finley seek to exploit him financially, speak ill of him to the press, and ask him to dishonor his father for whom he was named by changing his first name to True, Vida Blue could not even summon the energy to recite platitudes about winning and the team.

The second half of Blue's comment in Clark's book is also intriguing. The Hunter he referred to was Catfish Hunter, who was Blue's teammate and was recognized as the ace of the A's pitching staff from 1972 to 1974, when the team won three consecutive World Series. Hunter had also become one of the game's first free agents following the 1974 season, and he signed a five-year contract for more than $3.2 million with the Yankees. Hunter was always the big pitching star on those A's teams, but Blue was clearly right that his 1971 season was better than any season Hunter ever had. Nonetheless, the resentment Blue felt at never getting the recognition he felt he deserved is almost palpable in this comment.

This resentment may have grown after they both retired. Hunter was elected to the Hall of Fame the first year he was eligible, but Blue never made it, falling off the ballot after four years. However, both conventional and advanced statistics indicate that Blue was essentially as valuable as Hunter. Over the course of their careers, Hunter won fifteen more games, but lost five more. Their ERAs were almost identical: 3.26 for Hunter, 3.27 for Blue. Hunter had significantly more complete games and shutouts, and he threw about a hundred more innings. However, Blue had a better ERA+, a lower FIP, and 1.9 more WAR.[88] You could probably make a good argument that either was the better pitcher, but if Hunter was a Hall of Famer, then Blue should have gotten much more consideration for the honor. Blue also had legal troubles late in his career that undoubtedly hurt his Hall of Fame chances.

The All-Star Game in July 1978 did not go well for Blue. Rod Carew led off the game with a triple. George Brett followed with a double, driving in Carew. Three batters later, Carlton Fisk hit a sacrifice fly, putting the American League up 2–0. The second inning was much smoother for Blue, but in the third, another Rod Carew triple led to another run. Blue left the game after that, having given up three earned runs on five hits and one walk in only three innings. Jack Clark did not have a good game either. In his only time at bat, he struck out against Yankee fireballer Goose Gossage in the eighth inning.

Midsummer 1978

In the middle of the summer of 1978, the Giants were still the big story in San Francisco, as they managed to hold on to first place well past the All-

Star break. For the first time since the mid-1960s or so, they were the talk of the city. This excitement was reflected in the number of people going to ballgames. The uptick in attendance at Candlestick Park was beginning to draw national attention. Talk of the Giants leaving had disappeared from the local and national media. Leonard Koppett wrote a long piece in the *Sporting News* lauding Giants owner Bob Lurie's acumen as a promoter: "After several years of such poor attendance that the team seemed headed for financial disaster, the Giants suddenly blossomed as divisional leader the first two months of the season, and their attendance doubled." Koppett concluded that the A's, not the Giants, were going to have to find another town in which to play: "Wherever the Giants finish in the 1978 standings, they have built solidly and regained their following. They have a future. The A's . . . have no future—in Oakland. It should be different in Denver."[89] We now know that Koppett was right about the Giants and wrong about the A's, but there would be no more talk of the Giants leaving for at least a few more years. If the Giants had not traded for Blue and had not gotten off to a hot start, attendance would have been down and the talk of the team leaving would likely have accelerated by the All-Star break.

While Mayor Moscone no longer had to worry about the Giants leaving, the political environment that would frame California politics for decades was beginning to take shape. Dead Kennedys and other San Francisco–based punk rock bands had begun to bring new music to radical politics in 1978, but one of the lasting dialectics of California in the 1970s was that it was home to radical left ideas, politics, and music but was also the place where the new right finally moved from the fringe to the center of American politics. This was fully realized with the election of former California governor Ronald Reagan—the longtime standard bearer for the polite face of the right wing of the Republican Party—to the presidency in November 1980, but the summer of 1978 saw a significant development in this regard as well.

The first major victory since Watergate of the conservative movement nationally occurred in June 1978 when voters in California overwhelmingly approved Proposition 13 by a margin of 65 percent to 35 percent. Even a majority of San Francisco voters supported the conservative initiative, which captured the anger many Californians felt about their steadily increasing property taxes. It froze those taxes at their 1976 levels and limited increases to 2 percent per year. When properties were sold, they would be reassessed at 1 percent of the sale price, with the 2 percent annual cap going back into place the following year.

Mayor Moscone and Governor Brown had both opposed Proposition 13 but had to comply with it once the voters approved the measure. Proposition 13 is not primarily a San Francisco story, but a California one. The idea for it came from Howard Jarvis, a Southern California businessman and antitax radical, as well as Paul Gann, an activist from Sacramento. Although many of San Francisco's political leaders and elected officials, including Moscone and Milk (who initially supported it), opposed the initiative, they were unable to stem the growing antitax fervor that would not just lead to Proposition 13 but would also be at the center of politics for at least the next generation.

Proposition 13, however, had an enormous, and alarmingly sudden, impact in San Francisco, as it did in most of California, but particularly in the state's biggest cities. In the weeks and months that followed the passage of Proposition 13, library hours were cut, park staff was reduced, and other services were slashed throughout cities in California, including San Francisco. Roger Kemp, writing on the early effect of Proposition 13, concluded, "The impact of this measure on local governments was not as severe as predicted but was still dramatic. The most immediate effect of the initiative was a local government revenue reduction of $7 billion. . . . Statewide, municipalities eliminated more than 3,000 positions. . . . Many of the public services provided by these positions were eliminated."[90]

Kemp also reported, "Local governments have had to reassess critical programs and redirect limited resources to meet priority services. Public library services, parks and recreational programs and cultural activities were most severely affected by the redirection of funds to other programs."[91] The damage that Proposition 13 did to San Francisco would be felt even more in the 1980s as AIDS, homelessness, fiscal crises that defined California for much of the rest of the twentieth century, and federal budget cuts created an even greater strain on the city's budget. The progressive victories of 1975 and 1977 in San Francisco were proving to be counter, at least for the moment, to the broader trends in California.

While Mayor Moscone and other city officials sought strategies for adapting to the new fiscal reality brought about by Proposition 13, another initiative—Proposition 6, an effort to curtail the rights of gay men and lesbians to work as teachers—that would appear on the November ballot was gaining support throughout the state. This was a reminder that San Francisco, where a gay supervisor could pass a gay rights ordinance with a vote of 10–1, was not always in step with the rest of the state or country. Many gay San Franciscans were aware of the amendment and were concerned about further efforts to limit their rights. Harvey Milk was an outspoken opponent of the initiative, but many San Francisco Democrats, including Mayor Moscone and Governor Brown, shared his view.

At this point in 1978, the issues that would make it such a pivotal year were beginning to emerge. Those same conditions were also making it possible for San Francisco–style punk rock to come into its own. Proposition 13 guaranteed that fiscal problems would persist in urban California, thus creating the physical and social ecology that made a movement based in roughly equal parts around anger, youthful despair, and cheap space possible, while also making it very hard for city governments facing cuts in state funding to implement progressive economic policies. The extremely political nature of everything in San Francisco, from crime to personal conduct, meant that it was natural for punk itself to become more political. The punks, both the musicians and those who just went to shows and bought the few records that were available, found themselves crafting a movement that reflected the San Francisco of the moment and that would have a surprisingly enduring impact on the city and its culture.

7

The Pennant Race

•••••••••••••••••••••

By mid-August, the pennant race had tightened quite a bit. The Giants had been in first place since May 14. They had been alone in first place for almost that entire time, and in a tie with either the Dodgers or the Reds for nine of those days. Although the Giants had enjoyed a strong run atop the National League West, they had never been able to open up a big margin over their division rivals. Between April 30 and June 28, the Giants won 36 of 54 games, for a winning percentage of .667. That run, which lasted about a third of the season, had lifted them from fourth place, four games behind the Dodgers, to three games ahead of the second-place Reds. Other than those fifty-four games, the Giants were not a particularly good team in 1978, playing at a .472 clip.

In the period July 2–20, the Giants went 10–9, but the Dodgers stumbled uncharacteristically as well, going only 9–9. On July 20, the day after a show at the Mab where a new punk rock band called Dead Kennedys played together in public for the first time, the Pirates rallied for a run on singles by Ed Ott, Bruce Kison, and Frank Taveras off of Terry Forster in the bottom of the tenth inning in Pittsburgh to beat the Dodgers 7–6. In Philadelphia, the Reds were busy losing to the Phillies by a score of 8–6. That same day, the Giants were in Wrigley Field, a good hitter's park, playing the Cubs. The Giants and Cubs had a bit of a slugfest, but Jack Clark drove in catcher

John Tamargo with a single off of Bruce Sutter in the top of the eighth to give the Giants a 9–8 lead. That might have been enough for the Giants to hold on for the win, but the game was called for darkness immediately after the hit. The two teams had to wait until July 28 when the Cubs were in San Francisco to finish the game. Even though the Giants had no official game results that day, losses by the Dodgers and Reds put the Giants three games up yet again.

In July and August, during what in warmer climes is referred to as the dog days of summer, the legacy of 1978, on and off the ball field, was beginning to take shape. More bad news trickled out from Jonestown, but events there still seemed very far away to most San Franciscans, including the city's political leadership. Harvey Milk, who was beginning to emerge as a national political figure, began to turn his attention to the threat of Proposition 6, the homophobic initiative that would be on the ballot in only a few months. Early polls showed the proposition would pass, writing antigay discrimination into law and threatening the livelihood of every gay teacher in California. Meanwhile, Dan White was increasingly frustrated on the board of supervisors and finding it stressful trying to raise a family on his modest government salary, Dead Kennedys brought increased attention to the city's vibrant punk rock scene, and the Giants began to tumble into the mediocrity that would define them for the next several years.

In early August 1978, it was not yet apparent where all this would lead. When the month began, the Giants led the Reds by half a game and the Dodgers by one and a half games. The race was very close, but the Giants were still in first. At that point in the middle of the summer, the Giants were emerging as the big story in San Francisco. One of the reasons that warning signs from Jonestown, the growing tension between Dan White and Harvey Milk, and even the important musical happenings in North Beach were not getting the attention they may have deserved was because for the first time in years, the Giants had won the hearts of San Franciscans. For many San Franciscans, 1978 up to that point was the summer of the Giants.

The national baseball media was beginning to recognize this as well. Ron Firmite, in an August 7 article in *Sports Illustrated*, captured the feeling in San Francisco about the Giants, one that had not been apparent in years: "Clearly Giant baseball is all the rage in the Bay Area again. In saloons and restaurants, on the floors of the brokerage houses, in the North Beach coffeehouses, in the parks and on the Bay, the most pressing question these days is 'what's the score?'"[1]

Another newspaper article described the Giants' revival in colorful detail as well:

> The Giants, resting in first place in the National League's Western Division, already have passed the million mark in attendance—the first time that's happened in seven years—and "Giants Mania" is sweeping the city.
>
> Transistor radios once again are tuned in to KSFO and play-by-play announcers Lon Simmons and Joe Angel. People all over town—young and old, rich and poor—are sporting orange and black Giants caps.
>
> "Go Giants" someone has spray painted, in orange paint, of course, on a bare concrete retaining wall near Fisherman's Wharf.
>
> The taverns, from Perry's on Union St. to Lefty O'Doul's on Geary and Reno Barsocchini's on Battery, are full of baseball talk. No. Make that Giants talk.
>
> Willie McCovey, who has been playing baseball here so long that Mayor George Moscone once described the powerful and ruling first baseman as a local landmark, "equivalent to the Golden Gate Bridge and cable cars" said the crowds this year are unlike any he has seen before.[2]

This report was not written in a local San Francisco paper whose readership would have included many Giants fans, but in the *Los Angeles Times*. If the Los Angeles papers believed that the excitement in San Francisco around the Giants was worth covering, then something significant was occurring in San Francisco.

The 162-game baseball season is long. In those days when teams had to win a division of six or seven teams to make it to the playoffs, the length of the season had a way of bringing the best teams to the top. In 1978, the Dodgers were the better team, and they proved it in three or four weeks between July 21 and August 16. The Dodgers were a very consistent team in 1978, with a winning record in every calendar month of the regular season except October, when they only played one game before the playoffs started. The Giants had a losing record after the All-Star break, but the Dodgers were better than .500 in both halves.

The Dodgers did not overtake the Giants on the strength of one great stretch. Instead, they continued to play very good, but not spectacular, ball from July 21 through August 16, going 17–10. The Reds, also showing that they were not going to fade away easily, won a respectable fourteen of twenty-six games over this same stretch. The Giants didn't exactly collapse during this period, but they also didn't keep up with the veteran-laden Dodgers or Reds teams. After the game at Wrigley that was suspended because of darkness, the Giants came back to the 'Stick and took two out of three from Pittsburgh, keeping them two games ahead of the Reds. A split of a two-game home series against St. Louis allowed the Giants to pick up half a game on the Reds, but now the Dodgers were only two games back.

The Giants were slowly losing ground. When the Cubs came to town, the Giants won the resumed game from July 20 but could only manage a split of the four-game series, leaving them clinging to a one-and-a-half-game lead over both Cincinnati and Los Angeles. Losing two of three to the Astros didn't help as the Giants prepared to host the Dodgers for a four-game weekend set beginning August 3. The Giants began that series half a game up on the Reds and two and a half games ahead of the Dodgers.

A Willie McCovey home run, eight and two-thirds tough innings from Jim Barr, and a walk-off single by Darrell Evans gave the Giants a 5–4 win in the first game on Thursday night at the 'Stick. On Friday night, Vida Blue, like Barr the night before, came within one out of a complete-game victory, again proving his value to the team. The 2–1 Giants win put Blue's record at 16–4. The Giants lost the next game 2–0 as rookie Bob Welch outdueled Ed Halicki, and lost again 5–1 as Bob Knepper had his worst outing of the year, giving up four earned runs while only retiring one batter. That loss put the Giants in a tie for first with the Reds, with the Dodgers still two and a half games back. A total of more than 193,000 fans packed Candlestick Park for that series against the Dodgers. Most would have preferred a sweep, but at least it was August and the Giants were still in first.

The Giants then split a two-game set with the Astros, this time in San Francisco. The race had now tightened even more as the Giants headed to Los Angeles for a four-game showdown. The Giants were in first with the Reds half a game behind and the Dodgers half a game behind Cincinnati. On Thursday, August 10, Bob Welch again shut the Giants down, holding them to two runs in eight innings, while Blue was not himself, getting lit up for seven earned runs while not making it out of the fourth inning. He walked three while giving up nine hits, including home runs to Dodger sluggers Ron Cey and Reggie Smith. The loss dropped the Giants into a first-place tie with the Dodgers, while the Reds were only half a game back.

On August 11, another loss to the Dodgers dropped the Giants out of that first-place tie and into third place, but Bob Knepper held the Dodgers in check the next day as the Giants, behind home runs by Bill Madlock and

Mike Ivie, beat Tommy John and the Dodgers 3–2 to get back into a tie for first place. The next day, another big hit by Jack Clark gave the Giants a 7–6 lead over the Dodgers in the top of the eleventh. In the bottom half of that frame, Joe Altobelli had to turn the game over to John Curtis and then Ed Halicki. The tall righty Halicki retired Steve Garvey and Dusty Baker on fly balls, and the Giants were able to hold on to a win they desperately needed. The Giants had gone down to Los Angeles and survived. They were now one game ahead of the Dodgers and one and a half games ahead of the Reds with the season a little more than two-thirds over. The Giants and Dodgers had played eight games against each other in a ten-day span, with each team winning four. The more than 207,000 fans who saw the southern half of those games were probably no more satisfied with a split than fans in San Francisco had been the previous weekend. Despite this hiccup, the Giants at 69–49 still had the best record in the National League. In all of the big leagues, only the Red Sox at 74–42 had a better record. The Red Sox were sitting on a nine-game lead over the Yankees and seemed to be comfortably running away with their division.

On August 16, despite losing the previous evening in Montreal, the Giants were still tied with the Dodgers as they prepared to play the Expos in the second game of a three-game series in Montreal. The game pitted two veteran lefties, Blue and Montreal's Woodie Fryman, against each other. The two pitchers were on top of their game. Blue ably handled a slugging Montreal lineup that included future Hall of Famers Andre Dawson, Tony Perez, and Gary Carter, as well as solid hitters Ellis Valentine, Larry Parrish, and Warren Cromartie. Blue gave up three hits and one run while striking out one batter for each of the eight innings he pitched. Unfortunately, Fryman was better, allowing only three Giants base runners, on one single and two walks. Fryman took a 1–0 lead into the bottom of the ninth before getting groundouts from catcher Marc Hill and pinch hitter Terry Whitfield. Larry Herndon then flew out to Cromartie in left, and the Giants did not see first place again in 1978.

The Giants had fallen out of first place because they had been a mediocre team for more than a month, while the Dodgers had shown that they were a championship-caliber team. However, the three months between May 12 and August 16 were the most exciting baseball the Giants played in the sixteen years between division titles in 1971 and 1987. During that time, which constituted more than half the season, the Giants were a good team, winning 57 percent of their ninety-one games. They were not, however, a great team. A .570 winning percentage is usually not good enough to win a division; this was particularly so back when there were only four divisions. The real reason the Giants were able to stay in first place so long is that the Dodgers and Reds both got off to slow starts. Nonetheless, spending more than half the season in first was an accomplishment for the Giants and one that energized a generation of fans caught in the midst of the worst years in their team's history. Those weeks in first place began to shake the team, the fans, and indeed the city out of the belief that the Giants were losers who could not succeed in San Francisco.

After losing to Woodie Fryman and falling out of first place, the Giants became almost another team. They managed to win the final game of the series against Montreal and the first game of a series in Philadelphia against the Phillies the next day, but from August 16 through the end of the season, the team went 20–22 for a .476 winning percentage. Vida Blue's record fell to 16–6 after losing to Fryman. Up to that point, he had been, with Clark, the player most responsible for the Giants' improbable run leading the National League West. After that game, Blue had four losses and only two wins over the rest of the season, although his ERA rose insignificantly from 2.67 on August 16 to 2.79 at the end of the season. Clark continued to hit, but the slugger who had driven in eighty-three runs in the first 120 games of the season only drove in fifteen in the remaining thirty-six games. Of course, wins and RBIs are dependent on what other players do as well. Clark was still a good hitter and Blue a good but not quite great pitcher during the last stretch of the season, but the rest of the team was no longer giving Clark the opportunity to drive in runs or Blue the opportunity to win ballgames.

On August 30, a 10–4 loss to the Mets combined with a Dodger win dropped the Giants two games behind Los Angeles. In the bottom of the fourth inning of that game, Willie McCovey singled, sending Jack Clark to third base. Moments later, McCovey dove back to first base on a pickoff throw and injured his shoulder. He did not play again until September 13, when he pinch hit. He started a game two days later, but after that he did not play again in 1978.

McCovey was not having a great year with the bat in 1978. Mike Ivie was, by that point, the better hitter, so in some respects the injury was not a major problem. Giants fans, however, did not feel that way. McCovey, while not close to being the dominant player he had been in the late 1960s and early 1970s, was still a valuable weapon. He was always a threat to hit the ball out of the park, and in games he did not start he was a reliable pinch hitter whose presence made opposing managers have to think through their late-inning strategy differently.

The forty-year-old first baseman was also the Giant most respected by his teammates and adored by the fans. With him out for the rest of the season, the writing was more or less on the wall for the Giants, as throughout September they gradually slipped further out of contention. From September 1 through the end of the season, the Giants posted a .414 winning percentage. The prompted Nick Peters at the *Sporting News* to observe, "The big question in the National League West this month is 'what happened to the Giants?' . . . All the good that had been done over the first few months of the season was suddenly slipping away. . . . There were looks of disbelief as players sat in silence during the uncontrollable dive."[3] The Giants were playing poorly in all aspects of the game, while Joe Altobelli's magic touch of calling on the right pinch hitter or reliever was no longer working either.

Harvey Milk Steps in It

The Giants were fading, but Harvey Milk was continuing to raise his profile. After passing the gay rights ordinance in March, Milk consistently voted with the other progressives on the board of supervisors and generally supported Mayor Moscone's agenda, but he had not yet authored any other memorable pieces of legislation. That changed on August 29 when San Francisco became the second city in the country to pass a law requiring dog owners to pick up after their pets.

Milk was the lead sponsor for the bill, which the board of supervisors passed unanimously on August 29. It was quickly signed into law by Mayor Moscone. The law itself was much like the one that had been passed in New York a few weeks earlier. Dog owners who did not comply by picking up their dog's waste would be fined ten dollars for a first offense. The amount of the fine would increase with each successive violation.

The "scoop the poop law," as Supervisor Dianne Feinstein dubbed it at the time, was a good issue for Harvey Milk. Shortly before the bill came to a vote, he held a press conference at Duboce Park, a small grassy area very close to the Castro, to publicize the bill. During the press conference, Milk said that San Franciscans could use whatever they wanted to pick up after their dogs: "some people using pie tins; some people using the *Wall Street Journal*."[4] After he concluded his comments, Milk walked off camera and accidentally stepped in a pile of dog feces. Of course, the location and the opportunities for Milk to do just that had been scouted by Milk's people in advance. That press conference was Milk at his best. He was funny, he supported his point with great visuals, and he even got a dig in at a conservative newspaper.

The issue may seem trivial in retrospect, but it was precisely the kind of idea around which Milk's broader progressive vision was built. In the 1970s, dog waste on the streets was one of those urban problems that was simply assumed to be a fact of life. Stepping in it was a regular occurrence for most city dwellers. The pooper scooper law, as it came to be known, was first passed in New York but best dramatized by Milk in San Francisco a few weeks later. It was a simple solution that had a huge impact on the many American cities that passed similar laws. With one simple law, streets were made cleaner and healthier, and in San Francisco a once major urban nuisance was all but eliminated.

This was also the kind of issue about which the downtown interests had very little concern. Dogs were more common in the residential neighborhoods such as the Castro, the Marina, West Portal, and Dan White's Excelsior than they were in the Financial District. By taking the lead on this law, Milk showed that city government could be put to work to solve simple but real problems that regular San Franciscans, regardless of race, ethnicity, or sexual orientation, confronted where they lived.

Although Milk was very much on the left, this vision was not simply ideological. Over the following decades, urban politicians on both the left and the right crafted political programs that sought to address seemingly minor issues that affected people directly in the hopes that this would contribute to safer and more pleasant cities. The leap from Milk's concern about dog poop to James Wilson's "broken windows" theory of crime fighting that was central to the urban governance approach of conservative mayors such as Richard Riordan in Los Angeles in the 1990s and, most notably, Rudolph Giuliani in New York from 1994 to 2001, was not a big one. Needless to say, Milk did not pepper his quality-of-life concerns with racism and intolerance as Giuliani so frequently did.

The Jim Bouton Game

When the Giants started their September 14 game against the Atlanta Braves, they were in second place, seven games behind the Dodgers and only very tenuously still in the race for the division title. The previous night they had lost to the Braves 5–3 in 12 innings. They had been stymied by a thirty-nine-year-old knuckleballer, as Phil Niekro pitched ten innings without giving up an earned run. However, the Giants managed three unearned runs on seven hits and one walk against the Braves ace. For perhaps the only time in baseball history, on September 14 the Giants found themselves facing a thirty-nine-year-old right-handed knuckleball specialist for the second game in a row. The pitcher that day was Niekro's teammate Jim Bouton. That game completed a very unusual decade-long journey for Bouton that began in Seattle in 1969 and was a surreal coda to the Giants' first-place run from earlier in the season.

Bouton is one of the most important and influential baseball players in history not for anything he did on the field, but for writing *Ball Four*. *Ball Four* is a journal of Bouton's 1969 season, which was split between the Seattle Pilots, a team that existed for one year before moving to Milwaukee and becoming the Brewers, and the Houston Astros, with a brief jaunt to the Pilots' Pacific Coast League affiliate in Vancouver. However, describing *Ball Four* simply as the journal of a big league pitcher is like describing Woodstock as simply a rock and roll concert. Bouton's book was groundbreaking and controversial but also irreverent, providing an honest look at the pettiness, boredom, frustrations, and fun of being a big league ballplayer in 1969. It helped transform sports journalism.

Ball Four made Bouton an outcast in the baseball world and a target of criticism from many in a very conservative business. Bouton had been a fastball pitcher with the Yankees in the early 1960s but injured his arm. By the late 1960s, he was trying to make a comeback by relying on his knuckleball. In 1969, he appeared in seventy-three games for the Astros and Pilots, all but two in relief, and his ERA was 3.96. He struck out a hundred batters while only walking fifty. That was a useful but not great year, and midway through the 1970 season, during which Bouton struggled, he was released by the Astros amid growing criticism of his book from the baseball establishment.

Bouton spent the following years writing, newscasting, and acting, even serving as a delegate for George McGovern to the 1972 Democratic Convention, but he never left baseball behind entirely. He pitched for the Portland Mavericks, an independent minor league team in 1975, and by September 1978 had made it all the way back to the big leagues with the Atlanta Braves.

He made a start that September against the first-place Dodger team that constituted his first big league appearance since 1970, but it did not go well. Bouton gave up six earned runs on six hits, including home runs by Rick Monday and Davey Lopes, and four walks in five innings. His next start was scheduled for the September 14 in San Francisco.

In his book about Bouton's 1978 season, Terry Pluto describes what happened next:

> It was another clear day; this time the game was being played in San Francisco's Candlestick Park, where there is always a nice breeze. It was good knuckleball weather.... Once again, Bouton started well, holding the second place Giants scoreless in the first two innings. San Francisco broke through for a run in the third.... This time, Bouton didn't lose control of his knuckleball in the crucial situations. Now he made the pitches to the spots which left the hitters spitting, swearing, swinging and missing. After six innings, he had allowed only three hits, two them being looping opposite field doubles.[5]

Bouton ended up going six innings, giving up one unearned run on three hits and three walks against the Giants, and picking up his final big league win as the Braves edged the Giants 4–1. Bouton struck out both Madlock and Ivie in the first inning. In the *Sporting News*, Nick Peters referred to the game as the Giants "suffering the ignominy of a loss to Jim Bouton and the Atlanta Braves" and called it an "embarrassing defeat."[6] After the season, Bouton retired from baseball for good, but it was becoming that kind of year for the Giants and for San Francisco.

The lineup Joe Altobelli made out a few weeks later on October 1 was not a strong one. The Dodgers had already clinched the division. It was the last game of the season, and many regulars were given the day off. Marc Hill, Mike Ivie, Willie McCovey, Bill Madlock, Johnnie LeMaster, Darrell Evans, and Larry Herndon were not in the lineup. Instead, players including Rob Andrews, Jim Dwyer, John Tamargo, Tom Heintzelman, and Hector Cruz combined for four singles, a walk, and a double against three Astros pitchers. When Astros reliever Mark Lemongello retired Tamargo, Cruz, and Heintzelman on fly balls in the ninth, the Giants season, their winningest since 1971, was over. It had been by most measures a successful one.

The Giants missed the postseason, but they had been in the middle of a pennant race for much of the year, including two months in first place. They had drawn more than 1.7 million fans for only the second time since the team had moved to San Francisco. There were a lot of positives to be taken away from the season on the field as well. Vida Blue had reestablished himself as one of the best pitchers in the game and was named the National League's left-handed pitcher of the year by the *Sporting News*. Bob Knepper had pitched well all year and given the Giants two strong southpaws at the top of the rotation. Jack Clark and Mike Ivie had both had excellent seasons and were likely to get better into the early 1980s. Clark joined Blue on the *Sporting News* All-Star Team. Darrell Evans and Bill Madlock were solid and dependable veterans. Joe Altobelli encountered some criticism as the season wound down and the Giants fell to third place but was named National League Manager of the Year by the *Sporting News*.

In the context of their time and place, the 1978 Giants had accomplished something extraordinary. During the 1970s, the two Bay Area baseball teams combined to win six division titles, five by the Oakland A's (1971–1975) and one by the Giants (1971). The A's went on to win three pennants and three World Series in 1972–1974. The Giants lost to the Pittsburgh Pirates in 1971, their only postseason appearance of the decade. Over the course of the 1970s some very good players played for these two teams. Ten future Hall of Famers appeared in a Giants or A's uniform during the 1970s: Gaylord Perry, Juan Marichal, and Willie Mays for the Giants, and Reggie Jackson, Rollie Fingers, Catfish Hunter, Billy Williams, Orlando Cepeda, and Rickey Henderson for the A's. Hall-of-Famer Willie McCovey played for both the Giants and the A's. From 1971 to 1976, the A's had at least three future Hall of Famers on their roster. The 1970–1971 Giants had four.

None of these division-winning teams or teams with multiple future Hall of Famers drew more fans than the third-place 1978 Giants. Of those ten Hall of Famers, only one, Willie McCovey, was on that 1978 Giants team. The 1,740,477 fans who poured into Candlestick Park that year represented the second-largest crowd to see any Giants team up until that time, and the largest since 1960. No A's team drew more than that from the time they began playing in Oakland in 1968 until they finally drew 2,287,335 fans in their pennant-winning 1988 season.

Most Giants fans in 1978 saw the Giants as having a bright future even if they did not win a tough division race that year. The starting outfielders, in addition to key contributors such as Ivie and Knepper, were twenty-five or younger. The rest of the starting pitching rotation was under thirty. Swingman Jim Barr, at thirty, was the oldest Giants starting pitcher of any note.

Relief standouts Gary Lavelle and Randy Moffitt were also under thirty, as was star leadoff hitter Bill Madlock.

There were also some obvious holes that the Giants needed to address. Neither Johnnie LeMaster nor Marc Hill could hit much. The Giants could have probably gotten by with one nonhitter at a defensive position, but with two the lineup was just too short. Opposing pitchers had to worry only about the first six batters, as the Hill-LeMaster-pitcher bottom third of the lineup was no threat at all. Additionally, while Terry Whitfield and Larry Herndon had both hit well in 1978, the Giants probably needed to upgrade at one of those outfield positions to contend in 1979 and 1980. Like all teams, the Giants could have used one more starting pitcher, particularly as The Count, for the second year in a row, had regressed. Despite all these reasons to be concerned, most Giants fans, including me, were hopeful—and wrong. The Giants had given their fan base a rare reason to be optimistic but had also revived a franchise and that franchise's relationship with its fan base, which was in pretty bad shape going into the season. This revival made a lasting impression on many fans well beyond what a third-place team usually manages to do.

Several factors came together for the Giants in 1978 that made them more than just an ordinary third-place team. There are many ways for a team to end up in third place with 89 wins and six games behind the division winner. Some play solid baseball throughout the season but spend very little time in first place. Others stay around .500 for most of the season but then get hot at the end when they have little chance of making the postseason. However, the 1978 Giants finished third by falling off in mid-August after spending nearly three months atop the National League West. This formula is the best one for generating interest and bringing fans to the park, because fans like to see their team in first place. The Giants remained in first and in a reasonably close race for the division title for so long that fans had reason to go to games and remain hopeful well into late summer. Thus, the team was able to sustain high attendance throughout most of the season.

When the Giants traded for Vida Blue in spring training, they not only added a top pitcher, but they showed that they were not content to be a mediocre team and were going to try to win. That is certainly how fans in San Francisco interpreted it and how the Giants presented it. The trade paid off, in 1978 at least, beyond what the team could have hoped. Blue had a great year, going 18–10 with a 2.79 ERA while finishing third in the Cy Young balloting and twelfth in MVP voting. Blue also brought both a winning pedigree and good energy to a franchise that badly needed both. In many respects, 1978 for the Giants was the year of Vida Blue, and fans responded to that.

Jack Clark was also a big part of the Giants' success both on and off the field in 1978. Advanced metrics place him as having the fifth-most WAR of any player and third-most of any position player in the National League. He also finished seventh in batting and hits, while leading the league in doubles and extra-base hits. After the season, Clark finished fifth in the balloting for the National League MVP. Overall, the Giants did not have a great offense in 1978, finishing seventh in runs scored. Without Clark, they would have been worse than that. The remainder of Clark's tenure with the Giants was complex, but in 1978 he was simply a hot-hitting twenty-two-year-old star with a bright future.

There was more to it than that. Clark was the first player developed by the Giants who became a star in the post–Willie Mays era. Perhaps because of his skill set—he was a good hitter with a better batting eye than Mays had but did not approach the Say Hey Kid's power and skill in the field or on the bases—or perhaps because he was white, Clark was not compared to Mays the way so many Giants prospects in the previous ten years had been. This also had an effect on fans who would never be satisfied with a young player if they were constantly comparing him to Mays. As long as the aging Mays was on the team or a very recent memory, it was very tempting to do that. Clark was different. He was drafted out of high school by the Giants a year after Mays had been sent to the Mets. This alleviated some of the pressure on Clark and allowed fans and team officials to see him in a more realistic light.

Clark's emergence as a star was one of the first positive stories, other than the return of Willie McCovey in 1977, of the post-Mays era. The team for which Clark was the hitting star in 1978 was the first good Giants team since Willie Mays had been traded. This demonstrated to the fans that the Willie Mays period was finally over and that it was possible for the Giants to be good despite no longer having the best player of the postwar era on the club. That created a new life for the franchise and allowed it to begin to redefine itself and its relationship to the city more generally. Equally importantly, it put an end to talk of the Giants leaving town, at least for a few years.

Harvey Milk and the New Year

As it turned out, the most exciting pennant race in the big leagues in 1978 was not in the National League West, but in the American League East. The Yankees and Red Sox, the two best teams in baseball in 1978, had ended the season with identical records of 99–63. They were scheduled to meet in Boston on October 2, the day after the season ended, for a one-game playoff. The winner would advance to the American League Championship Series; the loser would go home. It was a very exciting game, as the Yankees came from behind to win 5–4. The game came down to the final out, as Yankee reliever Goose Gossage, probably the best of his generation, got Red Sox legend Carl Yastrzemski to foul out to third baseman Graig Nettles with the tying and winning runs on base. That Yankee-Red Sox matchup is most famous for the clutch three-run home run by light-hitting Yankee shortstop Bucky Dent, or as he is still known in New England, Bucky F**king Dent.

Up and down the East Coast, Yankee and Red Sox fans were following the game on radio and television. Jewish fans of both teams faced a particular challenge because the game fell on Rosh Hashanah, the Jewish New Year and one of the holiest days in the Jewish calendar. In New York, Rosh Hashanah has long been a day off for all public and independent school children, but not in San Francisco. Back then, taking a day off for Rosh Hashanah required phone calls to school, explanations to teachers and friends, and the like. My mother's secular views, lack of childcare, and belief in education meant that my brother and I were in school that day instead of ducking out of services early to watch the game, as we should have been doing.

It is not clear how Harvey Milk spent his last Rosh Hashanah on earth. He may have gone to shul, taken a few moments of reflection, or found some time to dip a slice of apple in some honey between meetings. It is unlikely that Milk did nothing to recognize the significance of the day, because he never forgot or sought to conceal his Jewish identity.

Milk occupies an enormous space in American history and in civil rights history because he was gay and played a groundbreaking role in gay liberation, but it is not possible to disaggregate his politics and his personality from his Judaism. San Francisco was not free of anti-Jewish sentiment in 1978. It was still a place where one heard phrases like "Jew him down" with some frequency and where Jewish businesspeople who were recent migrants to San Francisco were often tagged as "pushy New Yorkers"—and everybody understood precisely what that meant. In general, low-level anti-Semitism was relatively common. San Francisco had long had a Jewish community, but the Jews who had deep roots in San Francisco tended to be very highly assimilated German Jews. These Jews often had anglicized names, spoke no Yiddish, at least in public, and were rarely very religiously observant.

Sharyn Saslafsky moved to San Francisco from New Haven, Connecticut, around the time Harvey Milk arrived in San Francisco from New York. The two became friends and political allies. Saslafsky described the Jewish community she encountered in San Francisco: "High reform, wealthy . . . I went to services . . . no yarmulkes, no tallits, nothing. It was uncomfortable." San Francisco was the kind of place, continued Saslafsky, where "the first time I asked for corned beef on rye they said 'With lettuce, onion, and tomato?'"[7]

Harvey Milk was not part of that San Francisco German Jewish world. Like many Jewish New Yorkers of his age, he was no more than two generations removed from the shtetls of Eastern Europe. Milk spoke some Yiddish and, in San Francisco, his New York–accented English immediately marked him as Jewish. This alone represented a break from San Francisco's more established Jewish community where, according to Saslafsky, "if you went to high reform . . . it was disallowed. Yiddish was not the language that was spoken."[8] During the 1960s and 1970s, when many thousands of young people moved to San Francisco looking for a new kind of life or a place to be gay without being harassed, thousands of Jews with backgrounds similar to Milk's came to the city. These migrants not only helped remake their new home but also remade the face of Jewish San Francisco. Gradually, San Francisco's Jewry became less dominated by German Jews and developed stronger ties to New York. The brashness, humor, and progressive politics that we took with us from New York stood in sharp contrast to the city's more staid older Jewish community.

Milk was not a very observant Jew, but his synagogue was Sha'ar Zahav, perhaps America's first predominantly gay synagogue. The rabbi there was Allan Bennett, the first openly gay rabbi in the United States. Bennett, like Milk, was not a native San Franciscan but had moved there from Akron, Ohio. Bennett and Milk's nephew Stuart Milk both described Milk as not traditionally observant but frequently interested in discussing questions about Torah.[9]

Milk's politics were also unmistakably informed by his Judaism and grew out of the same left-of-center, rights-oriented New York Jewish progressive context that launched many twentieth-century progressives. Bennett told

me, "Any Jewish identity of his [Milk's] was not so much a religious identity as a cultural and political identity. I don't think he would have articu-
lated his values as religious values."[10] Nonetheless, Milk's progressive values
and rhetoric were very much those of the post-Holocaust Jewish American
left. Milk was not a baby boomer. He was born in 1930, before World War
II, and was old enough to have remembered that period and to have been
aware of the Holocaust while it was occurring. As a gay Jewish man, Milk
likely felt the memory of the Holocaust very profoundly, as gays and lesbians were also targets of Hitler's genocidal regime. Saslafsky told me, "Never
again . . . ran through Harvey in so many different ways. . . . He was keenly
aware of the possibilities that exist out there that never again could happen."
She added that the progressive Jewish tradition "was just a part of who he
was . . . going through him as a Jewish man."[11]

Milk's biographer Randy Shilts describes a scene in 1962 when Milk's
lover invited a German friend to dinner. At that dinner which occurred while
Milk was living in New York, according to Shilts, "Milk quickly turned the
conversation to the Holocaust. What did the guest think about Buchen-
wald? When Joe's friend said he didn't know about the death camps, Harvey flew into a rampage. 'How could you have lived in Germany and not
known what was going on? . . . Were you deaf? Dumb? Blind? Huh?' Joe was
now convinced Harvey had a persecution complex. Harvey told Joe he was
anti-Semitic."[12] Shilts relates that anecdote as a way to show Milk's quick
temper and impatience, but Milk's reaction to having a German guest in his
home only seventeen years after the Shoah was similar to how many American Jews would have reacted. It is not hard for me to imagine Milk's words
coming out of the mouths of my own parents and grandparents or the parents and grandparents of many of my Jewish friends.

Milk's post-Holocaust politics are also evident from his speeches and
other comments. In perhaps his most famous single speech, delivered at the
Gay Freedom Day parade in 1978, he used a very clear reference to Hitler:
"We are not going to sit back in silence as 300,000 of our gay brothers and
sisters did in Nazi Germany. We are not going to let our rights be taken away
and then march . . . into the gas chambers."[13] Milk was rarely hesitant to
make comparisons between Nazis and those who sought to limit the rights
of gay people.

As early as 1973, during his first campaign for the board of supervisors,
Milk similarly drew on what he had learned as a post-Holocaust American
Jew to frame his thinking about the struggle for gay liberation: "If there

comes an oppression as there did in Germany for the Jews, it won't matter where we were different in our economic thinking. Hitler didn't care if the Jew was an ultra liberal or a conservative. He was Jewish and he went into a concentration camp. We're in bed together . . . by the fact that we're all homosexuals. If we don't understand that, we're in trouble."[14] Milk's comments, drawing on his understanding of twentieth-century Jewish history, demonstrate that his desire for gay solidarity and for a gay political identity was based in substantial part on his own Jewish identity.

Milk also differed from many on the left who were fifteen or more years younger than him and born after the war. There was little room in Milk's politics for reflexive anti-Americanism. Unlike some of the more radical hippies and most of the punk rockers hanging out a few miles northeast of the Castro at the Mab or the On Broadway, Milk did not see the United States as simply an evil force in the world. He channeled that feeling into a patriotic appeal for gay rights. That 1978 Gay Freedom Day speech ended with Milk speaking directly to antigay bigots in extremely patriotic tones:

> Let me remind you of what America is. . . . Listen carefully. On the Statue of Liberty it says "Give me your tired, your poor, your huddled masses yearning to be free." . . . In the Declaration of Independence it is written "All men are created equal and they are endowed with certain inalienable rights." . . . And in our national anthem it says "Oh, say does that star-spangled banner yet wave o'er the land of the free." For . . . all the bigots out there: that's what America is. No matter how hard you try, you cannot erase those words from the Declaration of Independence. No matter how hard you try, you cannot chip those words from off the base of the Statue of Liberty. And no matter how hard you try you cannot sing the "Star Spangled Banner" without those words. That's what America is. Love it or leave it.[15]

In the 1970s, this was powerful and unusual rhetoric for a progressive. During Milk's time, conservatives actually said things like "America, love it or leave it," and "Go back to Russia" to people who demonstrated in support of civil rights, feminism, or gay rights, or who protested against the war in Vietnam. From conservatives, these words were meant to shut down dissenting voices and stop protest. From Milk, these words were unexpected and empowering, particularly for a group of people, gays and lesbians, who in many cases were fighting for basic rights that are guaranteed by the Constitution. Like many in the civil rights movement, Milk saw the gay rights struggle as about winning equality and the rights the Constitution gives to all Americans.

There is also a timelessness to Milk's appeal to America values. These same sentences would not have been out of place in 1920 at a labor rally, in 1965 at a civil rights rally, in 2017 at a rally against banning refugees, or at virtually any other time in American history. In many respects, Milk was a sui generis leader helping to craft a new civil rights movement as it unfolded, but he was also part of a longer American progressive tradition.

Pier 39

Two days after Rosh Hashanah, on October 4, Giants fans were not happy that the Dodgers, rather than the Giants, were in Philadelphia to play the Phillies in game 1 of the National League Championship Series. Closer to home, Dianne Feinstein was joined by several businesspeople, city officials, and media representatives on San Francisco's waterfront. The president of the board of supervisors, who had long been a supporter of business interests and more development, was there to cut the ribbon for a major new San Francisco destination.

Over the last fifty years, Dianne Feinstein has been a constant presence in politics. She served on the San Francisco Board of Supervisors from 1969 until late 1978, as mayor from that time through the end of 1987, and as a U.S. senator from 1992 to the present. As senator, she represents all of California, but she has always maintained a special connection to her hometown. In October 1978, however, her political longevity could not have been predicted. Feinstein had already run for mayor and lost in 1971 and 1975. Although she was president of the board of supervisors, because of her two failed campaigns for mayor, she had no clear path to higher office. Feinstein was respected but not yet recognized as the tough and charismatic politician that even her many detractors know her to be today.

Perhaps that is why, at this event on October 4, the president of the board of supervisors, and the most powerful female elected official in San Francisco history, was clad in a one-piece vintage men's bathing suit. Feinstein wore a bathing suit presumably because she was presiding over the ribbon cutting of Pier 39, a waterfront shopping and dining project aimed at revitalizing that part of town, and to make good, after a fashion, on a promise she had made that she would wear a bikini to the opening of Pier

39. Feinstein's decision to wear a bathing suit was a reflection of stereotypes about gender that were still very strong in 1978, but it was also a little bit of a reflection of San Francisco's late 1970s offbeat image.

Pier 39 was the brainchild of Warren Simmons, a pilot, entrepreneur, restaurateur, and developer. He had spent five years advocating for Pier 39—an actual pier, albeit a decrepit one—to be rebuilt and turned into a kind of seaside mall. Pier 39 is close to Fisherman's Wharf, which by 1978 was also a bit rundown but still a popular tourist destination, and not far from Ghirardelli Square, the chocolate factory that had been converted into a tourist attraction with restaurants, an ice cream parlor, shops, and outdoor entertainment.

Simmons had spent years working to get the approvals for Pier 39. He is said to have presented a slideshow to countless neighborhood groups, and even informal gatherings of people from the community, as well as to the board of supervisors and all the relevant committees. This is probably true, but Simmons also was a political player who contributed to campaigns and sought to build relationships with key political actors in the city. One of his new tenants at Pier 39, for example, was to be a baked potato cart run by a member of the board of supervisors and his wife. The *San Francisco Bay Guardian*, a left-of-center publication, had mentioned this forthrightly in its September 28 issue: "San Francisco Supervisor Dan White has been out lobbying on behalf of Warren Simmons North Point Pier, Inc., where White holds a potentially lucrative lease and intends to sell potatoes from a fast food operation called the Hot Potato."[16] White defended himself, claiming, "I don't think my office precludes me from testifying as a private individual,"[17] but this activity was corrupt and did not go unnoticed by law enforcement. According to Shilts, "Simmons gave White a concession for a fried potato stand to help augment the sparse $800 monthly salary supervisors earned. . . . The FBI started a probe into Dan White's connections with Simmons to see if the concession was a payoff for political favors."[18]

Dan White's mishandling of the politics and money around Pier 39 was further evidence of his limited political abilities. Many local politicians act in ethically challenged ways, but the more skilled ones are less blatant about it. White traded a vote on Pier 39 for the right to operate a small business on Pier 39. That would have made it pretty easy for investigators looking to find a quid pro quo. Additionally, what White got in exchange for his vote was the right to run a small business that might have been lucrative but also would have been a lot of work. These were not the actions of a man, even a less than ethical one, who truly understood how the business of politics worked.

Pier 39 was the antithesis of what Harvey Milk was trying to do in San Francisco. Milk sought a city where the needs of ordinary people in ordinary neighborhoods were paramount. Pier 39 was an effort to bring people from the other parts of San Francisco, and beyond the city, to shop, eat, and spend a day in an area that was almost entirely artificial. It was in San Francisco but certainly not of San Francisco. The critique offered by San Francisco literary figure Horace Schwartz summarized this sentiment: "It [Pier 39] is the Zsa Zsa Gabor of shopping centers—beautiful, lifeless and totally mercenary."[19] Many progressives feared that if a prodevelopment politician, like Dianne Feinstein, ever became mayor there would be more Pier 39–type developments. However, in October 1978 it seemed premature to worry about that happening anytime soon.

Tourist-oriented malls, whether indoor or outdoor, like Pier 39, now dot much of urban America, as they have for the last few decades, but in 1978 they were relatively new. While Pier 39 quickly became a destination for tourists to San Francisco who did not want to experience the real city, it was also somewhere for locals to go. Pier 39 was a long ride on the 30 Stockton even from our place in Cow Hollow, but it was also a reasonably fun way for my brother and me to spend a weekend day, particularly if it was not baseball season or if the Giants were out of town. There was ample junk food, a lot of other kids, and goofy street performances to watch. We rarely bought anything at the baked potato stand, preferring to spend whatever money we had on less healthy options. However, my friends and I knew whose family owned the potato place. Whenever we peeked inside the booth and saw a middle-aged woman working there, we told each other that she was Dan White's wife.

Pier 39 was a shining, vibrant symbol of the San Francisco that punk rockers hated. Warren Simmons, Dianne Feinstein, and others who supported the seaside mall had a plan for San Francisco that would threaten the infrastructure that made punk rock possible. Developers and the politicians who supported them looked at unused industrial spaces, abandoned buildings, and empty apartments not as the incubators of an important new cultural movement, but as the home of future malls, luxury apartments, office complexes, and, yes, a baseball stadium.

Between the time Dianne Feinstein cut the ribbon at Pier 39 in her bathing suit and thirty-two years later almost to the day when the Giants hosted the Texas Rangers in game 1 of the 2010 World Series only a few blocks further south on the city's eastern coast, San Francisco's population grew by almost a third, as the city redefined itself as the center of the global tech boom. With that redefinition came a bevy of shiny office buildings and condominiums, many not far from Pier 39. There are parts of the city, for example the Outer Sunset and Outer Richmond districts, that physically still look very similar to how they did in 1978. The northeastern and eastern flanks of San Francisco are not among them.

The area between Pier 39 and the new ballpark, where the Giants moved following the 1999 season, is one of the neighborhoods where the new San Francisco is most clearly on display. Pier 39 is no longer new and is now left almost entirely to particularly unadventurous tourists. However, a few blocks to the south the Ferry Building, which underwent a major renovation in 2003, draws both tourists and locals, including many tech workers from nearby offices. It offers great views and a broad array of high-end food shops and restaurants, and even a few actual ferries stop there. The farmers market that is held outside the Ferry Building on Thursdays and Saturdays is a popular hangout for many locals and visitors.

Although it would have been almost impossible to foresee what the waterfront would look like in the twenty-first century and the other changes that were coming to the city, by late 1978, Moscone's pledges to fight development and put resources into the neighborhoods were becoming harder to keep. The opening of Pier 39 was a reminder that the contestation and division of the mid-1970s had not yet been resolved and that the future of San Francisco was still unknown.

8

A Month Like No Other

. . . .

As November 1978 began, political questions about 1979 and beyond remained, but some things were breaking the right way for San Francisco, particularly progressive San Francisco. A few weeks earlier, the Yankees had come back to beat the Dodgers in the World Series. While the Yankees were hardly beloved in San Francisco, there had always been strong connections between the Bronx Bombers and San Francisco. Numerous players with roots in the Bay Area, including Joe DiMaggio, Lefty Gomez, Tony Lazzeri, Frank Crosetti, and Billy Martin had starred on or contributed to great Yankees teams. More importantly, by winning the World Series, the Yankees had kept the championship away from Los Angeles, so at least Giants fans upset about their team falling out of first place in the late summer didn't have to suffer through the sight of the Dodgers winning the World Series. A few days after the conclusion of the World Series, Mayor Moscone filed his papers to run for reelection in 1979. This was not a surprise, but in many political circles speculation about who would challenge the mayor was increasing, with Supervisor Quentin Kopp emerging as the most likely challenger.

After a long campaign on both sides, Proposition 6 was lagging badly in the polls, likely to fail statewide, and sure to be handily defeated in San Francisco. If Proposition 6 was rejected, it would represent the first major defeat for an antigay initiative in the United States and maybe, just maybe, a sign that the tide of antigay sentiment nationally was beginning to recede. It would also be an impressive demonstration of the growing political power of gays and lesbians, particularly in San Francisco. Defeat of Proposition 6 would also catapult Harvey Milk, the politician most identified with efforts to defeat the initiative, to even greater fame and a larger role in national gay politics.

On the first day of November, Congressman Leo Ryan, a Democrat from San Mateo County just south of the city, declared his intention to go to Guyana to find out what was happening with Jim Jones's Peoples Temple. There had been many rumors about troublesome goings on in the Peoples Temple since the group had decamped from San Francisco to the jungle of Guyana in July 1977, but these had increased in recent months and weeks.

Ryan's proposed trip to the Peoples Temple compound in Guyana immediately raised concerns from Jonestown, as Jim Jones and those around him did not want any powerful politicians nosing around on fact-finding missions. Ryan sent Jones a frank telegram dated November 1, 1978, that began, "In recent months my office has been visited by constituents who are relatives of members of your church and who expressed anxiety about mothers and fathers, sons and daughters, brothers and sisters," but in the next sentence Ryan added, "I have listened to others who have told me that such concerns are exaggerated." The congressman also asked Jones, "Please consider this letter to be an open and honest request to you for information about your work which has been the center of your life and purpose for so many years."[1]

Five days later, Ryan received a letter from Mark Lane, the Peoples Temple attorney. The tone of the letter is partly the indignation of a good lawyer, but the exhaustion of an attorney who has a difficult client is also evident. Lane begins by asserting that Ryan has been "briefed by persons hostile to the People's [sic] Temple and the project in Jonestown" and then offers to provide another side of the story to Ryan. Lane then proceeds to ask that Ryan delay his trip until he can join Ryan and Jones in Guyana, concluding by vaguely threatening that the Peoples Temple might have to accept an offer of refuge from one of "two different countries, neither one of which has entirely friendly relations with the U.S."[2] Even at the time it was not hard to see the defensiveness and concern in Lane's letter, which sought to dissuade Ryan from making his visit. Lane's efforts failed, as Ryan continued planning the trip.

The Peoples Temple was continuing with its own plans, including an ongoing presence in San Francisco. Although Jones had been gone for well over a year and over a thousand members had gone to Guyana with him, the Peoples Temple had not altogether disappeared in San Francisco. Neither had its fund-raising base. Accordingly, as late as early November 1978, the Peoples Temple was planning a gala at San Francisco's Hyatt Regency to raise money for the Peoples Temple Medical Program in Jonestown. The gala, called simply and grandiosely "A Struggle against Oppression," was scheduled for December 2.

The master of ceremonies for that event was to have been Willie Brown, the progressive assemblyman who had a long relationship with Jones and the Peoples Temple. No other politicians were scheduled to be speakers, although Jones was still influential enough to secure Dick Gregory as a special guest speaker. Moreover, two of the scheduled speakers were attorneys for the Peoples Temple, reflecting both Jones's diminished convening power and the growing feeling within of embattlement within the Peoples Temple.

The invitation to the gala includes a list of seventy-eight prominent people referred to as "endorsers." Most of those individuals were local elected officials or members of progressive organizations. There were no statewide elected officials, members of Congress, or state legislators among the endorsers. Mayor Moscone had also distanced himself from his former housing authority chair and was not listed in the program. However, three people who were progressive members of the board of supervisors were among the endorsers. Carol Ruth Silver, Ella Hill Hutch, and Harvey Milk continued to lend their names to Jim Jones's cause even by late 1978 when the problems in Jonestown were significant enough that a Democratic congressman was preparing to investigate.

On November 7, Congressman Ryan was easily reelected, beating his Republican opponent, Dave Welch, by 25 percent. Nationally, the Republicans picked up fifteen seats in the House of Representatives and three in the Senate in the midterm election, reflecting discontent with President Jimmy Carter. Despite that, progressive voters in San Francisco and leaders such as Milk and Moscone had a few things to celebrate. Governor Jerry Brown, a native son of San Francisco who had taken a strong position against Proposition 6, was easily reelected, defeating Republican challenger Evelle Younger by 20 percent. In his hometown, Brown outpolled Younger by more than three to one. Brown's big win was expected months in advance, but the failure of Proposition 6, while not quite a surprise, was different from what only a few months before many had thought would happen. The initiative lost by 16 percent and more than 1.1 million votes statewide.

The resounding defeat of Proposition 6 belied how close the race had felt for much of 1978. During that summer and into the fall, Proposition 6 looked almost certain to pass. Most polls showed it winning by a clear majority. In late August, the well-respected Field poll showed Proposition 6 winning by a margin of 61–31. As the November election approached, the polls began to tighten. Another Field poll done in late September showed the race to be within the margin of error.[3] One of the reasons for this was that California's Democratic Party leadership came out strongly against the initiative. By late September, the San Francisco political establishment was mobilizing against Proposition 6. At a September fund-raiser described as "the largest fund-raiser for a gay cause ever held in San Francisco," George Moscone described Proposition 6 as "the most outrageous distortion of what this country stands for I've ever seen."[4] Moscone had made his views clear on the bigoted initiative months earlier in a May statement: "I am staunchly opposed to the Briggs initiative. This dangerous measure would strike at the heart of our democracy and sanction wholly unjustified discrimination against gay citizens."[5]

That September event was attended not just by the city's progressive politicians like Moscone but by centrists such as Dianne Feinstein and even Republicans such as State Senator Milton Marks and conservatives like Supervisor Dan White. All eleven members of the city's board of supervisors opposed Proposition 6. Another San Franciscan, Governor Jerry Brown, on his way to an easy reelection victory, also opposed the bill, and he persuaded President Jimmy Carter to urge voters to vote against it at a rally in Sacramento on November 3.

Jerry Brown was (and is) a progressive Democrat, so his opposition to this initiative surprised few. However, one of the biggest blows against Proposition 6 occurred on November 1, only six days before the election, when Brown's predecessor in the governor's mansion stated his opposition to Proposition 6 in an opinion piece in the *Los Angeles Herald Examiner*. If in the late 1970s Ronald Reagan and Jerry Brown opposed something, it had little chance of passing. The two were ideological opposites who agreed on very little. Given that the final vote was not very close, Reagan's opposition to Proposition 6 may not have made the difference, but it was still very important.

The effort to defeat Proposition 6 gave Harvey Milk the opportunity to build new coalitions. One of these was with the punk rock community. San Francisco's uniquely politicized punk rockers were also against Proposition 6 and held a benefit at the Mab to raise money to defeat it. Among the bands that performed were Crime and the Offs. The master of ceremonies was Harvey Milk. In 1978 there were very few politicians anywhere in the United States who would have participated in an event in the most famous punk rock club in their city, but Milk did. There were also very few cities, perhaps none other than San Francisco, where punks would have visibly acted in such a progressive way on gay-related issues.

The event was called "Nix on Six: Save the Homos." This title captured much about punk rock politics of the era. While the punks were clearly on the progressive side of the issue, the approach to politics was also a bit edgy, even offensive. "Save the Homos" not only uses an offensive term for gay people, but it also makes a joke by playing on the "Save the Seals" and "Save the Whales" slogans of the era. "Nix on Six" was not just a one-off event but was a reflection of another characteristic of punk rock in San Francisco. San Francisco punk was relatively supportive and accepting of LGBT people at a time when that was considered very unusual. In describing a punk scene in San Francisco where "acceptance [of gay people] was 100 percent," Howie Klein said, "I don't think there was any real homophobia, and when there was it was from somebody who wasn't from the scene. It was from some outsider who washed up in San Francisco and wound up at the Mabuhay."[6] Klein also pointed out that it helped that several important figures in the San Francisco punk world—including Klein himself and at least equally importantly Dirk Dirksen, who, among other things, decided who could play at the Mabuhay—were gay. Ginger Coyote affirmed this, saying simply that the "majority of punks were gay friendly."[7]

There were other gay people involved in punk in 1970s San Francisco as well, including artists, writers, members of several well-known bands, and fans. Many were probably drawn to the movement because they were already outsiders in their own communities and because punk was considerably more open than most corners of society. Daniel Nicoletta, a prominent photographer, activist, and longtime San Franciscan, offered his take on these early days of punk in a 2018 interview: "There was queer ideation there [in early punk], but it was super cautious." Nicoletta added that as a gay man then, he experienced punk as "an unpacking of identity politics. In other words, 'Yes, you're queer. So what?'"[8]

Part of what framed punk culture was that categories were never quite clear in San Francisco, certainly with regard to music but to other things as well. On a quotidian level, in the late 1970s, many bands that could have been described as punk had very different sounds. For example, Tuxedomoon and Dead Kennedys sound nothing alike, but they were both considered punk by many at that time. Going back further, and looking beyond San Francisco, it is easy to see that the Ramones or the Sex Pistols were punk, but what about the MC5, Iggy Pop, or even David Peel and the Lower East Side? Which hippie bands were still genuine, and which had become simply corporate rock? In other words, there is an awfully big grey area that today is fodder for good conversation and debate, but at the time these communities and genres overlapped substantially.

In San Francisco, this was significant in a number of ways, primarily because of the dynamic between punk and gay San Francisco in 1978 and immediately afterward. In the late 1970s there were relationships and overlap between punk rock and gay San Francisco that were part of the emerging city. "Nix on Six" may have been the most visible of these, but there were more. Punk promoter and writer Howie Klein was a friend of Harvey Milk's. Tuxedomoon performed at the Gay Community Center on Grove Street. After the assassinations, when the leader of San Francisco's gay community was killed and the new mayor took a distinctly antipunk approach and was considerably more supportive of the police than her predecessor, the links between the two groups strengthened. Nicoletta described this as a time when "the more radicalized queer identities saw the punk movement as allies and vice versa."[9]

To a great extent, this also reflected an implicit understanding between two outsider groups that were trying to find a place for themselves in San Francisco. Punks and gays shared a need for a tolerant San Francisco and, probably more importantly, struggled against some of the same obstacles, notably police harassment. Punk began at a time when LGBT San Franciscans were just beginning to feel their own political power, including through the election of Harvey Milk, so in this regard the alliance was natural.

Milk's visibility in a significant win for gay people, after several tough defeats in other parts of the country, made him a bigger national figure than he already was. According to Frances Fitzgerald, "The defeat of the Briggs Initiative was a personal triumph for Milk. . . . In addition the campaign brought him statewide and even national coverage. In a movement that had no well-known leaders Milk began to stand out as the most effective spokes-man for gay rights."[10]

Milk had not been in office a year and was already building a national reputation that could, when necessary, be translated into a national fund-raising base. Milk and Moscone were political allies, so challenging the mayor in his upcoming 1979 reelection bid was out of the question. However, fol-lowing Moscone as mayor or running for a congressional seat should one become open suddenly seemed very possible for a man who had yet to com-plete his first term, or even his first year, as supervisor.

The defeat of Proposition 6 was also a victory for San Francisco, where almost 75 percent of votes were cast against it. That was the strongest no vote of any county in the state. In San Francisco, more people voted against Proposition 6 than voted for any politician on the ballot—for example, 164,073 San Franciscans voted against Proposition 6, but only 155,156 voted for Jerry Brown in the race for governor, the highest-profile race in the state. The nearly three-to-one margin against the antigay initiative was a victory for Milk, but it also made clear that at least with regard to gay rights, the progressive forces in San Francisco had won. Although there were (and are) still pockets of homophobia and intolerance in San Francisco, the election results showed that running against gay rights, or equality for gays and les-bians, was a losing political strategy in San Francisco. More than forty years later, that truism still holds.

In 1978, the national consensus lagged behind San Francisco quite a bit, so back east and in more conservative parts of the country, the defeat of Proposition 6 only solidified San Francisco's reputation as a place of "kooks" or "the land of fruits and nuts," to use two of the epithets that the unenlight-ened applied to our town back then. However, more thoughtful people saw a city that was in the forefront not just of tolerance and social change but of a new political movement.

Herb Caen, who advocated strongly against Proposition 6, was in the lat-ter group: "How in the name of Anita Bryant can we prejudge a person, find him guilty of an uncommitted crime and take away his livelihood sim-ply because of his sexual preference? . . . Bigots don't worry about homosex-uals as long as they're in swishy drag and speaking in exaggerated lisps. This new breed, highly visible in SF, is a different matter. . . . They're taking the fall for you in November, and if they go 'down the tube' as an entire group, guess who could be next?"[11]

Words like this were being written in other parts of the country, but not by sixty-two-year-old straight men who were deeply embedded in the establishment politics of their city like Caen was. Caen's views were tolerant, and his allusion to burgeoning gay political power was prescient (although his language is very dated), but these ideas also reflected what had become the mainstream politics of San Francisco by the middle of 1978. The city was indeed still contested, but there were already some indicators of who was going to win.

The significance of the defeat of Proposition 6 is not easily overstated. Today we have grown accustomed to LGBT Americans winning electoral and legislative battles, particularly in solidly Democratic states such as California, but in 1978 that was not the case. This was before the phrase "marriage equality" had entered the political lexicon, when almost no gay activists even had the temerity to suggest their single-sex relationships should have equal legal footing as that between a man and a woman. It was a time when most city police departments, although this was beginning to change in George Moscone's San Francisco, still believed that officers could beat up gay men with impunity and when very few gays or lesbians were out at their places of employment or even to their parents. The days when the Democratic Party would align almost totally with LGBT rights were in the distant future.

This was the context in which Proposition 6 was defeated in an effort led by San Franciscans. Ronald Reagan undoubtedly weighed in with a timely and influential "No on Six" statement, and President Carter had told a crowd at a rally in Sacramento for Brown and the Democratic ticket to vote against the initiative, but it was a gay San Francisco legislator, San Francisco's mayor, and a governor who was a San Franciscan who had led the fight against it.

When looked at through the lens of 1978, Brown's strong position against Proposition 6 seems even more impressive. In 2018, California's Democratic governor, who amazingly was none other than Jerry Brown, could take strong pro-LGBT positions knowing he was only helping himself politically, but the situation in California in 1978 was different. Brown was a popular governor, but California was far from the solidly Democratic state it has become in recent years. After Brown was reelected in 1978, no Democrat was elected governor of California until 1998. Additionally, Republican candidates for president carried the state in 1980, 1984, and 1988. Similarly, today President Carter's statement against Proposition 6 looks progressive and reflects well on the Democrat who served one term in the White House, but at the time, Carter had to be persuaded by Brown to make this statement. The video of the incident shows Brown assuring the president that because he and Ronald Reagan had also opposed Proposition 6, it was "safe" for the president to do so as well.

With the election over, Governor Brown back in Sacramento, and Proposition 6 safely relegated to a resounding defeat, San Franciscans could turn their attention to other matters. For devoted Giants fans, the hot stove league was underway as we discussed possible trades and tried to figure out how the Giants might benefit from free agency, then only in its second real year. We hoped the Giants might pick up one of the big name free agents, such as Pete Rose, whose bat would be valuable and who could play several different positions. We also hoped that the Giants could sign star lefty Tommy John away from the Dodgers. Neither of those things ended up happening, as Rose landed with the Phillies and John with the Yankees. The Giants were also in the running to land Twins first baseman and perennial batting champion Rod Carew in a trade, but that didn't come to pass either.

Moscone and Milk Finally Get Their Break

By early November, given the shoddy ball the Giants had played in most of September, few but the most intense fans were paying much attention to trade rumors and the hot stove league, but the city's politics were getting very interesting. A few days after the election that saw Proposition 6 soundly defeated, progressive San Franciscans got another break. The most conservative member of the board of supervisors, citing family reasons and financial need, resigned, stating "What is happening is that neither my family is being taken care of as they should be, nor are my constituents. . . . The people of San Francisco need full time legislators, and the supervisors should have a full time salary."[12] This was a huge break for Mayor Moscone and for progressive supervisors such as Harvey Milk. Dan White had been one of the more dependable votes against the mayor's progressive agenda. He had cast the only vote against Milk's gay rights ordinance, although he had supported Milk's dog poop law. White had also been a reliable vote for the downtown business interests that consistently opposed Moscone's agenda.

According to San Francisco's statutes, when a member of the board of supervisors had to leave office before finishing his or her term, the mayor could appoint someone to finish out that term. Because White had resigned three full years before the next election for his seat, which was set to occur in 1981, whomever Moscone appointed would have plenty of time to build a political base and have a good chance of being elected in 1981. Additionally, that person would be in that seat for the duration of Moscone's first term in office as he prepared for his 1979 reelection bid, thus ensuring the mayor would have one more dependable vote on the board.

In November 1978, George Moscone was the most progressive mayor of any major city in the United States. Soon he would have a working legislative majority. San Francisco was poised to become the national standard for progressive governance. Moreover, Moscone's commitment to a neighborhood-based progressive vision was shared by several key allies, not least of whom was Harvey Milk. For Milk, the timing of White's resignation could not have been better. He was in a great position to build on his growing national reputation following the defeat of Proposition 6 by working with the mayor on a range of policies. Replacing White with a progressive would make it much easier to turn those proposed policies into law.

Dan White's decision to resign therefore resounded well beyond his district in the southern part of San Francisco. Through one hasty decision, White had seemingly changed San Francisco politics profoundly. For example, a progressive majority on the board of supervisors would probably have elected a board president who was to the left of Dianne Feinstein and who would work with Moscone to remake San Francisco. This was very exciting to many progressives, people of color, gays and lesbians, and others, but it elicited the opposite reaction from real estate and business leaders as well as from social conservatives. For the latter groups, White's resignation raised the specter of stronger rent control laws protecting tenants, commercial rent control, limits on building and construction, stronger environmental regulations, more police reform, and a city government in which straight white business leaders would find themselves with a lot less influence.

Events in San Francisco during the rest of November ensured that Moscone never got to work with his progressive majority on the board. By the end of the month, San Francisco politics would again be transformed in a way that would redirect the city's trajectory forever. The Moscone progressive majority might have fallen apart, not lasted long, or otherwise had a minor impact, but there is a good chance that it would have led to a San Francisco that looked very different today. We will never know.

Within a few days of White's resignation, San Francisco began to unravel in earnest. By November 15, Jonestown and the Dan White saga had become the two major local stories in San Francisco. Readers of the morning *Chronicle* the next day might have been amused by perhaps the ultimate California-in-the-late-1970s headline: "Brown and Ronstadt—Rumor Denied." The article describes how Governor Jerry Brown had denied rumors that Linda Ronstadt had rejected his marriage proposal, but the separate articles about Dan White and the Peoples Temple that were also on the front page were not so light or funny.[13]

The article about Dan White reported that the erstwhile supervisor had decided that he wanted his old job back. Apparently, he had rescinded his resignation due to evolving political and financial circumstances. *Chronicle* reporter Marshall Kilduff's article began, "Dan White declared yesterday that he had changed his mind and now wants to return to his Board of Supervisors seat he abruptly resigned six days ago." Kilduff also reported that the mayor "said he would not oppose White's change of heart and returned the letter of resignation." The article went on to describe the political impact of White's new decision as well as some of the legal questions that had bearing on what might happen next.[14]

White's legal argument was that he had submitted his letter of resignation to the mayor and not to the clerk of the board of supervisors, as the law specified that he needed to do. The letter White submitted to the mayor was then forwarded to the clerk from the mayor's office. White had hoped that this technicality meant that his resignation would not be official. However, the City Attorney ruled against him. Five days before the assassinations, while still believing he might be reappointed by Mayor Moscone, White penned a letter to the city attorney, George Agnost, stipulating that "at no time did I instruct my staff to deliver a letter to the Clerk of the Board of Supervisors nor was I made aware of the fact that the letter was obtained by Mr. Boreman [the clerk] in the matter described above until today."[15] That same day, Boreman also sent a letter to Agnost, explaining that

on Friday, November 10[,] . . . various persons in the office were heard to be stating that Supervisor White had just resigned. . . . Upon hearing this information I proceeded to the office of Supervisor White, but the office was not occupied. I then proceeded to the office of his administrative assistant in room 250 where I asked Denise Apcar if it was true that Supervisor White had just resigned. She indicated that it was and handed me a copy of the resignation letter which bore Mr. White's signature. I immediately took the copy to my office, affixed the date time stamp and retained it in my file for the Board meeting of Monday, November 13.[16]

The evidence was clear that White had intended to resign but was now trying to find an obscure technicality that would negate his resignation. Fortunately for White, Agnost decided that although the supervisor had indeed resigned, Mayor Moscone could reappoint him if he wanted. White's declaration that he wanted his old seat back, as well as the mayor's initial indication that he would consider giving in to White and reappointing him to his old seat, set off a political firestorm in San Francisco and introduced significant tensions between the mayor and one of his closest progressive allies, Harvey Milk. In a private meeting, Milk appealed to his political ally on the grounds that White had frequently blocked or voted against progressive legislation favored by Moscone, including the gay rights ordinance. When that didn't work, Milk played hardball by making it clear that he would not work to deliver the gay vote for Moscone in 1979 if White, who was even by then broadly disliked among gay San Franciscans, was reappointed to the board. This political appeal was a reflection of growing gay political power in San Francisco. It also worked, as the mayor agreed to appoint someone else. Milk had seemingly persuaded Moscone not to reappoint White, but the mayor wanted to make sure he could do that on his terms, and perhaps even avoid making an enemy of White.

This version of events has become accepted by many and was the same story Randy Shilts told in his 1982 biography of Harvey Milk: "The news that George Moscone was going to actually reappoint the former police officer [White] shocked Harvey, who quickly set up an appointment with the mayor. Milk reminded George that White had been the swing vote in many of the 6–5 defeats that the mayor's proposals had suffered in the board. Beyond that, White was the only city politician who had stepped forth as an active anti-gay spokesperson. You *are* up for reelection next year, Harvey goaded, and reappointing the city's major anti-gay politico is no way to lock up the gay vote."[17] This scene is also depicted in the 2008 film *Milk*.

The encounter may have happened, but people close to both Milk and Moscone have disputed this. Rudy Nothenberg, who was deputy mayor at the time, told me over lunch in 2018 that Moscone's decision not to reappoint White "took all of two seconds," adding that the opportunity to appoint somebody other than White "gave him a chance to get six votes on the board. What idiot would refuse that?"[18] Carol Ruth Silver, who was a close ally and friend of Milk's on the board of supervisors and a reliable vote for Moscone's progressive initiatives, told me something similar: "George was never going to do it [reappoint White]." However, Silver also noted that White "blamed Harvey and me for persuading George not to reinstate him. . . . When we heard Dan had resigned we were delighted."[19] Thus, although Milk may not have had a major role in Moscone's decision, White most likely thought he did, and that sealed Milk's fate.

As White mustered his resources to pressure Moscone to change his mind, Shilts notes that it was apparent White was no longer the neighborhood politician he had once been: "Many of White's original supporters had grown disenchanted with the novice politician, since White seemed much more interested in currying favor with police, business and real estate interests than with his blue-collar constituents. When White held a press conference to pressure Moscone into reappointing him, he was flanked not by neighborhood activists, but by officials from the Board of Realtors and the Police Officer's Association."[20]

White probably overplayed his hand by doing that. By aligning himself so closely with downtown interests who already opposed the mayor, White inadvertently demonstrated his weakness in his own district, and he displayed his lack of political acumen by appearing in public with the very people with whom he should have been making an agreement in private before he impetuously decided to resign. A year away from a potentially close reelection campaign, Moscone was not concerned about angering conservative forces who did not have much influence over likely Moscone voters. Instead, he wanted a progressive majority on the board and needed to maintain good relations with Milk's gay base and other progressives throughout the city. Therefore, the mayor was unmoved by the press conference or by White's other appeals. Together, Milk and White framed the decision for Moscone as one that on one hand might anger gay voters, and on the other might anger police and the real estate lobby. Milk was pushing an open door, but he had outplayed White, leaving Moscone no choice but to recognize that.

The political contretemps regarding White's future that led to the terrible events of later that month raises a question that has never been satisfactorily answered: Why was Dan White such a bad politician? The entire episode of White's resignation, the retraction of his resignation, his frustration around not being appointed to the seat he had just resigned, and then his decisions in the following days and hours were made possible by his extremely bad political judgment or, less generously, his stupidity.

White's fundamental political mistake was to resign without first speaking to those around him who could have helped him. He seemed almost unaware of the value his vote on the board had to police, real estate, business, and downtown interests until after he had left the board. For those interests, replacing White with a Moscone loyalist could have been devastating, particularly for the police who needed White's vote on an impending issue regarding a federal consent decree that would have mandated the integration of the police department. The rank and file police officers opposed this decree and were relying on White's vote to ensure the Board would not support its integration. The police as well as moneyed San Francisco interests would have done a great deal to keep White's vote if given the chance. Therefore, if White had spoken to those business and real estate leaders about his legitimate financial concerns before stepping down, it is almost certain that somebody would have patched together some consulting work, business opportunity, or other way to get him the financial support he needed to stay in office. Had White done that, he never would have been in the losing position of resigning and then pleading for his job back. White had made some effort to do that, notably by getting his family potato stand on Pier 39, but even that was a clumsy attempt that also appeared to many as a form of bribery.

Carol Ruth Silver summarized White's mishandling of this situation: "[He] made one mistake [on the board] . . . resigning when he was in a financial crisis. He should have gone to people who supported him and asked them for help . . . [but] he saw himself as this macho guy who could solve all his problems."[21] Busch concurred that White was not a good politician, other than having skills as a street campaigner, but he also argued that White was someone who, despite his image in conservative San Francisco, never really succeeded at, or even stuck with, anything: "He was a good retail politician. He was good on the streets, shaking hands . . . but he was not a good politician. If you look at his career, he was a cop who quit. He was a fireman who quit. He was a supervisor who quit. Dan White really was way overrated and had never really accomplished much of anything."[22]

Busch's anger toward White has subsided somewhat over the decades, but it is still strong. Nonetheless, the former press secretary and baseball executive made an important point. White's defenders in the courthouse but also on the streets and in the schools and workplaces of San Francisco sought to portray him as a model citizen and highly accomplished man who, as many of my schoolmates argued at the time, "only made one mistake." Busch presents a different picture—one of a man who was unable to follow through on commitments or stay with something when it got difficult.

Art Agnos represented part of San Francisco in the state assembly during the time White was running for office and serving on the board of supervisors. Agnos's recollection of White echoed that of Busch: "He was politically inept. . . . On the surface he was an attractive guy, nice looking. He could speak reasonably well—all-American boy. He was the captain of the football team. However, he had no training in politics. . . . He had no idea [about politics]. . . . He couldn't keep up with it."[23] Nothenberg was less charitable toward the man who murdered Moscone and Milk than either Busch or Agnos: "He was not very smart. He was way out of his depth. . . . He was very young, very uncertain, not very smart . . . an ideologue I suppose, although I don't know if he understood that term."[24]

Agnos, Silver, Nothenberg, and Busch all had different political views than White. Quentin Kopp was different. He shared some of White's conservative views but claims to have never built a strong relationship with his younger colleague, who could have learned a lot from Kopp. Instead Kopp, although not quite sharing the anger expressed by former Moscone aides Busch and Nothenberg, described Supervisor Dan White as being "like a fish out of water trying to find a home" during the year they served on the board of supervisors together. Kopp also told of how White had not quite understood the culture of the board and had done things like put flowers on members' desks to try to make a good impression.[25]

Jonestown

Next to the article in the morning paper on November 16 about White deciding that he wanted to remain in his job was a piece by Ron Jarers titled, "Peoples Temple Shuts Doors on U.S. Visitors." Writing from Georgetown, the capital of Guyana, Jarers reported that a group of the Concerned Relatives had traveled to Guyana but been refused entry into the Jonestown compound in the jungle. The piece noted without much optimism that "Congressman Leo J. Ryan received a tentative and very limited invitation to visit the 2700-acre project founded last year 100 miles from Georgetown by the Rev. Jim Jones."[26] As explained in the article, the invitation to Ryan stipulated that he travel alone. This was an unusual and disrespectful way to treat a member of Congress. Ryan must have known that something was very wrong in Jonestown. Readers of the *Chronicle* could not have missed that conclusion either.

San Franciscans could not have known it yet, but the two horrific events that would make 1978 such an extraordinary year were both racing toward their denouement. On November 17, Congressman Ryan arrived at Jonestown. He had not given in to Jones's demand that he travel alone. Instead, he brought Don Harris and Bob Brown from NBC, Greg Robinson from the *San Francisco Examiner*, and an aide, Jackie Speier. Ryan had done his homework and was well briefed. He had come to Guyana to get answers and was not going to be easily swayed by a Potemkin tour of the jungle outpost.

Nonetheless, he almost was. Tim Reiterman and John Jacobs describe how, following a ceremonial welcome meal in Jonestown, Ryan "bounded onto the stage and took the microphone with aplomb." They continue: "Ryan waited until the applause died. 'I'm glad to be here,' [he said]. . . . Sounding as friendly as a political stumper, he said, 'This is a congressional inquiry and . . . from what I've seen there are a lot of people here who think this is the best thing that happened in their whole life.'"[27] The next day, November 18, did not go quite as smoothly for Jones, as he sought to conceal much of what has happening in Jonestown from the visiting congressman. By the end of the day, several people had approached Ryan asking for his help in getting them out of Jonestown. Ryan naturally agreed to assist them.

Despite his best efforts, Jones had been unable to persuade Congressman Ryan that everything was copasetic in Jonestown and probably knew that his project had little chance of survival if more people were able to escape to the outside world. Reiterman and Jacobs describe Jones's reaction to the inevitability of these departures: "Disappointment was a mild word for Jones's facial contortions. . . . This once-eloquent man appeared lost for words. The once-charismatic minister could not muster the animation to turn around followers who had believed in him and loved him." They add that "the presence of outsiders constrained Jones: he could not harangue over loudspeakers, summon up hostile peer pressure or threaten with his security detail."[28]

Ryan had come to Guyana to find out what was really taking place in Jonestown, and to bring some answers and perhaps even peace of mind to the Concerned Relatives. He had considerably more concerns, and information, than Lieutenant Governor Mervyn Dymally had when he had visited Jonestown previously. It was evident that Jim Jones was going to have a more difficult time spinning Ryan than previous visitors or other powerful California politicians. This is one of the reasons Jones sought to limit Ryan's delegation. Ultimately, Jones's arrogance got the better of him, as he presented the visiting congressman with a collection of lies that he hoped would be believed, rather than presenting Jonestown more modestly. The approach Jones chose would have raised doubts from any sophisticated observer, but for the first hours of Ryan's visit the deranged demagogue was successful.

Despite Ryan's initial response, by the time the congressman arrived in Guyana, Jones had played out his hand. He had not been an influential figure in San Francisco politics in over a year and was three years removed from his greatest political triumph, the assistance he provided to George Moscone in his 1975 runoff election victory. In politics, three years is a very long time, particularly in a city like San Francisco that by 1978 had grown accustomed to community and church leaders emerging and disappearing with some frequency. As word trickled out from Jonestown, increasingly in the form of testimonials and affidavits from people who had escaped, and as the Concerned Relatives began to seek more attention, it became very difficult for Jones to fool anybody anymore.

As the fantasy that Jones had constructed over many years—a fantasy that he had used to recruit and deceive thousands of people—began to collapse around him, the cult leader whose relationship and understanding of reality was growing more tenuous by the hour was faced with several options, none of them good. He could have seen Ryan off and hoped that the United States government would let the matter drop. Indifference from the U.S. government was unlikely, although not unimaginable. Jones could have tried to reason with the congressman to temper his growing suspicions. Jones could have told anybody who wanted to leave his dystopia that now was the moment. The embattled cult leader could have fled somewhere and lived the rest of his life off of the millions of dollars he had stashed in bank accounts around the world—money that had once belonged to the mostly poor members of the Peoples Temple.

Jim Jones pursued none of these options, instead choosing an almost unfathomably evil course of action. First, Jones decided that he could not permit Ryan to leave Guyana and report his findings back to the United

States, so as Ryan and his party were preparing to board a plane to take them back to Georgetown, the capital of Guyana, Jones ordered his private security forces to shoot and kill Ryan's entire delegation as well as the handful of Peoples Temple members seeking to flee with Ryan. The assassination of Ryan and his delegation made it clear that Jones himself had no intention of leaving Guyana alive. The only survivor of that shooting was Jackie Speier, a twenty-eight-year-old aide to the congressman who was badly injured. Speier was able to make it to the plane, get medical help, and eventually have an impressive career of her own in politics, serving in both chambers of the California state legislature between 1986 and 2006. She has been a member of the U.S. House of Representatives since 2008.

It was then that Jones's descent into homicidal madness moved into high gear. Realizing that there was now no future for Jonestown or the Peoples Temple, Jim Jones ordered his most loyal supporters to round up everybody in the compound and force them to drink cyanide-laced Flavor Aid. Those that refused were shot and in most cases killed. In a few hours, a community that had once offered hope to many, albeit probably falsely, was turned into a pile of hundreds of dead bodies of all ages, genders, and ethnicities.

The killings in Jonestown are now relatively well known to most Americans, although sometimes as little more than an obscure and horrific piece of history, but they remain largely misunderstood. They are frequently described as a mass suicide, but being forced at gunpoint to drink poison is not quite the conventional definition of suicide. Those who refused to drink the poison were shot and killed, suggesting that this was a mass murder more than a mass suicide. Oddly, the most enduring way Jonestown persists in the culture is in the phrase "drinking the Kool-Aid," meaning that somebody is a true believer in some idea, cause, or person. It is relatively common to hear people use that phrase who only know hazy, if any, details of its morbid provenance. However, that phrase itself misrepresents what happened in Jonestown. Many of those who drank the poison had long lost faith in the maniacal and murderous Jones, but faced with no choice at all between drinking the poison and being shot, they chose the former. Additionally, it wasn't even Kool-Aid into which the cyanide had been mixed. It was Flavor Aid, a cheap Kool-Aid knockoff. Until the very end, Jones's avarice was present.

The massacre at Jonestown was major national news. The *New York Times* lead story on November 20 was "Guyana Official Reports 300 Dead at Religious Sect's Jungle Temple." The *Boston Globe*'s banner headline was

"300–400 Found Dead in Camp of Cult That Killed Lawmaker." The *San Francisco Chronicle* had a special above-the-masthead headline "400 Dead in Guyana." Sadly, most of these headlines underestimated the actual death toll, which ended up exceeding nine hundred.

As the years have passed, Jonestown has become a cautionary tale about cults, and for some, of where the excesses of the 1960s lead. It has also entered the national consciousness as one of those strange and horrible stories that seem almost impossible to explain, but in San Francisco—the city where the Peoples Temple had been headquartered before the creation of the Jonestown outpost, that had been home to many of the victims, and where Jim Jones had been an influential political figure—the impact was even more complex, devastating, and threatening.

John Jacobs reflected what the world saw: "A ghastly, well-rehearsed ritual of murder and suicide. Nowhere were people more horrified than in San Francisco, where this world tragedy was also a local story, where the victims were not nameless faces or crazed cultists but friends and neighbors. 'When I heard the news, I proceeded to vomit and cry,' Moscone said."[29] Moscone's reaction to the news from Guyana was shared by many San Franciscans, but we could not know that the next few weeks would test our city as never before.

Monday after Lunch

It was the first Monday after Thanksgiving vacation. Most of us sixth-graders were not happy about being back in school after the long weekend, but at least lunchtime gave us forty-five minutes or so to scarf down our food (mine was probably a sandwich of leftover turkey on rye with Russian dressing) before running off to play touch football or basketball on the outdoor concrete play area of our school. My first class after lunch was science, taught by an earnest and friendly nun who was also a wonderful and committed educator. When class began, Sister Schroeder entered the room with an ashen look on her face. She told us in somber tones that she had an announcement and then reported that Mayor Moscone and Supervisor Harvey Milk had been assassinated. Sister Schroeder was certainly old enough to have remembered the assassinations of President John F. Kennedy, Robert F. Kennedy, and Martin Luther King in the 1960s. Most of us had some recollection of the failed attempt to shoot President Ford in San Francisco a few years before, but this was the first assassination of a major political leader that we experienced directly.

If you are Jewish and attend Catholic school for ten years, you encounter questions about that experience with some frequency well into middle age. The truth is that I had a great experience at my Catholic school, Stuart Hall for Boys. Stuart Hall prepared me well academically for high school and allowed me to forge lifelong friendships. The teachers and administration did not tolerate any anti-Semitism, so my brother and I were mostly shielded from a sentiment that I knew was present in some of my classmates. Despite having political views on many topics, notably abortion rights and LGBT equality that are more or less diametrically opposed to those of the Catholic Church, I have warmer feelings for the church than most left-wing secular Jews do, and I am grateful for the education and start in life that I got at Catholic school.

There were, however, times when I was acutely aware of how different my background was from most of my classmates, even the numerous Asian Americans and white Protestant kids among them. Seconds after our science teacher made the announcement, more than one of my classmates expressed happiness that "they killed that f*g." That was very much one of those moments. The divisions that were so acute in San Francisco then, and had expressed themselves so violently on that late November day, were on display in my middle school classroom. The school did not shut down or cancel classes for the day. We continued our afternoon classes, not getting the full story on the assassinations until we got home.

By Monday evening, the basic chronology of events had become clear to all of San Francisco and much of the country. That morning the mayor was prepared to appoint Don Horanzy, a forty-two-year-old community leader and loan officer at the Department of Housing and Urban Development, to White's seat. Moscone's press statement described Horanzy as having "a superb record of community leadership, and a proven ability not only to get along well with all the diverse ethnic populations of District 8, but with merchants, tenants and other social and economic classes as well."[30] That press statement was never released.

As the reality that Mayor Moscone was not going to reappoint him to his position on the board of supervisors began to sink in, Dan White became increasingly hostile, bitter, desperate, and ultimately violent. He was angry at the mayor for refusing to reappoint him and blamed Harvey Milk for influencing Moscone's decision. White's anger at Milk was fueled by White's homophobia and growing personal dislike for his former colleague. It is also likely that White was unhappy about how Milk, not him, had emerged as the star of the new group of members of the board of supervisors. However, White was right in his presumption that Milk had either helped influence Moscone or, at the very least, was pleased with the mayor's decision.

Most politicians in White's situation, upon realizing that they were not going to be reappointed to the board of supervisors, would have either found a seat in the state legislature for which to run or turned to friends in the real estate business for help in finding a way to make a very good living outside of politics. Unfortunately, this is not how the twisted and murderous mind of Dan White worked. At around 10:40 A.M. on November 27, he crawled through an open window at City Hall, thus evading the metal detectors that would have been set off by the loaded weapon he carried with him. Then he went to the mayor's office and demanded to see the mayor.

When White appeared at the mayor's office, Moscone made the fatal, but human, decision to invite him in. Corey Busch reflected upon this decision and noted that Moscone's political style and character ended up costing him his life:

> You really had to know George to understand his hesitancy in saying he wasn't going to reappoint Dan White. It was the same kind of personal characteristic and the same kind of caring for other people's feelings that brought George to have Dan come into his office that morning. . . . Ninety-nine out of 100 mayors, forty-five minutes before he's going to have a major press conference to announce an appointment to the board of supervisors, is going to tell his secretary to tell this guy, who's been nothing but a pain in the ass, "Sorry," but George said, "No, the guy's hurting and I want to talk to him."[31]

Nothenberg shared his old colleague's view of Moscone's decision on that Monday: "I think that George probably felt he owed White an explanation or something, and so they went into the back room. There was some whiskey around. George must have thought this was gonna be a good gesture."[32]

After shooting Moscone at point blank range three times, White walked down the corridor, asked to see Harvey Milk, and shot him five times at a similarly close range. Both men died almost instantly. In the hours following the assassinations, Dan White turned himself in to the police.

According to the law, the death of the mayor meant that the president of the board of supervisors would take over as acting mayor. Suddenly the 6–5 vote in January for president of the board in which Milk had backed Gordon Lau and White had supported the winner, Dianne Feinstein, took on even greater importance, especially as in the days that followed the assassinations Feinstein quickly consolidated her support to ensure that the board would make her acting mayor until the 1979 election.

Feinstein had been a familiar face to people who paid attention to politics in San Francisco since the late 1960s, and she would remain an important political figure well into the twenty-first century, but that day her calm demeanor in the face of these tragic and somber events began to convince the people of San Francisco that the city would survive and move forward. This made an impression that helped Feinstein forge her new political identity and ultimately help her restart her political career.

Early that Monday morning, Feinstein's political future seemed to be moving in a very different direction. Before the assassinations occurred, Feinstein had told several members of the press corps that she would not be seeking reelection to the board when her term expired in 1981.[33] Feinstein knew that Don Horanzy, the progressive whom Moscone was planning to appoint to White's seat, would likely prevent her from getting the six votes she needed to remain president of the board and did not want to return to simply being a member of that legislature. Given that the 1981 election was almost three years away, it is possible that Feinstein was not even planning to finish her current term. Feinstein was increasingly looking like a vestige from a different, more moderate, and less divided San Francisco. Feinstein, whom former San Francisco mayor Art Agnos told me "could be the luckiest politician in San Francisco," not only likely would have lost her position as president of the board if Horanzy had been seated, but she may have gotten her position in the first place due to a political deal made shortly after the 1977 elections.

In the years preceding the 1977 elections, the presidency of the board of supervisors generally, by custom but not legal requirement, went to the candidate who had received the most votes in the previous election. Because of this arrangement, Feinstein had served as the president for two years following her first-place finish in the at-large elections for supervisor in 1969 and again following her first-place finish in 1973. In 1977, the candidate who received the most votes in any district race was Quentin Kopp, then a conservative Democrat, who represented several neighborhoods in the southwestern corner of the city. Kopp had been serving as president of the board following the 1975 election, in which he was the top vote winner citywide.

As he explained it to me, he believed that he "should have, under custom and practice, been president [of the board] and I would have . . . [However,] Feinstein was bereft. Carter had been elected president. She thought in '77 she could get a job in the Health Department in Washington. . . . She was through, finished. John [Barbagelata] came up with the idea of restoring her self-image by letting her be president of the board in exchange for her endorsing me in 1979 against George for mayor."[34]

Speaking more than forty years after the deal was made, Kopp concluded by saying, "What a mistake." However, at the time, the deal made sense for everybody. Feinstein had twice run for mayor and had not done particularly well either time. Kopp was a rising star in the city who was more conservative than Moscone, and Feinstein as well, but not quite so much as Barbagelata. Kopp had been president of the board of supervisors during the first two years of Moscone's mayoralty. Unlike the candidate who had narrowly lost to Moscone in the 1975 runoff, Kopp was a lawyer and something of a policy wonk. He probably would have been a strong candidate against Moscone in 1979, or at the very least had reason to believe he would. Needless to say, once Feinstein became acting mayor, the deal was off. Kopp ran for mayor in 1979 anyway, but against Feinstein, losing in the runoff by eight points.

By late 1978 it seemed that Feinstein's career was at a dead end and that her brand of centrist politics was not likely to resonate in a city that was increasingly polarized and where progressives, led by Mayor Moscone, were in the ascendancy. All of that changed very suddenly with the assassinations. Only a few hours after telling the City Hall press corps of her plans to retire from politics, Feinstein, who earlier that day had rushed to Harvey Milk's office after hearing gunshots only to find that when she checked for the slain supervisor's pulse her finger went through a bullet hole, found herself faced with the unenviable task of announcing the deaths to the people of San Francisco. She began her remarks by saying, "As president of the board of supervisors, it is my duty to make this announcement. Both Mayor Moscone and Supervisor Harvey Milk have been shot and killed."[35] The crowd responded immediately with gasps of shock and sorrow and audible sobs.

The events of November 27 left two of San Francisco's political progressive stars dead and revealed the man once viewed as the hope of conservative San Francisco to be a deeply disturbed murderer. Three of the city's most intriguing political careers were destroyed that day. And one career was made. Dianne Feinstein did not set out to use the deaths of Moscone and

Milk as a way to build her reputation or become a national figure, but that is what happened.

When Feinstein made the announcement that Moscone and Milk had been killed, she spoke from the heart. Her voice expressed the sadness and horror she felt at these events. Her voice and body language also expressed a strength for which many San Franciscans were grateful. It was not obvious, based on what had happened between November 15 and November 27 of 1978 that San Francisco would survive or that the city would ever return to anything approaching normal, but Feinstein's words, deportment, and strength helped us begin to believe that it might.

John Burton, a friend of George Moscone's who has held elected office and leadership roles in the California Democratic Party almost continuously since 1975, described in a 1987 interview what Feinstein meant to San Francisco after the assassinations: "After that thing with George and Harvey, her style and her actions had a soothing effect. She helped bring the city together at a time when the people of the city wanted to be brought together. At that time in history, she uniquely fit the position of mayor."[36] Nothenberg, who served in City Hall under both Moscone and Feinstein, echoed this sentiment: "Dianne inspired confidence from the moment she took over. Even though she and George were not on friendly terms, she said she would honor his legacy and kept his staff on for a long time. . . . I think she was a rock."[37]

Feinstein's political career was given a new life by the tragic events of November 27. She would remain mayor through 1987, winning election to a full term in 1979, defeating a recall attempt in 1983, and being elected to a second term later that year. By 1984, she was on the short list to be Democratic presidential nominee Walter Mondale's running mate, a position that instead went to New York congresswoman Geraldine Ferraro.[38] In 1990 Feinstein was the Democratic Party's nominee for governor of California and was elected to the U.S. Senate in 1992. Feinstein's impressive political accomplishments are not all due to her becoming mayor in 1978, but if that had not happened, it is likely that she would have not made it beyond local politics in San Francisco. Moreover, had she not handled that day and those immediately following with such dignity and aplomb, her career probably would have taken a very different direction.

Only a month or so before the murders, the *San Francisco Bay Guardian* ran a few articles about the modest scandals surrounding Mayor Moscone and the possibility that he would not seek reelection in 1979. One of the articles speculated about who might run for mayor if Moscone did not run or was seen as vulnerable. The piece listed nine possible candidates, including two members of the board of supervisors: John Molinari and Quentin Kopp. Despite being president of the board of supervisors, Dianne Feinstein was not mentioned as a contender.[39] A few weeks before that, an article in the *Chronicle* titled "No One Yet Taking on Moscone" reported that "Supervisor Dianne Feinstein and Chief Administrative Officer Roger Boas, were quick to declare themselves out of the contest," adding "Feinstein also said she probably won't run for supervisor again when her current term expires in 1981."[40] That is a good reflection of the state of her political career on the eve of the assassinations.

Feinstein's political career was stalled in 1978 not just because of her third-place finish in the 1975 mayoral election, but because of the emergence of new voices in San Francisco politics, including within the city's Jewish community. The most important of those Jewish voices belonged to one of her colleagues on the board who had moved to San Francisco from New York as an adult. The dynamic between Dianne Feinstein and Harvey Milk reveals a lot about how San Francisco was changing in the late 1970s and continued to change during the rest of the twentieth century.

Harvey Milk and Dianne Feinstein were not the only Jewish politicians in San Francisco in 1978. Supervisors Carol Ruth Silver and Quentin Kopp were also Jewish, but Feinstein and Milk had higher citywide profiles. And although Milk and Feinstein were both Jewish, they represented very different strains of Jewish San Francisco. Even within San Francisco's relatively small Jewish community, there was tension between those groups.

Jewish identity is almost always complex, and sometimes in San Francisco it feels more complex. Feinstein was a product of that. Her father had been a prominent Jewish doctor, but her mother never seemed to acknowledge her Judaism. Jerry Roberts writes that Feinstein's mother "told her children she was Russian Orthodox" and quotes Feinstein herself as saying, "My father thought my mother was Jewish. But she wasn't."[41] According to Roberts, Feinstein also celebrated Easter.[42] That is significant, because while some secular Jews may exchange gifts on Christmas or even have a tree of some kind, Easter is different. Easter is a Christian holiday that is associated with the death of Jesus and therefore ties into one of the most enduring and vicious anti-Semitic tropes—that the Jews killed Jesus. Accordingly, celebrating Easter signifies assimilation of a much higher order, even in America.

Feinstein's family had roots in Russia but had always been understood to be part of the city's elite German Jewish community. This perception was bolstered by her marriage to her second husband, Bert Feinstein, a prominent German Jewish doctor. Dianne Feinstein had also attended the Convent of the Sacred Heart high school, the sister school of the Catholic boys school I attended through eighth grade. Moreover, she did this in the 1950s. This was a gesture toward assimilation that would have been hard to imagine for New York Jews like Harvey Milk. Even in the 1970s, my family back in New York could never quite understand my mother's decision to send my brother and me to Catholic school.

One of the differences between these two groups of Jews is that while there was always a degree of class-based resentment toward affluent German Jews in San Francisco, by the 1970s the more direct anti-Semitism was reserved for Jews like Milk. This was particularly acute in the late 1960s through 1980s when Jews from families like Milk's—Yiddish speaking with roots in Russia, Ukraine, Belarus, and Poland—began to remake the face of Jewish San Francisco. These Jews came from many places in the East or the Midwest, but the largest group of them naturally came from New York.

The 1970s in San Francisco was a time when "New York" was often used as an epithet in phrases like "pushy New Yorker" or in descriptions of people as having manners like a New Yorker. When those phrases were used, it was always clear that despite New York's extraordinary ethnic diversity, the speaker was expressing distaste, or worse, for Jews. Milk undoubtedly both encountered and understood the meaning of remarks like that after moving to San Francisco. As Helene Myers writes of Milk, "He was a New York Jew; for that particularly hypervisible Jewish type, geographic distinction and ethnoreligious identity are not easily separated." Milk made no effort to conceal either his Judaism or his New York roots. Myers then quotes Milk's friend Sharyn Saslafsky as saying, "He wasn't a religious Jew, but he was always proud of being Jewish. . . . He always had a sense of pride that he came from New York."[43] Saslafsky's description of Milk reflects how many New York Jews see their hometown and their ethnicity. It is certainly the view that my mother, a Jewish New Yorker who came to San Francisco around the time Milk did, held and passed on to her sons.

Unlike Saslafsky, Daniel Nicoletta is not Jewish, but he knew Harvey Milk well. Nicoletta began working in Milk's camera store in August 1975 and eventually grew close to the man to whom he was initially drawn due to "the coolness factor exclusively." Nicoletta elaborated: "I was politically naive at that point. . . . I was just responding to the friendliness of the guy. . . . He took a genuine interest in me." Over the course of their friendship, Nicoletta spent many hours talking with Milk, although Milk did most of the talking. Much of their conversation was about arts and culture, not just politics, but Nicoletta also got a very good sense of what drove Harvey Milk and of how his Judaism was central to that. "When you look at his overriding themes," Nicoletta explained to me, "his Judaism is there, particularly when it came to one of his go-to's, which was that whole analogy of these people have a shopping list. . . . Generally there was always a . . . reference to the Holocaust and what could happen if we're not careful. . . . What you get as a friend is that's his belief system on a molecular level, so of course his Judaism is gonna come through." Based on his deep personal knowledge of Milk, Nicoletta also said, "I never got the sense that it was expedient. It was always where he was authentically coming from."[44]

Given that, there is another angle to the assassinations that is rarely mentioned and very difficult to prove. Many things happened on November 27, 1978, but one of them was that an outspoken left-wing Jew who spoke with an unmistakable New York accent and more than occasionally invoked the memory of the Holocaust was killed by a man who had built a political career, albeit a modest one, by being a voice against diversity and the changes that were occurring in San Francisco at the time. There is no proof that White was an anti-Semite or that Milk's religion was one of the reasons White killed him, but it is certainly plausible. White frequently spoke about not wanting to be "forced out of San Francisco." Given what happened in November 1978, that phrase is generally seen as evidence of his homophobia. It was, but it may also have reflected his fear of other groups as well—for example, hippies and Jews.

Busch, a keen observer of San Francisco politics who was close with both Moscone and Milk, indicated that this anti-Semitism may have been one of the factors driving White's dislike for Milk: "Dan White . . . really resented Harvey for a lot of reasons, amongst which was the fact that he was gay. The Jewish thing was very possible too."[45] However, Charles A. Fracchia Sr. did not agree, asserting, "[San Francisco] was the most amenable place for Jews to live. I saw no signs of anti-Semitism. . . . I would say that it was not a Jewish, New York basis to this."[46] Silver, who is Jewish, echoed the Catholic Fracchia's view: "I never felt that the assassination was about anti-Semitism."[47]

Although the entire city was shocked by the assassinations, Harvey Milk's district, particularly the Castro, felt it most acutely. Within hours of the assassination, a candlelight vigil was organized, as thousands of gays and lesbians, as well as other supporters of Milk, marched from the Castro down Market Street, the city's main thoroughfare, to City Hall. San Francisco's gay and lesbian community was one of the biggest in the country, as young gay people came there from all over the United States (and in some cases beyond) because they believed they would be freer to be their true selves. Harvey Milk was the spokesman for that community. The connection he had with them was much greater than that of most local elected officials with their constituents. My supervisor back then was Dianne Feinstein. Almost nobody in my immediate neighborhood felt any real connection with her, but Milk was different.

There were about 60,000 people in each supervisorial district in 1978. Therefore, many of Milk's constituents either knew him, had some previous contact with him, or had met him campaigning or at a community event. Most gay people in the Castro were probably at most two degrees of separation removed from Milk, so the connection was intense. The impact of the assassination, therefore, was immediate and profound. When asked to describe the reaction to the assassinations, Allen Bennett, who as rabbi at Sha'ar Zahav was a spiritual leader of the city's gay community in 1978, responded, "Anger is obvious from the marches and the candlelight vigils . . . [and] the White Night riots and so on. The despair . . . Harvey was a flash in the pan. . . . He showed up. He blew up like a firework, casting light and noise wherever he went. He was not only entertaining. He was illuminating. . . . The despair got channeled into 'How do we coalesce? Where do we pick up?' . . . If nothing else, that's what he would have liked."[48]

After the murders, almost the entire city was engulfed in grief, confusion, and anger. The assassinations had occurred fewer than two weeks after Jonestown. Many San Franciscans were still only beginning to process that tragedy when White killed Moscone and Milk. The killings in Jonestown had dominated news coverage in San Francisco, since they had occurred just over a week earlier. Therefore, few San Franciscans other than political insiders were paying attention to the dispute that pitted Dan White against the mayor and his ally Harvey Milk about whether or not White would get his seat back. That comparatively minor piece of political intrigue had receded from the consciousness of most San Franciscans, but not that of Dan White.

On the evening of November 27, Dennis Richmond, the anchor on Channel Two news, began his broadcast by summarizing what many were feeling as they processed the day's news: "Good evening. To outsiders, and even to some San Franciscans, it must appear the city has gone a little insane. Just as everyone is beginning to come to grips with the mindless murder-suicide of over nine hundred members of the San Francisco–based Peoples Temple, word screams out over the radio, the television, the newspapers that another tragedy is upon us."[49]

Herb Caen's column in the next day's *San Francisco Chronicle* captured the powerful sentiments confronting many who were trying to make sense of what had occurred in their city over the previous fortnight:

> The vocabulary of grief and disbelief stretches only so far. The ghastliness of Guyana exhausted the pitifully few words at our command. At the end of a week of incredible headlines, all of us were left stunned, exhausted, overwhelmed by the flood of bloody "senseless" information.
>
> And then came the shock waves of yesterday.
>
> The Mayor, a good man, dead. The Supervisor, a good man, dead. Their suspected killer, we had been told many times by his supporters, was a good man too.

Caen concluded that day's column with this:

> As I look out over the city that George Moscone and Harvey Milk loved, a flag is slowly being lowered to half staff. Two valuable, invaluable, irreplaceable people are dead, their families and friends grief-stricken. Hundreds are dead in Guyana, leaving tears and misery in their wake. The phones are suddenly silent and the streets quiet. A pall settles over the holiday hills. Monday's mourning broken only by the siren that has become the sound of the city. What is there about November? What is there about San Francisco?[50]

The poet Lawrence Ferlinghetti, who had been a major literary figure in San Francisco since the 1950s and remained one well into the second decade of the twenty-first century, wrote a poem a few days after the assassinations called "An Elegy to Dispel Gloom." The poem sought to express the sense of gloom that had descended upon the city, while also urging people not to give up hope. The middle part of the poem describes all the places in San

Francisco (a diverse list familiar to any native) where a "breathless hush is in the air" following the murders, but it ends by imploring San Franciscans,

> Do not sit upon the ground and speak
> of other senseless murderings
> or worse disasters waiting
> in the wings.
>
> Do not sit upon the ground and talk
> of the death of things beyond
> these sad sad happenings.
> Such men as these do rise above
> our worst imaginings.[51]

Caen and Ferlinghetti both reflected the growing sense that something in the city had gone very wrong. Commenting on the events almost forty years later, Charles A. Fracchia Sr. confirmed this notion: "The feeling was just horrible. . . . It ranked as unbelievable. You had this thing in Guyana. You had the shooting, the assassination. . . . Some people said, 'I'm getting out of here.' . . . There was tremendous consternation. . . . It was a real apocalyptic feel."[52]

Writing more than thirty years after the killings, David Talbot summarized the feeling in the city similarly:

> In the days after Jonestown and the city hall assassinations, San Francisco sleepwalked under a dark canopy of clouds that seemed like it would never lift. The city was racked with despair. The San Francisco Suicide Prevention center received twice its normal number of phone calls. Rev. Cecil Williams fielded a flood of calls at his Tenderloin church from distraught people who feared that they, and the city itself, would never recover from the multiple traumas. The *Examiner*'s Washington, DC, bureau reported that San Franciscans visiting the nation's capital were bombarded by questions about their dark-starred city.[53]

A special report in the *Washington Post* was one of the first news reports to place these tragedies in a continuum of political violence in and around San Francisco: "Today this western mecca is shocked by a series of acts of violence unparalleled in recent American history. . . . These deaths appear part of a pervasive atmosphere of terrorism that has enveloped the region since the early 1960s."[54] The article then listed a spate of violent events, including the kidnapping of Patty Hearst by the Symbionese Liberation Army, the attempted murder of President Ford in September 1975, the attempt to bomb the home of Dianne Feinstein, an attack on John Barbage-lata, and threats to state senator Milton Marks. This quickly became how most of the country processed the killings in Jonestown and City Hall. There was clearly something to this argument, but for many San Franciscans it didn't quite resonate.

San Francisco's reputation as a kooky city where the excesses of the various political, social, and cultural movements of the late 1960s were taken to their extremes was entrenched well before November 1978. The mid-1970s was a time when people in the rest of the country made frequent jokes about the city and its northern suburbs in Marin County. San Franciscans were made fun of because of what we ate and the coffee we drank, our views about gay people and alternative medicine, and our appearance. In other words, we were considered slightly nutty because we cared about where our food came from, preferred to grind our own coffee beans, used a filter rather than a coffee maker, and believed that discriminating against people because of who they loved was wrong.

It didn't help that the governor of our state was a son of San Francisco who declined the ornate governor's mansion and other trappings of the office, preferring instead a modest apartment and equally modest Plymouth driven by his security detail. He also had the crazy idea that we should use satellite technology to facilitate communication. That idea earned Jerry Brown the nickname "Governor Moonbeam," given to him by longtime Chicago columnist Mike Royko.

Despite some initial resonance, the view that the tragedies of November 1978 were due to what the rest of the country saw as the weird and far-left character of San Francisco at the time is at best an incomplete, and in some respects a completely backward, interpretation of what occurred.

On the surface, this explanation make sense. The Peoples Temple was part of San Francisco and fits well into the context of other cults, communes, and religious movements that flourished in the city in the decade or so preceding the killings in Guyana. Moreover, at least some of the people involved in the Peoples Temple were former hippies or others who had come to San Francisco in the 1970s seeking something before stumbling into Jim Jones's bizarre messianic cult, although far more were low-income African

Americans desperate for a better life. It is also unlikely that a character like Jones could have become a politically influential figure in many cities the way he did in San Francisco. He successfully hoodwinked, and exploited, the liberal political ascendancy in the city in the years before he left for Guyana. In that regard, the Peoples Temple is very deeply a San Francisco story.

There is, however, another much less San Francisco side even to the Peoples Temple. Jim Jones was not a San Franciscan, nor did he migrate there as a young man in the late 1960s. Jones was from Indiana and did not move to California until the early 1970s when he was in his forties. Although the Peoples Temple was a unique brew of Christianity, radical politics, and a cult of personality, it had its spiritual roots as much in the Christian revivalism of the nineteenth and early twentieth centuries as it did in the San Francisco excesses of the 1960s and 1970s. If one wanted to understand the environment that created Jim Jones, studying the history of evangelism and hucksterism in the Bible Belt would be a much better starting-off point than examining the culture of post–Summer of Love San Francisco.

Regardless of whether or not Jim Jones was uniquely a product of the San Francisco of the era, the sheer scale of the Jonestown tragedy meant that its impact on San Francisco was huge. This was not simply a few people with a suicide pact, or even twenty members of some obscure cult killing themselves. It was the biggest murder-suicide in history. The killing of more than nine hundred people required logistics and precision on an almost military scale.

Although many of those who died were not from San Francisco, San Francisco was the place in the United States with which the Peoples Temple was most identified. Many San Franciscans, particularly those who were African American, knew people who had died or were one or two degrees of separation away from people who had lost their lives in Guyana. Even for San Franciscans with no ties to the Peoples Temple, the reminders of connections between the murders and our city were apparent. If you look closely at the photos from Jonestown, you can see a child or two wearing a Giants cap; those caps look to me like the same ones given out on Cap Day at Candlestick Park in 1977 or so. The former Peoples Temple building on Geary Street was a physical reminder of the mass murder in Guyana until the 1989 earthquake damaged it. It has since been replaced by a post office.

The Peoples Temple is now mostly remembered for its ghastly final days, but until mid-1977, Jim Jones had been a political player and service provider in San Francisco. Many progressive politicians—most visibly George Moscone but also Willie Brown, Mervyn Dymally, and to a lesser extent Harvey Milk—had ties to the Peoples Temple, benefited from its volunteers and perhaps other sometimes less-kosher forms of support during close elections or otherwise gained from a political alliance. After November 1978, few had the psychic energy to probe those relationships from either the legal or political perspective. By then, Jones, Moscone, Milk, and hundreds of others were dead. Nonetheless, it remains an unfortunate reality that, at least with regard to the Peoples Temple, San Francisco's progressive legacy and the ugliest of all the tentacles of the bizarre years of the 1970s were intertwined.

Some on the right have sought to further politicize the Jonestown killings by exaggerating the links between Jones and progressive San Francisco politicians such as Moscone and Milk but also Willie Brown, who became a powerful, progressive speaker of the California Assembly from 1980 to 1995 before being elected mayor of San Francisco in 1995 and again in 1999. The speed with which some of the right-wing media began this line of attack was ghoulish. In the December 8 issue of *National Review*, only a few weeks after the murders, an editorial titled "Guyana Holocaust" began by asserting "The most notable thing about cult leader Jim Jones and his People's [*sic*] Temple sect is the amount of liberal and leftist support this lunatic and implausible messiah managed to attract." The piece continued: "Apparently all you need in order to attract support of that sort is the word 'people's [*sic*]' in your logo. . . . The group, to be sure, was interracial—more bait for the big-shot liberals—and hundreds of its adepts died without regard to race or color, an egalitarian triumph."[55] The kernel of truth is significant. Jones indeed enjoyed strong relations with many progressive leaders, but in addition to tone of the article—which was smug and deeply insensitive not to the politicians but to the families of the dead—this analysis implies an almost magical leap from these relationships to the complicity of those politicians in the mass murder Jones committed. Moscone, Willie Brown, and others who benefited from their ties to Jones certainly should have scrutinized the Peoples Temple more closely and probably should have known by at least late 1977 that something very strange was going on there, but by then most of the Peoples Temple members, including Jones, had left town. The failure of so many politicians to do this scrutiny even earlier, when it would not have been too late, is unfortunate, but it hardly makes them complicit in the terrible crimes Jones went on to commit.

There were also some people who either were appallingly duped by Jones or simply refused to accept what they were seeing. California's lieutenant governor, Mervyn Dymally, visited Jonestown in late 1976 and reported positively about the Peoples Temple project in Guyana. In a letter six months later, Dymally shared his enthusiasm with Mayor Moscone:

> It was an experience that I will never forget. There they were, young and old, black and white, all working together to build a new community in the heart of the jungle. In that virgin forest, the members of the Temple are raising beef cattle and pigs, and planting cassava (a tropical food similar to the yam). They are building homes, repairing tractors and heavy machinery, and building roads.
>
> What was more inspiring was the support, commitment and high morale of the people there.
>
> It is a project that all Californians can be proud of and I hope some day your busy schedule will permit you to visit Jonestown as I did.[56]

Moscone did find time to travel to Europe to promote San Francisco in 1978, but the mayor chose not to go to Jonestown either to investigate what was occurring there or for a Potemkin tour. Dymally's association with Jones did not hurt him politically. He lost his bid for reelection in November 1978, but that election was held a few weeks before the killings. Dymally then went on to serve six terms in the U.S. House of Representatives and, after a decade or so out of office, three terms in the California Assembly. Dymally was clearly duped by Jones and displayed extraordinarily bad judgment in continuing to say positive things about him when, at the very least, he should have been suspicious about developments in Guyana, but the heavily African American constituency that elected Dymally a total of nine times after Jonestown did not see him as guilty of those crimes as some on the right seem to suggest.[57]

In 2014 the *National Review* was still trying to make this point. That year, an article titled "The Unburied Truth about Jim Jones" used a review of a fictional treatment of the tragedy to argue, "It is, after all, an inconvenient story, in which a Communist community, led by a committed Marxist and '60s Bay Area radical, came to a horrifying end. . . . Following the mass suicide, the mainstream media spun the story into one of religious fanaticism rather than leftist fanaticism."[58] This article was written in 2014, but it redbaits in a way that harkens back to the Cold War, which was alive and well in 1978, when conservatives sought to connect anybody to the left of the conservative wing of the Democratic Party to the atrocities committed by Communists in every corner of the world. Jones may well have been driven by "leftist fanaticism," at least for a while, but that has little to do with the nonviolent, deeply American, progressive values of Moscone, Milk, and other San Francisco Democrats in the 1970s.

In a more accurate and fuller description of the events, with the provocative title "The Left's Great Crime: Jim Jones, Marxist Mass Murderer," George Russell offered a more balanced but nonetheless conservative critique of the Jonestown tragedy. In this article for *Commentary*, he reminded readers, "Jones was friends with other radical showmen and ideologues like Dennis Banks of the American Indian Movement, the implacable Communist Angela Davis, and her friends and acquaintances in the Black Panther Party led by Huey P. Newton, the very essence of lumpenproletariat insurrection. Jones and his Temple followers were allies of San Francisco's left-wing mayor, George Moscone, and the nation's first openly gay politician, Harvey Milk, whose campaigns Jones supported. In return, Moscone named Jones head of the San Francisco Housing Authority."[59]

These conservative efforts to attack Milk, Moscone, and others because of their associations with Jones miss another very important point. It was not only progressives, or even Democrats, who had misread Jones. In 1976, Milton Marks, a Republican state senator, who incidentally had finished fifth in the first round of the 1975 mayoral election, sponsored a resolution in the California State Senate calling for that body to "commend the Reverend Jim Jones and the Peoples Temple for their exemplary display of diligent and devoted service to and concern for their fellow man, not only in this state and nation, but throughout the world."[60] This demonstrates that as late as 1976, Jones—despite his involvement in progressive politics—was still seen by many, even some Republicans, as a minister simply trying to help the needy.

There is another aspect of Jones and the Peoples Temple that conservative critics simply ignore. While Jones positioned himself on the left and supported progressive candidates, he also used the Peoples Temple as a somewhat traditional social service agency, providing assistance to children and seniors, organizing a singing choir and sports teams, even helping with drug rehabilitation for addicts and with other needs of low-income communities in big cities. For these reasons, from about 1973 to 1977, Jones was not just a religious political figure in San Francisco but was part of the broader community of social service providers. The paradox is that we now know that while he was doing this, he was leading a church that was, in reality, a cult, and that he was abusing his congregants financially, emotionally, sexually, and otherwise.

One way to see the breadth of support for the Peoples Temple in San Francisco and beyond is through an extraordinary document created by the Peoples Temple in its later years called simply "Statements about Rev. Jim Jones and the Peoples Temple." This document was a collection of statements or endorsements from dozens of prominent people. These statements were divided into different categories, including "medical profession," "legal profession," "education," "law enforcement," "religious leaders," "the media," "governmental and political leaders," and "civil rights." In addition to containing endorsements from several progressive politicians, the document quoted numerous professionals with either little or no political profile endorsing the work of the Peoples Temple in various areas. It also included a quote from Edward M. Davis, the tough-on-crime, conservative chief of police of the Los Angeles Police Department: "The Peoples Temple has done a fantastic job for us in the social parts of the City. After considering the outstanding work of the church, your kind words take on a special significance. I hope I will continue to merit both your support and your respect. . . . Thank you again, Reverend Jones, for imparting the spirit of God and human fellowship to your congregation. We are deeply indebted to you for your hard work. With God's help, we will both continue to help men live happier and more rewarding lives."[61]

The "governmental and political leaders" section included statements not only by liberal California politicians but also by national politicians and several prominent Republicans, including Milton Marks, Congressman Lawrence Coughlin of Pennsylvania, and Don Clausen, a Republican member of Congress who represented a district north of San Francisco that included the town of Ukiah, where the Peoples Temple had been based before moving to San Francisco. Joseph Alioto, who had preceded Moscone as mayor of San Francisco, was a big city Democrat who was never accused of being a radical or even particularly progressive, but even he had very kind things to say about Jones: "I have known Pastor Jones a long time and fully agree with the testimonials he has received about his great integrity and of the spirit of brotherhood and love that he has brought to his parishioners and to all those with whom he comes in contact. He is also to be commended for his compassion and his deep understanding of the refugees from Vietnam, and for setting an example to the community by adopting Korean War orphans.[62]

The moment when it should have been obvious to everybody that Jones was a dangerous cult leader and megalomaniac who had veered far away from the principles he claimed to hold is not clear. By the spring of 1978, statements made by the Concerned Relatives or Deborah Layton should have been taken much more seriously, but to suggest that by 1975, or even 1976, politicians such as Moscone, Willie Brown, or Milk should have known the full truth about Jim Jones or known what was going to happen two years later is neither fair nor realistic.

Despite this, those conservatives who portray Jones as a product of radical leftism are not entirely wrong. Jones's politics were on the far left; he had ties to many progressive politicians as well as to celebrity left-wing figures of the era such as Angela Davis, Dennis Banks, and Huey Newton. Additionally, until Leo Ryan went to Guyana, criticism of Jones from San Francisco's liberal political class was very muted. However, Jones's ties to progressive San Francisco are also sometimes overstated. While it is very possible that Jones committed election fraud in support of Moscone in 1975, John Barbagelata's assertion that the fraud was enough to swing the election, an assertion that many on the right have come to take at face value, is very difficult to prove.

Barbagelata went to his grave believing that the 1975 runoff had been stolen from him, as noted by George Cothran in *SF Weekly*: "Until his dying day, March 19, 1994, former Supervisor John Barbagelata swore that Jim Jones and members of the People's [*sic*] Temple stole the 1975 mayoral election from him by double- and triple-voting under dead people's names, giving the coveted seat of chief executive to Moscone."[63] However, the fact that Barbagelata continued to believe this does not mean it is true.

A review of the numbers suggests that the claim, while based in the reality that voter fraud occurred in the 1975 race, is not true. The election was very close, but Moscone won by 4,316 votes. Moscone received 101,528 votes and Barbagelata 97,212. There is no reliable data other than raw numbers from that election, but of the roughly 200,000 votes cast, based on census data and voter registration and participation histories, it is likely that no more than 20 percent of the voters in that election were African American, although that number was probably closer to 15 percent. Writing the day after the runoff, Michael Harris of the *San Francisco Chronicle* estimated that Moscone won 80 percent of the African American vote—meaning that at most 32,000 African Americans, some legally and some perhaps not, cast their vote for Moscone.[64] If Jones's intervention was indeed enough to make a difference, that would mean one out of eight African American votes for Moscone, and more than one out of ten African American votes overall, were cast illegally. That is voter fraud on a sufficiently massive scale that it would likely not only have been noticed and halted on the day of the election, but also would have required extraordinary organization and coordination. Volunteers and campaign staff would have had to know about it and help conceal it. Hundreds of election workers would have had to willingly look the other way, and a proactive effort to keep the media from finding out about the fraud would have been required. It is extremely unlikely that all occurred.

Art Agnos, who supported Moscone in that 1975 election, described Jones's role in the political life of San Francisco in the mid-1970s: "[Jones] endeared himself to them [Willie Brown, Moscone, John Burton and Phil Burton] through superb political organizing and bringing people to rallies, demonstrations, and all that stuff. . . . He would deliver the troops for elections, for getting out the vote, for whatever was necessary that required a large number of volunteers, so the political world was fascinated with this guy."[65]

When asked directly about the role of voter fraud in Moscone's victory, Agnos was dismissive: "That stuff didn't happen. . . . He energized the black community and organized it."[66] Carol Ruth Silver, another Moscone ally from 1975, shared Agnos's view: "I have no indication that is the case. Every politician who narrowly loses an election is tempted to say that." However, Silver also conceded that "Moscone was a friend of Jim Jones [and] . . . did get some political help [from the Peoples Temple]."[67]

Rudy Nothenberg served as Moscone's field director in the runoff against Barbagelata and was therefore in a position to know what the Peoples Temple was doing in that election. His response to me when asked about how Jones did or did not help Moscone in 1975 was similar to those offered by Agnos or Silver, but it included somewhat more detail:

I was pretty closely associated with that campaign. For the last month, I was the director of the get-out-the-vote effort in which the Peoples Temple sent some troops. The thought that they were in some way critical to George's election is absolutely preposterous. On election day we would get two hundred people maybe or so, and I had two thousand people on the street.

They would come, and we would send them to the housing projects and tell them to get out the vote. If there was any impact on that, it would be very marginal because turnout in the projects was low anyway.[68]

After the election, Nothenberg went on to be deputy mayor during Moscone's time in office, so he may not be the most completely objective observer, but that does not mean he is dishonest. Following the assassinations, he served as budget director and later chief administrative officer under Mayor Feinstein, a position he held during the mayoralties of Art Agnos and Frank Jordan as well. Nothenberg served four different mayors and was viewed as a man of integrity. Moreover, it is extremely unlikely that Feinstein would have appointed someone who had engaged in election fraud on behalf of Moscone to such a senior position, so Nothenberg's words should be given a substantial amount of credence on this question.

The claims of Nothenberg, Agnos, and Silver run counter to the right-wing narrative that has gotten a surprising amount of traction among those who still care about elections from 1975, but the right has offered little hard evidence to support its assertions. Instead, the accusation is generally more of a circumstantial one, based on the idea that Jones supported Moscone, that Jones was, we now know, a sleazy and murderous person, that the election was very close, and that Barbagelata believed the election had been stolen. Additionally, while the charge that Jones stole the election for Moscone is probably an overstatement, it is very likely that Jones engaged in election-related activities that ranged from simply providing volunteers to ones that were probably fraudulent. Thus, the charges that Moscone was close to Jones and that Jones probably violated election law were true. Moscone then compounded this mistake by giving Jones a position in his administration. However, the story there is not quite that simple, because while Moscone made a mistake in appointing Jones to the San Francisco Housing Authority, that was not exactly the most powerful position in the mayor's administration. Jones wanted something more important, but Moscone delayed and finally gave him a position in the housing authority.

From May through July 1976, correspondence between the new mayor and the cult leader who helped him get elected (which is mostly from Jones to Moscone) shows an increasingly frustrated Jones pushing Moscone, with very limited success, for more appointments for members of the Peoples Temple and for an influential appointment for himself. A May letter from Jones to Moscone included a list of 12 Peoples Temple members, along with a brief description of their credentials, for whom Jones was trying to find jobs in the new Moscone administration. In addition to two- or three-line summaries of their credentials, Jones also listed the ethnic background of some of his candidates. For example, Jim McElvane was listed as "Black," Noreen Talley as "Caucasian," and Linda Amos as "Jewish." Reading this list is chilling, as five of the twelve, including McElvane, Talley, and Amos, were all later killed by Jones in Guyana.[69]

Moscone's reluctance to staff his administration with members of the Peoples Temple did not discourage Jones, who continued to use his usual mixture of flattery and pleading to try to get what he wanted. In a June letter, after he had been offered the position in the housing authority, Jones continued to lobby for his members. He concluded one letter by writing, "I enjoyed our conversation and appreciate your empathy, and your open-minded, constructive approach. I sincerely hope that Peoples Temple will be able to play a significant role in helping you achieve the vital aims of your administration."[70]

A month later, Jones redoubled his efforts to get Amos hired in the administration as a social worker, describing her as "brilliant in her work" and telling Moscone he would "certainly consider it magnanimous on your part if you would do what you can . . . on Ms. Amos' behalf." There were not too many Peoples Temple members who were Jewish and well-educated, so placing Amos in Moscone's administration would have been very helpful for Jones. The preacher ended his letter with more flattery: "All of us in Peoples Temple appreciate the job you are doing, mayor. In our minds you are this country's most enlightened civic leader."[71] Amos was not appointed by Moscone and was later killed in Guyana at the time of the mass killing, although not at the Jonestown site.

The Milk-Jones relationship was not quite as complex. Milk and Jones were both left-wing San Franciscans in the early and mid-1970s whose paths crossed a fair amount. Milk had spoken on occasion at Peoples Temple and had lent his name to a few Peoples Temple–related events. Milk's politics were deeply grounded in the notion that it was important to build coalitions, because he recognized that the gay liberation struggle could only succeed with support from other progressive groups. Therefore, it is not surprising that he at times worked with Jim Jones who, by the early 1970s, was one of the most visible civil rights leaders in San Francisco. Little is known about whether Milk felt uncomfortable around Jones or suspected that something was very wrong at the Peoples Temple, but by the time Milk was in elected office, Jones had faded from the San Francisco political spotlight.

Despite this, there is at least some evidence that by 1978 Milk recognized something was very strange, even dangerous, about Jim Jones. Art Agnos recollected, "In early '77, I happened to be at Peoples Temple. There was some kind of a city political rally. . . . All the city fathers were there. I'm a legislator. I'm there for the first time sitting in the Peoples Temple. Harvey's next to me. He's now elected as a supervisor. . . . He says, 'Stay away from him [Jones]. There's something wrong with him.' . . . We were listening to him . . . on a shortwave radio [from Guyana] where he was ranting. I said, 'Is this guy crazy or what?' He [Milk] says, 'Stay away from him.'"[72]

One key difference between Jones's ability to influence Moscone and Milk is that Moscone needed Jones a lot more than Milk did. Milk's electoral base, and the district from which he was ultimately elected, was largely white and gay. Jones's ability to mobilize large numbers of African Americans was, therefore, much less pertinent for Milk. Peoples Temple members handing out flyers on Market and Castro or going door to door on Nineteenth Street and Noe or Sanchez would not have been effective not only because they were not of that community but also because they were unlikely to be conversant in the issues that were of central import to Milk's gay electoral base.

Conservative assertions such as "Jones provided conscripted 'volunteers' for Milk's campaigns to distribute leaflets by the tens of thousands" and "Milk returned the favor by abusing his position of public trust on behalf of Jones's criminal endeavors"[73] written many years after the deaths of Milk and Jones resonate with right-wing audiences, but they are based on some questionable assumptions. Milk did not need, and in a real political sense could not have used, the volunteers Jones provided. When Milk finally won an election, it was not by a close margin, as he outpolled the second-place finisher in that 1977 supervisor race by a margin of 30.5 percent to 17.9 percent, receiving almost 2,500 more votes than Terrence Hallinan. Moreover, by the time of that 1977 election, Jones and many of his followers had already left San Francisco. While Milk was clearly too close to Jones at various points in the 1970s and lacked the prescience to understand how dangerous and evil Jones was, by the time Milk joined the board of supervisors, his attention was elsewhere, and he was no longer running any interference for Jones.

By the fall of 1978, it was apparent that politicians in San Francisco should have cut ties with Jones, and many already had. Still, had Moscone responded more quickly to the warnings raised by the Concerned Relatives earlier in the year, it is not clear what he could have done. Once Jones and his followers left San Francisco for the jungle of Guyana, the events that led to the mass killings had been set in motion. Despite this, it is not reasonable to think that in a close political campaign in 1975, candidate Moscone should have turned away support from a weird but progressive preacher because of something that would happen three years later.

The conservative argument that Jones's mass murder belongs to the catalogue of atrocities committed in the name of left-wing causes alongside those of Stalin, Pol Pot, or the Kim dynasty in North Korea is powerful, although Jones was a piker compared to those genocidaires. Asserting that politicians who accepted his help or stood with him at a fund-raiser a year or more before the killings are complicit in those killings is absurd and an offense to the politicians in question as well as to the victims.

Dan White

The murders at City Hall encapsulated the tension between the old and the new, the radical and the reactionary, the forces of change and the fear of change that had been part of the gestalt of the city for most of the 1970s. It is possible a similar event could have happened somewhere else in the United States in 1978, but it didn't, if for no other reason than no other city—not Los Angeles, not New York, not anywhere else—had any gay elected officials who could become the target of the bigotry and anger that, at least in part, motivated Dan White.

While the assassinations may have only been possible in San Francisco, it should be remembered that the gay former hippie from New York and the progressive mayor who had embraced the new, radical, tolerant, and in the eyes of some, weird, San Francisco were the victims. They were the ones who died that day. Their killer was not some wild-eyed, drugged-out, long-haired cult member, but a short-haired former police officer with deep roots in conservative San Francisco.

Dan White was the criminal whose actions brought the city to its knees on November 27. White, however, was not a product of radicalism, hippies, or drugs. He was a son of the conservative neighborhoods of western San Francisco. As David Talbot wrote, "Dan White was no denizen of the city's wacky fringe but a wholesome-looking product of the Catholic Church, US

Army and San Francisco police and fire departments."[74] White's political antecedents were not to be found in the Summer of Love, radical activism, or even the cult underworld of Charles Manson and Jim Jones. White's politics had their roots in the right-wing politics of Anita Bryant, George Wallace, and the southerners who threw rocks and otherwise abused young African Americans in the 1960s simply for trying to go to school. It was reactionary intolerance, not radical counterculture excesses, that drove White to crawl through that window in City Hall on that fateful Monday. Attributing the City Hall murders to the alleged excesses of the 1960s is blaming the victim.

When Dan White began his campaign for supervisor in 1977, he was in his early thirties, was a pretty good retail politician, and was positioning himself to be part of the next generation of conservative leaders in San Francisco. John Barbagelata did not run for the board of supervisors in 1977, which left an opening for a well-spoken, charismatic, Catholic conservative. White could have filled that role, but there was always a darker side to White. His campaign, "Unite and fight with Dan White," was probably chosen in substantial part because it rhymed, but it also suggested that the answer to the city's problems lay in fighting. Left unsaid, but understood, was that more conservative, whiter, and straighter San Francisco should be uniting against the city's newer and less conventional residents.

That idea was made more explicit in campaign literature in which White stated, "You must realize that there are thousands upon thousands of frustrated angry people such as yourselves waiting to unleash a fury that can and will eradicate the malignancies which blight our beautiful city."[75] The anger in that statement is hard to miss, while the phrases "unleash a fury" and "eradicate the malignancies" are quite startling and laden with violent imagery, threats, and historical resonance.

Over time, Dan White has come to be remembered for the assassinations and for the relatively light sentence he received. During the trial, attorneys Doug Schmidt and Steven Scherr claimed, among other things, that White had been suffering from depression, and they presented his increased consumption of unhealthy sugary snacks as part of the evidence of this. This became known as the Twinkie defense, although his lawyers never used that phrase in the trial. Beyond that, history has not been kind to Dan White, as he has become something of a symbol for violence, reaction, and homophobia.

At the time, however, views of White were much more divided. Many liberals and gays felt anger, fury, and hatred toward White. He was not only a political assassin, but he had killed a person of unique historical import to the gay rights movement. Despite his legal defense, White was not some deranged and delusional loner, but an angry political opponent and bigot. That, at least, was how a good proportion of San Franciscans saw him.

Not everybody, however, saw White that way. David Talbot describes how many in the police department viewed White's actions as justifiable, even heroic:

> When word [of the murders] reached the Hall of Justice, the reaction was different. Scattered cheers broke out on the fourth floor, among the police inspectors who had felt betrayed by Moscone. The jubilation soon spread throughout the SFPD network. Moscone and Milk were dead and a member of the cops' family, Danny White, had done the job. The Notre Dame Fighting Irish song crackled on the police radio, then 'Danny Boy.' . . . The San Francisco Police Department was deeply implicated in the murders of Moscone and Milk. Dan White was not carrying out SFPD orders that morning in City Hall, but he was carrying out the department's will. He was no longer on the force, but he was one of them: their star ballplayer, their political representative, their brother. He knew all about the cops' murderous feelings towards the city's liberal leadership. He felt the same way. They had the will, he had the willpower.[76]

Talbot demonstrates the polarization of assessments of the assassinations, but he also suggests that the killings of Moscone and Milk were not simply political assassinations but almost a coup in which a police department not happy about having its wings clipped and being forced to govern in a more tolerant way manipulated an emotionally distraught former colleague into killing the mayor, knowing he would be replaced by a more conservative successor. There is no way to prove this or anybody's motivations so many years later, but that is a reasonable description of the events themselves.

The police ire was aimed at least as much at Moscone as at Milk. Milk may have been the target of police homophobia, but Moscone was the mayor and used his power to integrate the police and to reform police culture. As Corey Busch argued, "The integration of the police and fire department is what cost him [Moscone] his life. . . . It happened because of what Moscone did. . . . That was his vision."[77] Moscone's efforts to reform the police department had included changing police policy with regards to gays, punks, and others, but perhaps most significantly the appointment of Charles Gain as chief of police. Gain was a reformer who had previously been the chief of police in Oakland. Gain helped implement Moscone's police policies, but he also pursued reforms of his own. Among the most remembered of those was his decision that police cars should be a softer and friendlier light blue rather than the formidable black and white they had been for years.

As early as the spring of 1976, fewer than 18 months into Moscone's mayoralty, the views many police officers held about their mayor were clear: "The police department becomes an easy political scapegoat to be manipulated and its member[s] sacrificed to satisfy the political whims of special interest groups in bids for re-election. Chief Gain, a member of the Moscone-Burton-Brown political machine[,] has conducted a psychological campaign designed to make men quit in anger."[78] This piece was written a year and a half before the assassinations, but the links are clear. Police resentment, resistance to reforms backed by minorities and gays, and the belief that everything Moscone did was a cynical political move were all ideas that helped drive Dan White to murder.

After he turned himself in, the police treated White more like a friend in trouble than an admitted killer. He received visits from friends on the force while in his cell, while others brought White meals from the outside so he wouldn't have to eat the unappetizing prison food. Much of the local media coverage of Dan White in the months following the murder was notably positive as well. The day after the killings, the *Palo Alto Times* headlined a profile about the murderer, "Daniel White Was Always Serving People-In Various Capacities." The article described White as "the pleasant supervisor" and described how he was "always serving the people, whether it be in elected office, public safety departments or dishing out French fries."[79] A *San Francisco Examiner* article from December 17 quoted Linda Nustari, who was described as "a deeply loyal family friend who visits and writes him [White]," as saying, "He is the warm gentle Danny I have always known, a man who could not hurt anyone unless he had lost his mind."[80]

The Death of a Mayor

The assassinations of Milk and Moscone occurred fifteen years, almost to the day, after the assassination of President Kennedy. It is possible to see these killings as bookends of the era of assassinations, although the assassination attempt against President Ronald Reagan in 1981 suggests that period was not quite over. In the eighteen years between 1963 and 1981, one president was assassinated; two more, Reagan and Ford, were almost assassinated; a presidential candidate, Bobby Kennedy, was killed in the midst of a campaign for the White House; and another, George Wallace, survived an assassination attempt that occurred midcampaign. Additionally, civil rights leaders Medgar Evers, Malcolm X and Martin Luther King Jr. were felled by assassins during these years as well. Other than Moscone and Milk, only King and Evers were killed by someone with diametrically opposed political views. The assassinations of Moscone and Milk need to be understood in this context as well. These two progressive men were killed by a conservative opponent who, through these assassinations, stopped the progressive movement in San Francisco, or at the very least set it back a decade. Sadly, Americans of that era grew accustomed to assassinations, but rarely were the motives and impact so political.

For these reasons, Moscone occupies an unusual place in political history. Outside of San Francisco he is known, if at all, as the man who was killed alongside Harvey Milk. Some San Franciscans have a better memory of him because he was briefly our mayor but also because the city's major convention center and a public park in the Marina District a few blocks from where he grew up are named for him. Cow Hollow and the Marina have changed a lot since Moscone—and a few decades later, I—grew up there. It is now home to affluent tech workers and other well-heeled professionals. Most probably don't know much about the man after whom one of their local parks is named.

Despite this, Moscone still stands out because he and Art Agnos are the only real progressive San Francisco mayors of the postwar era. Those interested in the political history of San Francisco must therefore reckon with the memory of George Moscone. Moscone served less than one full term as mayor and was hamstrung by an uncooperative board of supervisors during that time, so he was unable to do all the things he would have liked. Additionally, like most chief executives, he spent much of his time in office responding to crises and events. During his first year as mayor, the efforts to prevent the Giants from leaving town and to settle a public employee strike took up much of his time. Similarly, in 1978 alone, the latest wrinkle in the struggle to keep the Giants in San Francisco, efforts to keep the city solvent and functioning after Proposition 13, and, in Moscone's last days, helping the city recover from the Jonestown killings all took a lot of effort and attention. But this is true of almost all mayors. Before she became mayor, Dianne Feinstein could not have imagined how the AIDS crisis would dominate her time in office. Nor could her successor, Art Agnos, have known that a major earthquake about halfway through his term would determine much of how he would spend his time in City Hall.

All this makes it very difficult to assess Moscone's legacy accurately. Because his death is now more than forty years in the past, not that many people are left who knew him personally. Those who are speak of him warmly. Most simply refer to him as "George," and even his old political opponents smile when they recall him, describing him as charming, friendly, and gregarious. Quentin Kopp, who spent much of 1978 preparing to run against Moscone the following year, reminisced about the softball game between the mayor's office and the board of supervisors that year. Kopp, who when I interviewed him in 2018 was a few months shy of his ninetieth birthday and looked like he could still give a softball a good ride, chuckled as he described how "Moscone was out in centerfield with his suit jacket off, but smoking a cigarette in between pitches." Kopp contrasted Moscone's behavior at that game with that of Dan White, who insisted on being captain of the supervisors team and, according to Kopp, acted like it "was the World Series."[81]

Carol Ruth Silver kvelled over Moscone when recalling his campaign for mayor in 1975, describing him as "movie star handsome . . . super charming to everybody." She added, "To the homeless lady on the street . . . to the pizza guy . . . [he was] always on, always charming, articulate . . . a very, very super person. San Francisco was lucky to have somebody of his caliber as mayor . . . a really class act."[82]

It is also part of the story that this handsome, charming, and gregarious man barely won his election as mayor and did not pass much major legislation during his almost three years in that office. Nonetheless, he was the first San Francisco mayor, and the first of any major city, to embrace a broad diversity of the kind that now defines progressive politics in the twenty-first century. By doing this, Moscone kept a promise that he had made during the campaign and that was instrumental in his ability to build a winning and diverse coalition. A flyer from his 1975 campaign boasted that he was "the only candidate with the courage to state from the beginning that he will demand the resignation of every member of every board, agency and commission in the City." It went on to proclaim how Moscone's "commitment to a new government—with appointments reflecting the diversity of San Francisco, and not with special interests—sets him apart from all other candidates."[83]

Moscone was also a straight white Christian man whose belief in the power of his own charm and personality may have cost him his life when he decided that Dan White, a discredited bigot who was also a straight white Christian man, deserved a personal explanation. Moscone benefited greatly, in part because of those demographic characteristics, by being able to function in both old and new San Francisco, but that skill does not make it easier to evaluate his time as mayor.

Moscone's major accomplishments as mayor were not primarily legislative. He passed little groundbreaking progressive legislation, nor did he implement budgets that radically changed San Francisco. Instead, his impact as mayor either took the form of how he handled crises or how he helped change the feel of the city; he was the one who struck the fatal blow against the straight white hegemon that had governed the city since the Gold Rush. Making sure the Giants stayed in the city and crafting a fiscal strategy following the passage of Proposition 13 are two major examples of the former. Beyond that, Moscone's legacy is harder to pinpoint. The bullets from Dan White's gun are largely responsible for that.

Had Moscone not been killed, he would have been up for reelection in 1979. He would not have coasted to victory and might not have won at all, but the campaign would have given voters an opportunity to reflect on Moscone's time in office and decide what they made of it. Had Moscone lost that bid for reelection, he would have been a failed progressive in a sea of generally more successful pro-business San Francisco mayors, not unlike Agnos a decade or so later, who was elected in 1987 and lost a bid for a second term in 1991. Had Moscone won a second term, particularly if he had strengthened the progressive majority on the board of supervisors that he was about to create when he was killed, he would have been able to cement his legacy by passing laws and leaving a bigger mark on the city. Instead, Moscone's legacy is largely in the agonizing category of what might have been.

In October 1978, *San Francisco* magazine asked Moscone to pen an article describing his approach to governance and reflecting on his first three years in office. Moscone's response reveals a mayor whose progressive idealism had been tempered by the difficult work of governance, particularly after the passage of Proposition 13:

If your routine approach to problem solving consists of inflammatory press releases, chest-beating on the six o'clock news and little else—then you can't really expect to hit on solutions that bring opposing parties together.

I don't think that's what the people of San Francisco expect from their Mayor. During the last three years, my philosophy has been to work with the diverse groups of this City, bring people together and hammer out a future for San Francisco that makes sense.

That kind of difficult, even tedious work yields results—but it may not be very exciting. The task of improving MUNI or making streets safer can't always compete with *Monday Night Football* for thrills. No one ever said that progress makes great copy.[84]

Moscone's evolution from a progressive candidate to a pragmatic mayor focused on the real challenges of governance is apparent in this writing. This change also represented the reality of city governance in California after the passage of Proposition 13. Freezing property taxes meant that the state had to cut programs, thus pushing those costs down to the local level. Cities, therefore, became more focused on raising and maintaining tax revenue instead of engaging in ambitious progressive projects. Moreover, a smart politician like Moscone probably knew that a declining quality of life in San Francisco, which would in large part be attributable to Proposition 13, would nonetheless hurt an incumbent mayor's chances for reelection.

Toward the end of the draft he submitted to the magazine, Moscone listed declining crime rates, a program to retain small businesses in San Francisco, increased large-scale retail development, improvements at the Port of San Francisco, and major projects such as Pier 39 and the Yerba Buena Center as his major accomplishments.[85] The Yerba Buena Center was to be a large convention center in the South of Market area. The goal of constructing the center was to bring more conventions to San Francisco and to revitalize the South of Market area, known in recent years as SOMA. Moscone was particularly proud of the project because despite its being initially backed by the development community, he had won broader support for it through community involvement. In December 1978, before work was completed, the board of supervisors voted to rename it the Moscone Center.

Because of the laws governing succession in San Francisco, Moscone's assassination meant that the new mayor would be someone not of his choosing and a person somewhat more conservative than Moscone. For this reason, the killing of Moscone, even more than that of Milk, had a direct ideological impact on San Francisco politics. Milk's replacement on the board of supervisors, Harry Britt, was a progressive gay man who voted on the board much the way Milk did and who sought to carry the gay rights mantle previously carried by Milk. Moscone's replacement, on the other hand, was of a different ideological stripe.

The dramatic nature of Moscone's death also overshadows the scope of Moscone's fifteen-year career in politics, which also included stints on the board of supervisors and in the California State Senate. Moscone came out of a very unusual time and place in San Francisco politics in which he was part of a cadre of local politicians—including Milk, Agnos, Willie Brown, Jerry Brown, Nancy Pelosi, John Burton, and Phil Burton—who were ahead of the progressive movement that began to overtake the Democratic Party sometime in the 2000s. Milk became a civil rights legend, and Agnos's one term as mayor of San Francisco looks more impressive with each passing year. Willie Brown went on to become one of the most important state legislators in California history and then to serve two terms as mayor of San Francisco. Jerry Brown is one of the most intriguing and important politicians in American history who never became president. The Burton brothers' mark on California politics is still felt today. Nancy Pelosi became Speaker of the House of Representatives and the most powerful woman in American history. Moscone's political legacy is largely forgotten among that group because he didn't live long enough to make the mark he wanted in San Francisco.

Two Weeks in November

The last two weeks of November 1978 were in turn frightening, painful, traumatic, and unbelievable for those of us who lived through them. San Francisco was a small enough city in 1978 that many of us knew Milk, Moscone, and White or were otherwise directly impacted by the killings. In addition, the impact of the Peoples Temple killings on San Francisco was enormous, as many African American San Franciscans were similarly close to one or more of the victims lying dead in the Guyanese jungle.

A column by Herb Caen late in 1978 captured how these tragedies had worked their way into many of the city's more quotidian corners:

Early in the '77 high school baseball season here, it looked as though the Opportunity High Cobras, coached by Ron Cabral, would burn up the AAA League. With Tim Jones pitching like a big leaguer, the centerfielder batting .566, the Cobras won their first six games—and then the team fell apart.

The Rev. Jim Jones' wife Marceline told Ron "Sorry to take your star pitcher away, but Jim and I, and of course our boy Tim, are moving to South America." . . . Other children of Peoples Temple members who were pulled off the team included Catcher Bill Oliver, Second Baseman Armando Griffith and Right Fielder Mark Sly. Wes Breidenbach, also a Temple kid, replaced Tim Jones as pitcher and proved a disaster. . . .

Tim Jones survived the Guyana holocaust, but Oliver, Griffith and Sly died there. Sly's father, Donald, was the man who tried to knife Congr. Leo Ryan in the Jonestown Camp. And Wes Breidenbach . . . was in the hit squad that killed Ryan and others at the Kaituma airstrip.

Ron Cabral, coach of the dark-starred Cobras. Well, he's now at Wilson High. . . . Around Wilson they talk a lot about a one time Wilson baseball All-Star—Dan White. . . . Circles within circles, until the mind grows dizzy.[86]

Those circles forced everybody in San Francisco to think about where our city was going and whether it could survive. Mike Ivie's grand slam in late May or that sunny day in June when Harvey Milk framed gay liberation as the next great American civil rights movement seemed a long way away. As 1978 wound down and San Francisco slowly began to process what happened in November, no consensus emerged from the still diverse and contested city, but we all knew that something had to change if we were to survive.

9

The Long Shadow of 1978

●●●●●●●●●●●●●●●●●●●●●●

For some in San Francisco, 1978 ended much as the previous year had. As they had done on December 31, 1977, the Grateful Dead performed a New Year's concert on the last day of 1978 at Winterland, only a few blocks away from the mostly abandoned Peoples Temple headquarters on Geary Boulevard. Once again, Bill Graham, the refugee from the Nazis who had come to San Francisco by way of the Bronx, descended onto the stage, this time at the stroke of midnight. The year that began with Graham riding a gigantic Harley-Davidson motorcycle through the air above the crowd at Winterland ended with the legendary promoter descending onto the stage riding what Dan Akroyd described from the stage as a "a ten-, no, a twelve-foot-long burning ember of marijuana."[1] Graham, dressed as Father Time, was not riding an actual joint but what from the old video appears to be a reinforced papier-mâché mock-up of one. The Grateful Dead played for about four or five hours that night. The Blues Brothers also performed. Special guests included one of the original merry pranksters, Ken Kesey, as well as John Cippolina, a mostly forgotten guitarist from the Summer of Love era who had been part of the influential San Francisco band Quicksilver Messenger Service.

When the Dead finished their three-song encore, playing their own "Casey Jones," a cover of Chuck Berry's "Johnny B. Goode," and the traditional "And We Bid You Goodnight," one of the most famous and important venues of the 1960s and 1970s closed its doors forever. Winterland had opened in 1966 and was the creation of Bill Graham, who had renovated a defunct ballroom into a famous concert venue. Winterland was only used in that capacity for about fifteen years, but almost all of the most famous bands of the era played there, including the Rolling Stones, Jimi Hendrix, the Allman Brothers, the Band, Big Brother and the Holding Company, the Grateful Dead, Pink Floyd, Jefferson Airplane, Grand Funk Railroad, Frank Zappa and the Mothers of Invention, Elvis Costello, Pink Floyd, Bruce Springsteen and the E Street Band, the Ramones, and the Sex Pistols. It is notable that Winterland, which for many is a symbol of the 1960s in San Francisco, was an active venue well into the 1970s. Like much of what is remembered as the 1960s, many of Winterland's most memorable moments actually occurred in the 1970s.

The Dead show at Winterland was not the only New Year's Eve concert in San Francisco. At the Old Waldorf in the city's Financial District, New York's best-known punk rock band, the Ramones, was the headliner. At the Mab, the Readymades, the VIPs, and Flight were playing for San Francisco punks who wanted to welcome the New Year with some local flavor. Most San Franciscans were relieved to see 1978 end. The final six weeks of the year had been traumatic for most of us and much worse for many. By December 1978, San Francisco looked like a much darker and more frightening place than it had a year earlier. It had become a city where political scores were settled with gunshots to the head, where hatred was so strong that many San Franciscans expressed sympathy not with the dead mayor and supervisor but with their killer, where an entire community could disappear into the jungle and die at the hands of a cult leader turned mass murderer, and where a new trend in music and fashion was seen by many as at best completely baffling and at worst dangerous and frightening.

The hope that many gay and lesbian, African American, and progressive San Franciscans had felt at the beginning of the New Year as Harvey Milk, Carol Ruth Silver, and Ella Hill Hutch took their seats on the board of supervisors had been brutally dashed by Dan White. That was the environment in which Dianne Feinstein, an experienced but still somewhat undistinguished supervisor, found herself when she became mayor late in the morning of November 27. She would stay in office for most of the next decade and have an extraordinary impact on the city. In a very real way, the San Francisco that the world knows now is Dianne Feinstein's San Francisco.

Feinstein quickly proved that she was both an able professional and committed to returning San Francisco to a more conservative and pro-business approach to governance. During Feinstein's years in office, the progressive economic and land use ideas of Moscone and Milk had no place in City Hall. Instead, Feinstein offered a modernized vision of the city's economy that was much like what previous centrist mayors such as Democrat Joseph Alioto or Republican George Christopher had offered. Feinstein rarely opposed a major development project, paid little attention to issues such as preserving low income housing, and always stayed close to the same real estate and business interests that had disdained her immediate predecessor.

Neighborhoods had been at the center of the progressive urban vision of Feinstein's predecessor George Moscone, but things were different during Mayor Feinstein's time in office. Feinstein returned to an approach to governance that led with downtown interests and often neglected the neighborhoods. During her years as mayor, downtown grew substantially, as Chester Hartman and Sarah Carnochan document: "Between 1978 and 1987, office space in the city, virtually all in downtown high-rises, grew from 59 million square feet to 74 million square feet."[2] In a series summarizing Feinstein's time in office as her term wound down in August and September 1987, a team of *San Francisco Chronicle* writers wrote, "San Franciscans will remember Dianne Feinstein as a strong leader but also as a mayor who favored downtown over neighborhoods, the Chronicle Poll has found. Residents believe Feinstein neglected the city's neighborhoods while she promoted a downtown building boom."[3] They also noted that

critics say the mayor allowed the building boom to go too far, creating traffic congestions and other problems. They also say she reneged on a promise, made in her first term, that the neighborhoods would not suffer from the rush to develop downtown. Suddenly neighborhood residents discovered that "their parking went kapooey, not because of increased density in the neighborhoods, but because increased commuter density downtown brought people looking for parking places," said slow growth advocate Calvin Welch. In addition, neighborhood shops were driven out by high rents that rippled out from downtown.[4]

Carol Ruth Silver continued to serve on the board of supervisors through 1989 and so was there during all of Feinstein's time in office. She described Feinstein as being "much more in bed with the development community [than Moscone had been]," adding, "She was for helping businessmen become bigger and better businessmen."[5] Nothenberg expressed a similar sentiment in describing the contrast between the first two mayors he served: "I think she gave less time and power to the most assertive anti-development folks than George did.... She was open to having more development.... Fundamentally what you gotta know ... [is] all politics in San Francisco is land use. That is a given. If you don't understand that about San Francisco politics, you don't know what the hell you're talking about."[6] Nothenberg's point about the centrality of land use to local politics is important, because Feinstein's positions on development were ultimately essential to how she governed and to progressive dissatisfaction with her. Those positions also laid the foundations, in some cases literally, for San Francisco in the twenty-first century.

Feinstein's positions on diversity issues were more complex and made more difficult because AIDS hit San Francisco very hard beginning not long after she became mayor. Feinstein had voted with Harvey Milk on the landmark gay rights ordinance, but she was a very divisive figure in gay San Francisco, most memorably because of her decision to close bathhouses frequented by gay men in San Francisco as part of her effort to limit the spread of AIDS. Despite this, Feinstein, unlike White or Barbagelata, had a baseline commitment to tolerance and diversity. She never race-baited or used homophobic language, and she was always a strong advocate of women's rights. Shortly after Feinstein became mayor, an article in *Ladies' Home Journal* citing her liberal credentials described how she had "marched against the Vietnam War, worked hard for civil rights and is deeply concerned with human suffering."[7] Feinstein's politics made it possible for her to craft a San Francisco where these two ideals—a commitment to a strong business community and business climate and an understanding that the city could not survive unless it was tolerant and accepting of everybody regardless of race, ethnicity, or sexual orientation—could coexist.

It is also significant that *Ladies' Home Journal* was a national magazine without a strong political bent, because for readers of media like that, Feinstein was clearly a liberal. Her views on feminism, gays, labor unions, and many other issues placed her unambiguously on the left on the national political spectrum. Moreover, as a Jewish woman, she seemed like a liberal to many outside of San Francisco. The issues where she differed from liberal orthodoxy throughout her time as mayor were ones that were important in San Francisco, such as how she sought to combat AIDS or her views on land use, but they did not read as conservative outside San Francisco. The San Francisco that emerged during the nine years Feinstein was in office reflects this dynamic.

That San Francisco, despite hard-fought and frequently competitive elections, is still recognizable today. San Francisco is a city that is home to a vibrant tech sector that has directly contributed to enormous growth in population throughout the twenty-first century, a rising cost of housing, and at times a palpable tension between older and newer, and richer and poorer San Franciscans. It is also a city that has some of the most progressive legislation in the country on environmental policies, living wages, LGBT rights, and tenants' rights and that has a governing class that is very diverse. The coexistence of these realities is a reflection of the consensus forged during the Feinstein years and cemented in the following decades. It is also why conservatives can with some credibility complain that San Francisco has been taken over by the far left, while progressives can feel that City Hall never fully reflects the city's progressive values.

Moscone did the hard work of changing the culture of San Francisco government and of bringing a government into power that reflected the diversity of the city. He frequently did this against strong political opposition, including that which he faced in his close 1975 campaign, but also against opposition from many powerful business interests. Moscone should be recognized for that, but Dan White murdered Moscone before he could finish his first term as mayor. In the slightly less than three years he was in office, Moscone simply did not have enough time to institutionalize these changes.

Thus, when Feinstein found herself assuming the mayoralty, it fell to her either to make diversity a permanent part of San Francisco governance or to reverse it. Although many on the left will always see her as too moderate, she chose the former and should be recognized for that. Nothenberg expressed this view in speaking about the similarities between Moscone and the woman who succeeded him. According to Nothenberg, when Feinstein became mayor, these changes "were reversible." He went on to say, "I think she came by it [commitment to diversity] honestly. I think those are her instincts. . . . Philosophically they [Moscone and Feinstein] were not all that different. Dianne was more moderate. She was far more cautious."[8]

Richard DeLeon astutely summed up Feinstein's tenure as mayor from a progressive perspective: "If the Feinstein administration is judged by the policy checklist of the progressive agenda, one would have to conclude it was a retrograde failure on nearly every point." DeLeon tempered this strong criticism by adding, "Feinstein's centrist political instincts may have been well adapted to the requirements of governance during this period of turmoil. . . . It was a politically necessary hiatus—one that achieved system stability at the price of policy backsliding."[9] While DeLeon's book persuasively outlines how Feinstein's politics with regard to land use, development, downtown interests, and the business community were clearly much more conservative than Moscone's, his words about system stability are important. First, it is a reminder that when Feinstein became mayor, many believed the city could not recover from the twin shocks of Jonestown and the assassinations. At that moment and in the months that followed, the system was not stable, and many feared that it would not become stable anytime soon. Second, the system that proved stable was a different one than before Moscone. The new system, which remains in place today, is one in which nonwhites and LGBT people have several permanent seats at the table and, even in the face of the twenty-first-century influx of tech money, a core set of progressive values around social justice, the environment, and civil rights still define San Francisco.

The presence of a Democratic mayor with Feinstein's pro-business but socially liberal profile contributed to the end of the Republican Party in San Francisco. Since John Barbagelata lost his narrow race to George Moscone in 1975, no Republican has made a meaningful bid for citywide office in San Francisco, and there have been very few Republicans elected to any office at all in the city. Other factors, such as the declining proportion of city voters who are white and the rightward drift of the GOP nationally, contributed to this as well.

Despite the role Feinstein played, the impact of 1978 did not fade away quickly. The 1960s notion that San Francisco was crafting a new way of living and helping society break its ties to repressive and conventional thinking was still believed by many San Franciscans when 1978 began, but the end of the year it was hard to avoid the view that those utopian ideas and experimentation were somehow related to the horror in Guyana and to the assassinations. That assumption may or may not have been true, but conservative and older San Franciscans at the time believed it to be axiomatic.

Even the great feeling the Giants had provided for much of the city had largely faded by December. The Giants had managed to stay in first place for most of the summer but were essentially an average team for the last four months of the season. During the last three months of 1978, following the end of the season, other than re-signing third baseman Darrell Evans, a key contributor and very solid player, the Giants did nothing to improve their team. Astute fans were beginning to temper their optimism about the Giants' future.

Given all this, it was possible to see 1978 as some kind of annus horribilis for San Francisco. The mayor and a leading progressive supervisor had been slain, and the man who had offered hope to an older, more conservative San Francisco was proven to be a demented killer. Hundreds of San Franciscans had been murdered in the jungles of Guyana. As the year wound down, it was apparent that the city could not have withstood any more loss, so it is worth considering the one dog that did not bark. The Giants had brought a measure of joy and even unity to the city in 1978. For much of the spring and summer, one of the stories pushing Jonestown out of the newspapers and ameliorating the growing political divisions was that exciting young Giants team.

The two days in 1978 that had the most impact on the development of San Francisco were November 18, when the Jonestown massacre occurred, and November 27, when White killed Moscone and Milk. It is possible that the third most important date of the year was March 15. That was the day the Giants acquired Vida Blue and very possibly changed the trajectory of their tenure in San Francisco and perhaps of San Francisco more generally. The trade was completed late enough that day that it did not make it into the next day's newspaper, but it was above-the-fold news on March 17. The headline on the top left-hand corner of page 1 of the *San Francisco Chronicle* announced, "Giants Get Vida—A's Closer to Denver."

Blue was a big enough star, particularly in the Bay Area, that the trade was major news and baseball fans did not need to know the last name of the player in question. There was only one Vida in baseball in the 1970s. The second half of the headline was equally important. Although the A's never made it to Denver and have managed to survive in Oakland through today, at times tenuously, the trade was quickly understood to show that if one team was going to leave the Bay Area, it was no longer going to be the Giants.

Blue went on to have an excellent year and led the Giants into contention. That season and the strong attendance that was part of it would have been much less likely without Blue. Blue never won a pennant for the Giants and was traded to the Royals four years later almost to the day, but the impact of acquiring Blue in 1978 was enormous. It didn't guarantee the Giants would remain in San Francisco, but if Blue had ended up in Cincinnati or New York and the Giants had finished in fifth place, it would have been much easier for the team to have left San Francisco in the years immediately following 1978.

If the season had not gone as well for the Giants, they very well might have left San Francisco by 1979 or 1980. This is impossible to prove, but the constant rumors and last-minute efforts to save the Giants of the previous years would have been tested again if the city hadn't rediscovered its passion for the team. Had the Giants played .410 ball and drawn fewer than 800,000 fans in 1978 as they had done for most of the preceding five years or so, they might have been on their way to Denver, Florida, or elsewhere—and as per the agreement Moscone made in 1976, the city would have signed away its right to sue to keep the Giants in town. That would have been another blow to a city already reeling—a blow from which San Francisco would have had a very difficult time recovering. The symbolism of the team leaving the city would have been clear and would have sent a message to the rest of the country while being a psychological punch in the stomach to San Francisco. Willie McCovey, Mike Ivie, Jack Clark, but most of all Vida Blue, stopped that from happening.

Even though the Giants remained in San Francisco, in many ways things got worse in San Francisco in the years immediately following 1978. Republican administrations in Washington and Sacramento during the 1980s meant cuts in services for cities such as San Francisco, but the biggest crisis to hit San Francisco in the years following 1978 was AIDS. AIDS had a national and global impact, but in the early years of the plague there were few places in the country that were hit as badly as San Francisco. The disease wrought a terrible toll on San Francisco's gay community, killing thousands and causing tremendous fear. This fear was not limited to gay people, as many straight people were afraid of getting the disease. In these early years of AIDS there was a tremendous amount of misinformation about the disease that contributed to an increase in homophobia in San Francisco and elsewhere. San Francisco was largely left to fight this public health crisis on its own as, for example, President Reagan never addressed AIDS in a meaningful way during his two terms in the White House and was well into his second term before he even said the word "AIDS."

The last major blow to San Francisco related to 1978 occurred on May 21, 1979, when the jury in the trial of Dan White returned its verdict. The trial had been relatively brief, lasting about three weeks. The facts of the case were never in doubt, so White's motivations, state of mind, and awareness of his actions were the main issues that were debated during the trial. On the day before what would have been Harvey Milk's forty-ninth birthday, Dan White was found not guilty of charges of murder, although he was convicted of voluntary manslaughter, a crime that carried a considerably lighter sentence than murder. Therefore, White was sentenced to only seven years and eight months in prison. At the time there were thousands of people in California's jails serving longer sentences for nonviolent drug offenses. This appallingly light sentence for a man who knowingly and in cold blood killed two people was, by any measure, a travesty of justice.

Many San Franciscans, particularly gay San Franciscans, wanted to see White get the death penalty or at least a life sentence. Instead, he almost literally got away with murder. San Francisco's gay community, seething at the injustice of the sentence, once again marched to City Hall. Fewer than six months earlier, many gay San Franciscans had marched somberly and peacefully from the Castro to City Hall following the assassination of Harvey Milk, but the march had a very different feel this time. On the evening of May 21, the sadness and sense of loss of six months earlier was replaced by anger, frustration, and the realization that in America's justice system, shooting and killing a gay man at point-blank range was too frequently still treated as a minor offense.

The march was anything but peaceful. In the evening of May 21 and the early hours of May 22, that day that would have been Milk's forty-ninth birthday, demonstrations around City Hall turned violent as gay men broke windows, torched police cars, and loudly and angrily protested the miscarriage of justice. There were extensive clashes between the police and gay demonstrators around City Hall and later that evening in the Castro. At City Hall, the police used tear gas, but the demonstrators did not back down. In the Castro, after first entering a gay bar, the police then moved to the streets and continued to assault people with their nightsticks. In the *San Francisco Chronicle*, Katy Butler described "a long furious night of burning and looting . . . an almost atavistic reaction to the Dan White manslaughter verdict." She continued: "Throughout Monday night, community leaders using feeble bullhorns tried desperately to harness the fury of the raging crowd. It was like trying to turn back the sea."[10] Over the course of the evening over twenty people were arrested and 124 demonstrators and 59 police officers injured.

Although the demonstrations at City Hall, which came to be known— in an unwitting echo of the dress rehearsals for mass murder in Jonestown— as the White Nights, consisted primarily of gay San Franciscans, others were there as well. For punk rockers whose politics ran toward leftist anarchy and who shared gay San Francisco's anger at the police department, this was an opportunity to turn their politics into action. Many made the short walk from North Beach to the Civic Center to join the demonstrations.

Michael Fox was hanging out at the Mab on the evening of May 21 when he heard what was happening at City Hall. He described his recollection of what happened next: "We all ran down by City Hall. A whole bunch of us got over there, and people were turning over cop cars, and a couple of them were on fire. . . . We just rushed in. And the cops didn't try to stop us. They were standing around watching us trash everything because they just let off f**king Dan White. . . . After that, it kind of broadened out. People [punks and gays] started talking to each other. . . . On that night, it was gays and punks flipping over cop cars, really pissed off."[11] Fox's comments about gay people and punks beginning to talk to each other, and riot together, reflects a strengthening of the ties between the two communities that was in evidence the previous year during the "Nix on Six" event.

The White Night riots were a reminder that tensions between gays and the police force were still very strong and that the two groups interpreted the events of November 1978 very differently. More chillingly, they were a reminder that the violence and divisions that so powerfully affected the city throughout the 1970s were still present. At the time, the events continued to raise questions about the ability of the city to survive and of the persistence of divisions that threatened to destroy San Francisco. It became clear within the next few years that the White Night riots were not the beginning of renewed divisions in San Francisco, but the last gasp of a reactionary police force—representing a dwindling political constituency that was losing its place in a rapidly changing San Francisco—and in many respects the real end of the tumultuous year that 1978 had been. Within a few years, Harry Britt, Harvey Milk's successor, would no longer be the lone gay elected official in San Francisco, more gays and lesbians would join the police force, and Dianne Feinstein, a propolice centrist mayor, would make it clear that the days of wanton police violence toward gay people, although maybe not punk rockers, were over.

Stuck in Reverse

The Giants also had some dismal years following the 1978 season. They won eighteen fewer games in 1979 than they had in 1978, and other than a decent year in 1982, they were a pretty bad team until they returned to contention in 1986. In 1987, they won their division with a ninety-win season, finally exceeding their 1978 mark. The Giants teams of the early and mid-1980s, again with the exception of 1982, were generally characterized by Jack Clark missing too many games due to injury and Johnnie LeMaster never hitting but nonetheless holding on to the shortstop job. Young players such as Tom O'Malley, Joe Strain, and Brad Wellman generally failed to contribute to the big league club. During those years, the Giants also rotated through numerous veterans, such as Manny Trillo, Champ Summers, Dan Driessen, Al Oliver, and Gene Richards, who had left their better years in other cities.

By the time the Giants made it back to the postseason (in 1987), the nucleus of that 1978 team had been traded away (Clark, Mike Ivie, Bill Madlock, Vida Blue, Bob Knepper, and John Montefusco), had left via free agency (Darrell Evans following the 1983 season), had gone to Japan and then to the Dodgers (Terry Whitfield), or had retired (Willie McCovey). The 1987 Giants had exactly one player, an aging Greg Minton, who had been on the 1978 team. Minton had pitched eleven innings for the Giants in 1978 before becoming a very effective reliever in the early 1980s. In 1987, he was expendable, pitching in only fifteen games for the Giants before being released on May 28, the ninth anniversary of Ivie's grand slam off of Don Sutton.

Much of the big decline the Giants experienced between 1978 and 1979 is attributable to the team's pitching being much worse in 1979 than it had been the previous year. In 1978, the Giants offense was not great, as they only scored 613 runs, seventh overall in the National League. In 1979, they scored 672 runs, good enough for eighth in the league. However, the pitching numbers tell a much starker story. In 1978, the Giants were third in the league with a 3.30 ERA. The team ERA rose all the way to 4.16, good enough only for eleventh out of twelve teams in the National League in 1979. That year saw a 6 percent increase in runs scored overall in the league, but that does not change the extent to which the collapse of the Giants pitching was behind their overall decline.

The starting pitching, which had been a major strength in 1978, all but imploded in 1979. Vida Blue's ERA ballooned to 5.01. Additionally, John Montefusco and Ed Halicki were both injured for much of 1979. Those two righties, despite being anchors of the 1978 pitching rotation and being under thirty years old, would never be good pitchers again. Bob Knepper went on to a fine big league career that would last a total of fifteen seasons, but 1979 also was an off year for the youngest member of the 1978 rotation.

Modern baseball analytics and understandings of pitching suggest an explanation for why the Giants had such a bad year in 1979, particularly compared with 1978: the Giants' starting pitchers were overworked in 1978. Joe Altobelli got very good seasons out of all four of his young starting pitchers, but none of them ever again pitched more innings or had a better season than they did in 1978. Had the pitching held up, 1979 could have provided an opportunity for the Giants. The Dodgers and Reds, who between them had won every National League West division title since 1972, were both in a period of transition, as many of their biggest stars were either aging or injured. The Reds team that won the division was a shadow of the Big Red Machine of earlier in the decade, winning only ninety regular season games before getting swept by the Pirates in the National League Championship Series. Although there was an opening for the Giants in 1979, they failed to take advantage of it, in part because during the 1978–1979 offseason the Giants did nothing to address their needs. They had gotten no offense from the shortstop or catcher position in 1978 but stuck mostly with Johnnie LeMaster and Marc Hill at those positions anyway. They needed another power bat in the outfield but instead added speedster Bill North. North played very well for the Giants in 1979, posting a .386 OBP while stealing fifty-eight bases in eighty-two tries, but given that Larry Herndon was a decent enough centerfielder who, like North, was not a power hitter, North was the right answer to the wrong question.

The Giants were unable to build on their 1978 success for another reason as well. Their farm system had finally dried up. The Giants' ability to draft or sign top prospects in the 1960s and 1970s was so good that even in 1978 they still benefited from young stars they produced from within, such as Clark and Knepper, as well as players such as Evans and Madlock, who had, indirectly, been acquired in exchange for young or unproven players. Evans was acquired for Willie Montanez, whom the Giants picked up from the Phillies for a young Gary Maddox. Madlock came to the team from the Cubs in exchange for Bobby Murcer, who had come from the Yankees in return for Bobby Bonds. In 1978, the Giants only had two players in their entire farm system who would go on to big league careers of any note, outfielder Chili Davis and catcher Bob Brenly, who both made it to the team in 1981. If the Giants had had a power-hitting outfielder, a decent catcher, or a shortstop ready to contribute at the big league level, or good prospects who could have been traded for those types of players following the 1978 season, they might have been in better shape in 1979.

There were some bright spots in 1979. Terry Whitfield, .287/.349/.396, and Darrell Evans, .253/.356/.391, had solid seasons. Jack Clark had another great season at age twenty-three, batting .273/.348/.476 and hitting twenty-six home runs. Mike Ivie continued to push Willie McCovey for playing time. McCovey had a decent season, hitting .249/318/.402, but Ivie emerged as one of the top young hitters in the league by hitting .286/.359/.547, including twenty-seven home runs in only 455 plate appearances. A puzzling midseason trade that sent second baseman Bill Madlock to the Pirates, where he helped them win the World Series, didn't help. The Giants ended up winning seventy-one games in 1979, and their attendance fell by 300,000.

Through the next few years, the team's position was never as precarious as it had been in the mid-1970s, but the Giants remained a small market team, plagued by low attendance, limited television exposure, and, therefore, the inability to generate enough revenue to pursue big money free agents, an increasingly important part of the game in the late 1970s. This made it very difficult for them to contend as the 1970s turned into the 1980s.

It didn't help the Giants' profile in San Francisco that while they were struggling to contend from 1979 to 1986, the 49ers, the city's football team, were emerging as one of the great teams of all time. Joe Montana, Ronnie Lott, Dwight Clark, and coach Bill Walsh led the team to Super Bowl victories in 1982, 1985, 1989, and 1990. Even when the Giants managed to win a pennant in 1989, the 49ers were still the highest profile team in town.

In the new century, that has changed dramatically. Beginning in the mid-1990s, the Giants became the marquee sports franchise in the Bay Area. For more than twenty years, Giants hats, T-shirts, and other paraphernalia have far outnumbered similar A's, 49ers, or Raiders gear. In 2016–2019, the Giants were briefly eclipsed by the Warriors, but the local basketball team has yet to prove as enduringly popular. Since moving to their new ballpark in 2000, the Giants have sold out almost every single game. Their beautiful park is now a destination for tourists and visitors, not just intense baseball fans. Beginning with their first of three World Series victories in 2010, the Giants reclaimed their position as one of baseball's most well-known and popular franchises, a position they had last held briefly in the first half of the 1960s.

Many events were turning points for the Giants as they changed from being an obscure unsuccessful franchise to one of the best and most popular in the game. In the off-season of 1992–1993, the team was believed to be moving to Florida before an ownership group led by Safeway magnate Peter Magowan bought the franchise, committed to keeping the team in San Francisco, and then signed Barry Bonds, the best player in the game at the time, as a free agent. Seven years later, the opening of the new ballpark was another turning point. Winning the 2010 World Series, the first since the team moved to San Francisco, brought the Giants more positive national attention than they had had in decades. However, the seeds of much of this were in that 1978 season.

In 1978, the Giants drew a million more fans than the season before, demonstrating that even a third-place team could be economically competitive in San Francisco. The exciting baseball they played that year helped them win a new generation of fans whose enthusiasm wavered over the next decade or two but whose loyalty did not. It took the Giants years to finally figure this out, but in the last decade or so, the brand that the Giants have successfully built has antecedents in 1978. The Giants are now a team that maintains strong ties to players from their past, including Hall of Famers Willie Mays, the late Willie McCovey, and Juan Marichal, other great Giant players like Will Clark and Jack Clark, and beloved players like Vida Blue, who had his best years elsewhere. They have been able to use the team's history to draw new fans and energize older ones. The roots of those moves were in both the decision to bring McCovey back as a free agent in 1977 and to trade for Blue in spring training of 1978. The Giants have also built an identity that is much more rooted in their unusual hometown than they did before 1978. Few teams were as fast to adapt to the new technology of the internet age as the Giants, whose enormous base of tech-savvy fans beginning around 2010 helped make them a national franchise again. Any team can have Grateful Dead night at the ballpark, but only the Giants can claim to be the favorite team of most of the members of that band. Penelope Houston or Jello Biafra Bobblehead Night and celebrations of the city's punk rock history have still not happened at the ballpark, but we can't rule it out.

That 1978 roster left such a lasting mark on so many Giants fans because they were in first place for half the season and had some wonderful players and some memorable moments, but their impact on the team, their fans, and indeed the city went beyond that. However, it took some time for that to work out. The years from 1979 to 1985 were better than the mid-1970s but still not easy for the Giants. The contrast between Mike Ivie's grand slam home run to put the Giants ahead of the Dodgers in a game in May 1978 and Joe Morgan's three-run shot that knocked the Dodgers out of the play-offs in 1982 reveals a little bit more about San Francisco in those years, and how the events in the city on, but mostly off, the ball field changed attitudes and perceptions. Today, devoted Giants fans who are under forty years old are more likely to remember Morgan's home run. For example, as long ago as September 1999 as the Giants prepared to play their last games at the 'Stick, the *San Francisco Chronicle* ranked Morgan's home run as the third-most memorable Giants moment at the 'Stick. The author of that piece, Henry Schulman, introduced the moment:

> For 40 years, people have flocked to Candlestick Park for different reasons. To cheer the Giants on to an important September victory during a pennant race. To idle away a summer afternoon reading a good book, enjoying a ballgame in the background. To drink in the true Candlestick experience on a June evening, which would mean buying three cups of hot cocoa: one to sip and two to use as hand-warmers. On Oct. 3, 1982, 47,457 people came to Candlestick for a far different purpose. They wanted to see that blue Los Angeles Dodger blood spilled on the turf.[12]

Schulman's interpretation is accurate. I cheered loudly for both home runs, but when Ivie hit his, the season was young enough that there was still room for hope, and the feeling in San Francisco was still optimistic.

Corey Busch, the Moscone press secretary turned Giants executive, suc-cinctly explained the difference between Ivie's and Morgan's blasts: "Ivie's grand slam was more in the context of hope for the team. . . . Morgan's hit was wonderful because it was payback. . . . It was very different. . . . Ivie's grand slam was very hopeful and very exciting, and it was forward think-ing. Morgan's home run was 'F**k you' [to the Dodgers]."[13]

As somebody who grew up hating the Dodgers, I was very happy to see the Giants knock them out of the race in 1982. But even as the ball left the park, something felt different. As great as it was to see the Dodgers' hopes ruined, we also knew that the Giants had been eliminated by Los Angeles the previous day and the Dodgers had won the World Series the previous year. Additionally, although Joe Morgan, the man who hit the home run, was a truly great player, he was not a real Giant in any meaningful sense.

Morgan—who was elected to the Hall of Fame in 1990, which was the first year he was eligible—played in the big leagues for twenty-two years, won two MVP awards, three World Series championships, and five Gold Gloves but did none of those things during the two years he was in San Francisco. Nonetheless, we loved Morgan for what he did to the Dodgers that day. The years following that Joe Morgan home run were not good ones for the Giants. They finished fifth in 1983 and in last place in both 1984 and 1985. In those years, we joked that the biggest highlight of the first half of the decade was when Joe Morgan knocked the Dodgers out of the playoff race, but it was always a joke that was on us as we recognized how pathetic our beloved Giants had become.

The four years and four months between the Ivie grand slam and the Morgan home run were critical ones for San Francisco that changed the mood of the city and probably made us more able to be the kind of bitter sports fans who take glee in their rival's defeat because our own victories were increasingly unimaginable. In the beginning of that summer of 1978, there was reason for hope in San Francisco. Although there was still division, anger, and even hatred on the political front, there was a new progressive mayor who appeared committed to calming racial tension. Harvey Milk was emerging as a man of principle but also a savvy politician who was committed to working with everybody in the legislature. Many thought of Jim Jones as a charismatic and powerful, if somewhat strange and off-putting, preacher and political figure, but he had left town a year earlier and appeared to be receding into history. Nobody had heard of AIDS, and there were Democrats in the White House and in Sacramento who seemed to care about cities. Things were still far from perfect in San Francisco, but there was reason to believe, or maybe just to hope, that after the upheaval of the early and mid-1970s, things were improving in San Francisco and we were moving toward a better city. Just like as Giants fans we had no idea how bad things were about to become for the orange and black, few San Franciscans in May or December 1978 thought things were going to get worse, but they did.

By the fall of 1982, assassinations, mass murder, the brutal early impact of AIDS, and President Reagan's attack on urban America had begun to make their impact not just on life in San Francisco but on the gestalt of what it meant to be a San Franciscan. This was also reflected in cultural trends such as the rise of punk, which, while often bitingly political and funny, was never a sunny and optimistic musical genre or cultural trend. In that context, it is fitting that a home run that hurt the Dodgers much more than it helped the Giants was the signature moment for the team in the early 1980s.

After Punk

Punk's moment was brief, and punks continue to argue about just how brief it was. By the early 1980s, punk was also in a rough spot. As Penelope Houston recalled, "By the time the '80s came around, a lot of people had gotten into heroin, and there was this kind of dark swamp [around punk]."[14] For some punks, the scene was over by the mid-1980s; for older punks, it was over by 1980; for many more, it was over about three years after they got started. There may be no more punk sentiment than announcing that by some purely subjective, but relatively early, date punk was over.

The question of when punk ended remains entirely subjective, as many believe that later bands such as Green Day were also punk. Nonetheless, central to the feel of punk was that it was short lived. Very few punk bands continued performing or evolving the way countless hippie bands did for decades after the 1960s. This is partially because the financial incentive was not there, given that punk was always much smaller, but it also reveals something about the nature of punk.

Fifteen years after the first Dead Kennedys concert, there was little direct evidence of punk left in San Francisco. The culture had moved on, whereas fifteen or even fifty years after the Summer of Love, the music of that era was still very visible in San Francisco. By the early 1990s, the fingerprints of punk were visible in music and fashion, but punk music itself was no longer easy to find. Some bands had adapted the tempo and some of the optics of punk, but usually without the attitude, humor, and energy. Similarly, hair colors, haircuts, and accessories that in 1978 shocked people were widespread by 1993 and are much more widespread today but are no longer thought of as punk.

Central to the legacy of punk is that, particularly in San Francisco, punks are not remembered the way hippies are. Punk arose in part as a reaction to hippie hegemony, and now when both hippies and punks are something from the history books, that hippie hegemony still drowns out punk. Joel Selvin attributed this to there being no punk equivalent of the Grateful Dead to continue waving the punk banner for decades while serving as a focal point for aging punks to reconnect and stay in touch as the years go by.[15]

Instead, Selvin added, punks became a "cultural archetype . . . a role model for people with certain attitudes." However, unlike other youth movements, Selvin argued, by its nature punk "has a certain orthodoxy that is always going to appeal to a limited minority."[16] Part of that orthodoxy was the near constant refrain that punk was over and that if you really wanted to be a punk, you needed to be here two weeks, two years, or two decades ago. That orthodoxy always limited punk and kept it from being a mass cultural trend while also ensuring that it stayed punk. For Selvin, the contrast was clear if somewhat overly dramatic: "Punk rock's a nihilistic, negativistic, exclusive message. Hippie is an inclusive, positive, encouraging message."[17] Henry S. Rosenthal, the drummer from Crime, offered a more practical analysis: "In the minds of the bands, we were what was happening at that time, but it was an illusion. . . . It was always a tiny little thing. . . . It was hard to get a foothold. Punk rock was never destined to be a mass cultural movement. It was esoteric. It was conceptual. It was art-based rather than music-based. It had an aesthetic that did not have mass market appeal."[18]

To people who identify as outsiders, including at the ballpark, punk has an enduring appeal. In game 1 of the 2010 World Series when the new San Francisco was on display for the world, there was no punk rock presence at the ballpark—but by McCovey Cove, a little off to the side because of the heavy police presence in his usual spot, Joe Dirt, a major punk figure in late 1970s San Francisco, was preparing to go after any splash hits that day. Dirt had a ticket but preferred to be outside in case anyone hit a home run into the bay, but that was not the only reason for his decision. When describing his passion for both punk rock and baseball to me, Dirt evocatively captured the feel of being a punk rocker in 1978 or 2010: "I've always been an outsider all my life even at the ballpark. I'm hated at the ballpark."[19]

10

Neighborhoods, Natives, and Those Hills

●●●●●●●●●●●●●●●●●●●●●

Every city dweller knows that the key to making a life in New York, Los Angeles, Chicago, Shanghai, Paris, London, Tokyo, or anywhere else is not to let oneself be intimidated by the sometimes overwhelming size of their city, but to experience it as a collection of distinct neighborhoods or villages. This was certainly true of San Francisco in the 1970s, and it may have been one of the reasons why the politics and culture were so dynamic, diverse, unusual, and occasionally violent during those years.

My San Francisco as a ten-year-old middle school student in 1978 was very small. I spent almost all of my time in an area confined by California Street to the south, Van Ness to the east, and Arguello to the west. The northern boundary of my San Francisco was the bay. This area covered maybe one-sixteenth of the city, but it felt very large to me. The corner of Clay and Van Ness, where we caught the Ballpark Express, was at the edge of my known San Francisco. The ballpark itself was in a part of the city I did not know well and to which I never went other than to see the Giants. Ghirardelli Square lay just outside the northeastern border of the San Francisco I knew. A trip there or, later in the year, to the newly opened Pier 39, where Dan White's potato stand stood, felt like a whole-day affair, with a thirty-minute bus ride on either side.

Even in that relatively small portion of the city where I spent most of my time in 1978, there was a lot of diversity and difference. The mansions of Pacific Heights where some of the richest people in the city lived contrasted sharply with the much more modest parts of Cow Hollow and the Marina, where working class Italian or Chinese families, many senior citizens, and the occasional single Jewish mother from New York lived side by side in smallish apartments that are always called flats in San Francisco. A few blocks south of the heart of Pacific Heights, the wealthy white neighborhood flowed into the northern reaches of the Fillmore–Western Addition neighborhood. The latter back then was lower income and heavily African American.

The hills of San Francisco also reinforce neighborhood boundaries and mean that what would otherwise be a fifteen-minute walk between, say, the Inner Richmond and the Castro, becomes a journey rarely done on foot. The Castro is a particularly hilly neighborhood, making it possible for it to feel farther from other parts of the city than it actually is. The distance from the western end of Broadway or Pacific, among the streets with the largest and most expensive homes in the city, to the more northern parts of Cow Hollow where George Moscone grew up and that as late as 1978 was still a modest, largely working- and middle-class area, is fewer than ten blocks. The hills, however, are so steep that even the walk down from Pacific Heights is daunting. The walk up is brutal. I know that from personal experience, because for almost my entire primary and secondary education, I took the bus to school rather than walk the relatively short distance from my home to my grade school and later high school in Pacific Heights.

San Francisco's microclimates further contribute to the sense of the city as a collection of distinct neighborhoods. It may appear trivial now, but it seems oddly relevant that the weather was almost always nicer in Harvey Milk's district than in much of Dan White's, or that Mike Ivie's clutch grand slam occurred in the warm and clear skies that were almost never seen in the working-class areas of the Outer Sunset or Outer Richmond. Similarly, the cold and near constant fog in those areas, even now, lends a sense of timelessness to the corner of Thirty-fifth and Kirkham or Twenty-eighth and Quintara.

Understanding this makes it easier to see how acute the tension and contestation was in 1978. For gay denizens of the Castro, hippies in the Haight and surrounding areas, and bohemians and punks in North Beach (who often lived side by side with that neighborhood's older Italian American community), it was tempting to see San Francisco as a city that belonged to an emerging culture, one of tolerance and progressive values. This was partially because these people had little reason to go to the Outer Richmond, the Excelsior, Bayview–Hunters Point, or even the Outer Mission. Similarly, people in the more conservative areas of San Francisco, despite living only a few miles from the Castro, only went there very occasionally. For them, the Castro felt almost as distant as the Lower East Side of Manhattan or rural Alabama. Penelope Houston, one of the most prominent punk singers of the era, echoed this sentiment, describing how in 1978 when she lived in North Beach, the Sunset and Richmond districts felt "like the ends of the earth."[1]

This is also one of the reasons why the Giants, despite their dramatic and fun 1978 season, could have remained peripheral to newer San Franciscans who were not baseball fans. The 'Stick was in a distant corner of the city where constituents of Harvey Milk or Dianne Feinstein before she became mayor had much reason to go unless they wanted to see the Giants or 49ers play. Mayor Moscone, on the other hand, had spent time there, not least because he needed (and received) the support of the African American voters in that area in his tough 1975 election campaign. Many of the victims of Jim Jones hailed from the same part of town where the Giants played, but the demented cult leader spent very little time among the Irish Americans in the Sunset or in the burgeoning gay community in the Castro.

Of all the extraordinary things that happened in San Francisco in 1978, and the impact those things had on national and even global culture and politics, from Harvey Milk to Dead Kennedys, perhaps the most extraordinary is that it all occurred in a forty-nine-square-mile city with fewer than 700,000 people. Today's San Francisco is still a city like no other, although for a very different set of reasons. Many are amazed to learn that the population, although considerably larger than it was in 1978, is still roughly one-tenth of that of New York City.

This context also makes it more difficult, but also essential, to see the events of 1978 as a cohesive story about San Francisco rather than three or more distinct ones. In the footage from, for example, the Castro or the Gay Freedom Day parade during the summer of 1978, there are almost no visible Giants caps, T-shirts, or jerseys. Similarly, you didn't see too much of the orange and black at the Mab. At more than a few punk rock shows in the early 1980s, mine was the only Giants cap in attendance. Even the "Steal Your Face" Giants jerseys and caps with the Grateful Dead's famous logo intertwined with the Giants' "SF" that are now seen at most Giants games and occasionally in other parts of the city did not appear until another decade or so. The paradox of 1978 in San Francisco is that the three distinct stories of culture, politics, and baseball seemed to have very little overlap at the time, but the San Francisco that has taken shape over the last forty years has its roots in the synergy of those three storylines.

There are many excellent books written about Jonestown, the rise of punk rock, or the assassinations during this period, but almost none of them mention the Giants. Similarly, even the studies of Harvey Milk or Jonestown rarely mention the rise of the politically radical punk rock movement in San Francisco that was happening at the same time. It was also extremely rare to see an openly gay couple or Mohawk haircuts and black leather jackets at the 'Stick in the 1970s. It is likely that in the minds of conservative San Franciscans, scary punk rockers and gay men making out in the Castro were lumped together as degenerate and related, but this is a mischaracterization in several ways. The two movements were mostly distinct, although people such as Howie Klein and bands such as Tuxedomoon bridged these communities.

One of the ways that San Francisco has always felt simultaneously very large and very small is that it is possible to spend days, even weeks, in a specific neighborhood and believe that it is San Francisco. A gay man who lived and worked in the Castro, an Irish American fireman in the Sunset, an African American in the Fillmore, a punk living in North Beach, or a squat South of Market could have experienced this and begun to lose sight of the larger city. On the other hand, it was just as easy for an ordinary San Franciscan in 1978 to pass through several of these neighborhoods in one day and experience firsthand the rather extraordinary diversity of the city. It is from that diversity that the impact of 1978 began to be felt.

San Francisco was also a very racially diverse city in 1978. The city's large Asian American and Latino communities as well as its still substantial African American population may, at first glance, seem not to be the primary actors in the stories that made 1978 a significant year for San Francisco, but they were. Most obviously, the Jonestown tragedy hit San Francisco's African American community very hard. While white San Franciscans like my family may have read and watched the news with a feeling of horror and shock, African American San Franciscans were much more likely to have had friends, relatives, or acquaintances who were victims of Jim Jones's descent into maniacal brutality.

The impact of the Peoples Temple tragedy on African American San Francisco was particularly acute and contributed to the ongoing decline of the city's African American population. Roughly 620 of the 918 people who died in Jonestown were African American, and 232 of those were from California. Additionally, many with roots in other parts of the country had lived in California, and in many cases San Francisco, for years after joining the Peoples Temple and before going to Jonestown.[2] African American Californians who died in Jonestown came from various parts of the state, including Los Angeles, but it is very likely a good proportion of those people were from San Francisco. It may not be possible to determine precisely how many of those African Americans were San Franciscans, but even if it is only a hundred, and it was probably a lot more than that, those deaths would have had a big and lasting impact on the community. The physical representation of that impact was the abandoned Peoples Temple headquarters on Geary that was more or less in the heart of the Fillmore District, a once heavily African American area that was already beginning to change by 1978. Additionally, Jones, although white, had his biggest social, political, and religious impact in African American San Francisco. The two politicians most associated with him were Lieutenant Governor Mervyn Dymally and Assemblyman Willie Brown. Both were African American.

The year began with the first Chinese American member of the board of supervisors being sworn into office. Today few remember Gordon Lau, but in early 1978, he was a rising political star and leader of the city's Asian American community. If one vote for president of the board had gone the other way, Lau, not Feinstein, would have been president beginning in January 1978.

For nonwhite San Franciscans, the battle for the heart of the city that ultimately played out between Harvey Milk and Dan White may have seemed like a fight among different white people, but again the impact of that struggle affected all San Franciscans. George Moscone had a very different vision for San Francisco—one in which lower income nonwhite communities would have had a much larger role in decision making—than his successor, Dianne Feinstein, did.

Many San Franciscans spent 1978 working, going to school, raising kids, pursuing personal goals, taking care of elderly relatives, or otherwise immersed in daily life. For them, baseball, punk rock, gay liberation, and politics may or may not have been central to their lives at the time. Nonetheless, the major events of November affected everybody in the city, threw our town into turmoil, and dominated our lives for a few months, but in some respects the legislative fights, events at the Mab, and fortunes of the Giants were initially unimportant to many, perhaps a majority, of San Franciscans. For many of us, 1978 was just another year, until it wasn't.

Feinstein, Moscone, and Punk

As mayor, Moscone had not done or said much about punk, but his daughter Jennifer frequented the Mab from the very early days of the San Francisco punk rock scene. Additionally, Moscone's progressive policies made it easier for punk to survive while it was very new. His efforts to reform the police relieved pressure on punks, while his views on development helped keep the spaces where punk bands performed affordable.

Dianne Feinstein was very different. Feinstein was mayor from the day of the assassinations through the end of 1987, a period that overlapped with much of San Francisco's punk rock era. Unlike her slain predecessor, Feinstein viewed the punk rock movement as a blight that was bad for business and would scare off tourists. She also cast herself, again in contrast to Moscone, as a law-and-order mayor who was not interested in challenging or reforming the police. Michael Stewart Foley explains: "For punks, Feinstein's rise to power amounted to a rude awakening. Mayor Moscone and his reformist police chief Charles Gain had generally tolerated the punks gathering at their usual hangouts: the Bagel on Polk Street, the Broadway Hotel, the Mabuhay and elsewhere. . . . But less than a week after Feinstein assumed power, the police started cracking down on the punk community. On December 1, they arrested Mabuhay owner Ness Aquino. . . . They also arrested random punks that night. . . . And that was just the start of what seemed like nightly harassment."[3]

Punks could be forgiven for feeling that they were singled out by the new mayor. Moscone and Milk were killed on November 27. Before the week was even out, Feinstein had begun this policy. Many in the city were grieving, tensions between police (and their supporters) and the gay community were extremely high, the city had barely begun to recover from the Jonestown tragedy, many San Franciscans wanted answers about what Dan White had done, and there was a feeling in the air that San Francisco was unraveling. But somehow Feinstein thought that punk rock was an urgent problem that needed to be addressed.

Accordingly, Feinstein became a villain for San Francisco punk rockers. Henry S. Rosenthal remembered, "She was definitely seen as not a friend of the punk movement. The tenor of everything changed. The city got meaner and less hospitable."[4] John Gullak of the Mutants recalled, "She shut down one of our shows. . . . The show was canceled because of the posters."[5] Michael Fox also remembered that after Feinstein became mayor, "things [for punks], they changed." He elaborated: "The punk scene got attacked. Almost every show got closed down before the show was over, by the fire department or the cops or whatever."[6] Almost forty years after his campaign forced Feinstein into a runoff in the 1979 election, Jello Biafra's contempt, even hatred for the former mayor has barely softened: "One thing that united punks of all stripes across the board was a deep anger and hatred towards the wicked witch of the west. She [Feinstein] was so petty and so mean and so cruel. . . . The police went completely out of control the moment she got in. . . . There were regular attacks on punk shows too. . . . It was no secret that the police actually hated us."[7] Foley describes Feinstein as being to San Francisco punks what Margaret Thatcher was to U.K. punks.[8] The analogy, while not exactly fair to Feinstein on substance, is very apt with regard to how punks felt about the mayor whose tolerance never extended to punk rock. Feinstein's aristocratic background, prudishness, conservative demeanor, and complete ineptitude with anything that resembled youth culture also contributed to these feelings.

Dianne Feinstein was no great progressive. That has been borne out by her more-than-twenty-five-year career in the U.S. Senate, where she has earned a reputation as being hardworking, moderate, and a good advocate for California. Feinstein, however, was also no Margaret Thatcher. The San Francisco mayor was clearly conservative by San Francisco standards but was a mainstream liberal Democrat by the national standards of the 1980s. Given this, it is irresponsible not to at least raise the question of whether misogyny—which was more present than many would care to acknowledge in a movement that was male dominated and fueled by no small amount of testosterone—contributed to punk disdain for Feinstein. Feinstein was also a Jew at a time when punk rockers, despite the protestations of bands like Dead Kennedys, were not above wearing and displaying swastikas. This was sometimes done in the alleged name of shock value or irony, but for a middle-aged Jewish mayor in 1978, that may never have seemed entirely plausible. It certainly didn't to at least one Jewish San Francisco teenager at the time either.

Despite these other possible influences on the anti-Feinstein feeling, she was no friend of San Francisco's punk rock community. In addition to the direct attacks and the tolerance of police harassment on punks, her vision for San Francisco, much of which was enacted during the nine years she was in office, was a stark contrast to that of George Moscone. It also created numerous problems for punks. For example, Feinstein's support for development meant that many of the buildings that had once included low-rent apartments, concert venues, and even squats were torn down and replaced with expensive residential or commercial properties. Additionally, Feinstein's coziness with powerful real estate interests contributed to rising rents throughout much of San Francisco.

When Feinstein ran for a term of her own in 1979, her major challenger was Supervisor Quentin Kopp, who challenged her from the right. The deaths of Moscone and Milk had sufficiently damaged the citywide progressive movement, so no established politician had the name recognition or fund-raising ability to wage a strong campaign against Feinstein. The third major candidate in that race was David Scott, a gay activist who had little experience and less chance of winning.

That was the void that helped make one of the most unlikely mayoral campaigns in San Francisco's history possible. It is a reflection of the devastating impact that Dan White's bullets had on progressive San Francisco politics that the progressive opponent to Feinstein and Kopp in that election was a punk rocker whose campaign was, in large part, but not entirely, a goof. Jello Biafra's campaign for mayor was not taken very seriously at the time and is usually remembered more for the candidate's funny ideas and style than for some of his less outlandish ideas. His proposals that men in the Financial District be required to wear clown suits during working hours, that police and gay activists swap uniforms, or that the city erect statues of Dan White all over town and raise money by selling eggs for people to throw at the statues were genuinely funny and demonstrated his punk sensibility. Other ideas he had regarding neighborhoods were indeed progressive. Some of these ideas were spelled out in a Biafra campaign flyer: "San Francisco's spirit must not be crushed in the name of law and order and tourist dollars. The current administration has stepped up what they call a 'cleanup' of the city. They give big business a free hand while the creative forces that make our city tick see a steady rise in harassment by the law. Should San Francisco lose its face and become just another cold, efficient American city? Not if the city fathers hear a loud enough NO." Much of that language could have come from a speech by Harvey Milk, or from Bill de Blasio during his 2013 mayoral campaign in New York. Most of that passage could be used today by progressive San Francisco politicians or activists concerned about the tech ascendancy.

Biafra also addressed issues such as police brutality that were very important not just to his core punk constituency but to people of color as well. Biafra proposed that police officers be elected to four-year terms and that they be allowed to patrol only the districts where they were elected. The idea would have been difficult to implement, but it was a reasonable proposal at a time when most cities were only beginning to wrestle with ideas like community policing or residency requirements for police. As Biafra pointed out to me, "Rodney King would still be alive if that was the law, and tens of thousands of young black kids wouldn't be in jail."[9]

Biafra's campaign was certainly funny and clownish, but as Selvin was quick to point out, "Jello was only partly kidding. . . . He was facetious, but there was some kind of community-oriented politics at the back of it that also represents the kind of thinking of the punk community."[10] Biafra's campaign crystallized the progressive political aspects of the punk movement. It was neighborhood based, radical, and ahead of its time, but it was also in your face and funny.

The absence of a more mainstream candidate to Feinstein's left is only somewhat due to the sad reality that in 1979 both the progressive mayor and the most well-known progressive voice on the board of supervisors were dead. It was also because neither Willie Brown nor Art Agnos, progressive legislators who would later become mayors, were quite ready for a citywide run. Other progressive members of the board such as Harry Britt, Gordon Lau, or Carol Ruth Silver were not well known enough or able to raise the money necessary to defeat Feinstein. Silver elaborated on this point when I asked her why there was no progressive challenger, other than Biafra, in that 1979 race: "[There was] kind of an exhaustion factor. I don't know who it would have been. . . . Whoever did it would have had to take the mantle from Moscone."[11]

Another reason no candidate emerged to challenge Feinstein from the left is that shortly after taking the job she had sought twice before, Feinstein moved to consolidate her power by securing the support of a majority of her colleagues to make her acting mayor through the scheduled 1979 election, and then she governed with one eye toward her coming reelection campaign. Feinstein did not quickly seek to undo Moscone's accomplishments, but honored his and Milk's legacies as much as possible—at least until she was elected to a term of her own. One way she did this was by appointing Harry Britt, Milk's chosen successor, to finish his term.[12] Britt was also gay and a progressive ally of Milk's. By appointing him, Feinstein diffused some potential opposition from Milk supporters. Additionally, she kept many of Moscone's appointments in place and let it be known that she was not going back to the days when the city was run by straight white men.

Most politicians thinking about their future recognized they had little to gain by being drubbed in the first round by Feinstein and Kopp, who, still smarting from Feinstein's failure to get behind his mayoral campaign earlier in 1978, ran as a more conservative alternative to Feinstein. This left an opening, albeit a small one, for Biafra. Feinstein was reelected in 1979, defeating Kopp in a runoff 54–46, but Biafra helped deny her a majority in the first round, making a runoff necessary. In the first round, Biafra came in fourth, with 3.79 percent of the vote. On the one hand, Biafra was badly beaten, but he did better than most fringe candidates with no experience and almost no campaign budget generally do. Biafra was never going to win that election, but he clearly won support from well beyond his punk rock fans and, amazingly, was the only progressive candidate to run for mayor of San Francisco in either 1979 or 1983.

Native San Franciscans

One of the unifying themes of all the central dramas of San Francisco in 1978, whether they occurred at the Mab, in the Castro, out at the 'Stick, in City Hall, or in the humid jungle of Guyana is how few of the principal players were native San Franciscans, which, according to local custom, is understood to refer to persons who have at least one, but preferably two, essential documents—a birth certificate stating that they were born in San Francisco and a high school diploma from a school within the city limits.

Most of the names that we remember from 1978—including Harvey Milk, Jim Jones, Quentin Kopp, Jello Biafra, Penelope Houston, East Bay Ray, Bill Graham, Vida Blue, Mike Ivie, and Willie McCovey—had neither. The only true native San Franciscans whose names were at the center of that year's stories were the mayor who was assassinated, the woman who replaced him, and the killer who shot him. George Moscone and Dianne Feinstein were born and raised in San Francisco. Dan White moved there as a child.

By 1978 part of what defined San Francisco was that it had become a magnet for people from all over the country, and soon the world, who were looking for something different. Few understood that better than that most famous of new San Franciscans, Harvey Milk. In his most famous speech, Milk urged young gay people who were facing discrimination at home to either "go to California [read San Francisco] or stay in San Antonio and fight."

Jello Biafra, Vida Blue, Harvey Milk, and Jim Jones were all born elsewhere and moved to San Francisco as adults. Blue grew up in modest circumstances in rural Louisiana and settled in the Bay Area because the A's drafted him while he was attending Southern University and A&M College in Baton Rouge. Jones came from a Midwestern Bible-thumping, revivalist tradition complete with faith healing, and devolved into being a murderer of historic proportions. Milk was a civil rights leader from New York whose life was cut short by assassin's bullets. Biafra was a punk rock trailblazer from Colorado who transitioned into a spoken word artist while continuing to be an astute social critic.

Biafra, Jones, and Milk had some other things in common as well. They all espoused some form of radical politics and were not exactly comfortable in the mainstream of straight Christian America, but their differences were also apparent. Jones was a political radical and religious charlatan who sometimes professed a belief in God while also promoting his own divinity. Milk was a secular Jew who according to his rabbi had never "cared two hoots about organized Judaism"[13] but whose politics were formed profoundly by the twentieth-century Jewish experience. For Biafra, religion was never particularly important.

None of them were native San Franciscans, but they all chose to go there during the 1970s, as did so many others. That is also part of the 1978 story in San Francisco. Years of being the place to which so many people moved who were not comfortable, or had little opportunity in Boulder, Colorado; Lynn, Indiana; Mansfield, Louisiana; or Woodmere, New York, began to make an impact on the city. Some of this was positive. Migrants like Biafra helped make San Francisco the center of an exciting and important cultural movement. Vida Blue helped bring excitement and winning baseball to San Francisco for the first time in years and may just have been instrumental in the team's remaining in the city. Gay people and hippies like Milk helped San Francisco become known as a center of tolerance and progressive values. On the other hand, Jones chose to move his Peoples Temple to San Francisco because he knew that the city's tolerant environment would provide fertile soil for his organization and his evil plans and that his rhetoric regarding equality and poor people would be welcomed in radical San Francisco of the 1970s.

The three natives—Feinstein, Moscone, and White—responded to the changes in their city differently, but all of them, like all native San Franciscans during the 1970s, had to process what was occurring in their hometown. Moscone embraced it all and developed a progressive vision for remaking San Francisco. He was able to strike a balance between the new tolerance, diversity, and values of San Francisco in the 1970s with the values he learned and the relationships he built in the streets of Cow Hollow and at Saint Ignatius while growing up in San Francisco. That balance got him all the way to City Hall.

Dan White reacted differently, opposing the changes and consistently trying to return to an older, more conservative San Francisco. Initially, he channeled these views into legitimate outlets by running for, and winning, elected office, but by the end of 1978 his frustration and bigotry had led him to kill George Moscone and Harvey Milk. However, as much as many San Franciscans may not want to recognize it, particularly today, White spoke and perhaps even acted for a number of San Franciscans. White is sometimes referred to as "the most hated man in San Francisco history."[14] This epithet makes for a good sound bite, but anybody who was in San Francisco in 1978, or even through the early 1980s, knows that this was not true then. If White holds that title, it didn't become his until several years after the murders.

The third native San Franciscan whose impact on 1978 was enormous was Dianne Feinstein. She is also the only one of these three who was not dead or in jail by January 1, 1979. Feinstein's post-1978 career is well known, but it would not have been possible if she had not been so adept at crafting a centrist image in a changing San Francisco. That same centrist image that led her to a third-place finish in the 1975 mayor's race made it possible for her to enjoy one of the longest and most successful political careers of any San Francisco politician ever. Feinstein, like Moscone and White, was very much a product of the San Francisco institutions that had run the city for decades. She was a graduate of Stanford University and the Convent of the Sacred Heart, one of the city's elite Catholic girls schools. Feinstein was younger than Moscone or Milk and only three years older than Carol Ruth Silver, but as Silver observed, "She seemed much older than she was. I thought of her as being older. . . . She was so much more formal. Always impeccably dressed and made up, always had the social graces. In her house was a huge formal dining table. . . . Everything was meticulously dressed and decorated—not a hair out of place."[15] However, as a Jewish woman trying to make her way in politics and whose instincts on issues of tolerance were, by the standards of the time, clearly liberal, Feinstein was also able to function, in fact thrive, in the emerging San Francisco.

Old San Francisco lefties will chafe at the notion that Feinstein was a centrist with some genuinely liberal views, but she clearly was. Feinstein was pro-business and a friend of downtown interests, but she was also pro-choice, tolerant, and never resorted to hate or division to win elections or to help her policy proposals succeed. In her years in the U.S. Senate, she has worked with Democratic presidents but has never sought to push them to the left. She has generally been opposed to Republican initiatives but has sided with the Republicans more than most Democratic senators. That is the very definition of a centrist.

Just as the history of countries is not simply that of wars, kings, and presidents, the history of San Francisco in 1978 was not simply about mayors, supervisors, demagogues, baseball stars, musicians, and killings. 1978 was a year when many San Franciscans whose names may not pop up in the history books ventured to the Mab to check out their first punk show, marched in the biggest Gay Freedom Day parade the city had yet seen, went to see the Giants during the almost three months they were in first place, quietly worked through the assassination of their mayor and one of their supervisors, mourned the death of somebody they knew in Jonestown or were themselves forced to drink the Flavor Aid on that dreadful day in the Guyanese jungle. Additionally, tens of thousands of people who lived in San Francisco knew no one who was killed in Jonestown and were neither gay activists nor angry at the changes occurring around them in their city. Regardless of whether they were adults or young people like me who were growing up in a much more unusual place than we could understand, these people could not help but be affected by the extraordinary occurrences in our city throughout the year.

These people are an important part of the 1978 story as well. Many of them, unlike the artists forging the punk rock movement or the ballplayers bringing the post–Willie Mays Giants respectability, were natives. The more than 1.7 million fans who poured into Candlestick Park to watch the most exciting Giants team in years included many older native San Franciscans who could still remember the old Pacific Coast League Seals, as well as a new generation of fans. There were also youths and children who never saw the

Seals, and may never have even seen Willie Mays. For these younger fans, the San Francisco Giants were the only team they had ever rooted for, but 1978 was the first time the team had rewarded them. From that group came lifelong Giants fans such as Charles A. Fracchia Jr., who described becoming a Giants fan in 1978 as "a religious conversion."[16] These women and men are now well into middle age, but they still get excited remembering Mike Ivie's big grand slam, can imitate Terry Whitfield's distinctive batting stance, and will always include Willie McCovey on any list of their two or three favorite players ever.

The best-known bands from the punk scene in 1978 may have included many people who had come to San Francisco as adults, but the crowds at the Mab and other places were made up largely of local people, many of whom were young, because the Mab and several other clubs allowed minors. While the focal point of punk rock may have been North Beach and a few areas South of Market, many young people brought punk back to their own neighborhoods, often after long rides home on the city's frequently inadequate public transportation system. There was resistance to punk, but over time these young fans spread the word to some of their friends, siblings, and neighbors, creating an environment where this new form of music could thrive and where many local bands emerged beginning around 1980. This guaranteed that the Bay Area would remain central to the punk rock scene and that punk's influence on San Francisco would endure.

Regardless of whether the events of 1978 affected us directly, all San Franciscans, individually and collectively, had to reckon with them and find a way to move forward. Some left San Francisco, perhaps to return to the same communities that had warned them about the crazies out in San Francisco, but most stayed. Although significant pockets of sympathy for Dan White remained for years in San Francisco, it was apparent that the city could not hold together if the kind of violence and killing that we all saw in November continued.

It may just be coincidence that following the murder of the mayor, a prominent member of the board of supervisors, and of hundreds of mostly low-income people of color who had fallen prey to a demonic huckster promising racial equality and spiritual salvation, San Francisco moved unequivocally toward becoming the most tolerant major city in America, and even the world. However, that is unlikely. A more plausible scenario is that the murders in City Hall and Jonestown persuaded us that we could only survive if we embraced our diversity and sought to give everybody more of a voice.

After 1980, politicians like White and Barbagelata all but disappeared from San Francisco politics. The San Francisco politician who came closest to the social conservatism that buoyed White and Barbagelata's political careers was Frank Jordan, a former police chief who served one term as mayor from 1992 to 1995. Jordan was pro-business, but was not intolerant, at least by national standards, and he did not propose to "eradicate the malignancies." He was also a Democrat. Other centrist mayors such as Gavin Newsom or Ed Lee have been close with business interests, but the core notions of tolerance are no longer contested in post-1978 San Francisco.

The Fog

There are moments and places in San Francisco, even today, when if I ignore the weight of the cell phone in my back pocket and don't look at the cars too closely it feels like 1978 again. One of these places is the Presidio, where my brother and I spent countless hours playing baseball in 1978 and where by the early 1980s my friends and I often went to pursue less wholesome activities. If I find an untrafficked spot with no new buildings around, then the smell of the eucalyptus trees, the afternoon fog, and the feel of the distinct Presidio mulch under my feet—more often than not shod in the same Chuck Taylors as those I wore in 1978, although a few sizes bigger—help me channel that year. Way out in the Avenues, particularly when it is foggy, sometimes only the age of the cars is a reminder of what decade it is. Deep in other neighborhoods, such as Bernal Heights, or standing on the beach looking out toward the ocean, it is also possible to feel this way.

There are other parts of the city that have either changed radically or that barely existed in 1978. Back then, Hayes Valley was the kind of area where the Peoples Temple might have rented some cheap apartments and stuffed as many members in them as possible. Today Hayes Valley is a trendy and affluent area with expensive restaurants and boutiques where tech millionaires can sip eighteen-dollar cocktails and anybody over forty feels old. Cow Hollow, where George Moscone and I both grew up, is unrecognizable as well. Unlike the South Beach area around the ballpark, this is not because of new construction, but because what was once a working-class neighborhood with a big Italian American population has now become a community of mostly well-off singles and young families who work primarily in the Financial District or the tech sector. I still go to Giants games whenever I am in San Francisco during baseball season. AT&T Park is a great place to see a ballgame, and not just because of the three World Series flags flapping in the breeze. The ballpark is new, but so is the whole area. It is a neighborhood that simply didn't exist in 1978.

All cities change as the decades go by, and most middle-aged men find it difficult to recognize the town in which they lived as boys. Nonetheless, the journey between the extraordinarily eventful, raucous, and transformative year that was 1978 and the San Francisco of today has been unpredictable, tumultuous, complicated, and profound. At first glance, much about San Francisco in this decade may seem unrecognizable for those of us who lived through that year, but spend a bit more time in San Francisco and it becomes clear that the city of today has deep roots in 1978.

Acknowledgments

Many people have been very generous with their time and intellect as I wrote this book. Dan Epstein, Bill Finan, David Jordan, Ken Sherrill, and Josh Wilker read early drafts and proposals, gave me feedback, and encouraged me to pursue this project. Janet Steen read several drafts and offered many valuable suggestions. Ester Fuchs from Columbia University first encouraged me to study urban politics when I was a graduate student in the early 1990s and has offered guidance and support to me in the years since. The late Bob Bailey helped me think about how to study the politics of San Francisco. Charles A. Fracchia Sr., of the San Francisco Historical Society, sat for a long interview and numerous follow-up discussions. He shared many memories from that era with me while I was writing this book and enthusiastically encouraged me to stay with this idea. I am grateful to Micah Kleit, Elisabeth Maselli, and the rest of the team at Rutgers University Press for their work with me on *San Francisco Year Zero*.

Many people who were involved in San Francisco politics during the last forty years were very generous with their time, including Art Agnos, Corey Busch (who provided a lot of insight into the Giants as well), Quentin Kopp, Rudy Nothenberg, Rich Schlackman, and Carol Ruth Silver. Allen Bennett and Sharyn Saslafksy helped me understand Harvey Milk and Jewish San Francisco in the 1970s. The staff at the George Moscone archives at the University of the Pacific and at the San Francisco Public Library's San Francisco History Center helped me find countless fascinating and valuable documents, photos, and other ephemera. People from the San Francisco

Municipal Transit Agency, the San Francisco Giants, the Utah State University Digital History Collection, and the Grateful Dead Archive at UC Santa Cruz also helped me find photos and flyers from 1978.

I never made it to the Mab or any punk shows in 1978, but many people who were there shared their memories of the punk scene then, including Jello Biafra, Jennifer Blowdryer, Jack Boulware, Ginger Coyote, Joe Dirt, Michael Fox, Penelope Houston, Howie Klein, Michael Lucas, Daniel Nicoletta, Raymond Pepperell (East Bay Ray), Henry S. Rosenthal (Hank Rank), and Joel Selvin. Tim Sternberg, John Yelding-Sloan, and many other people with whom I attended punk shows in the early 1980s offered memories and advice on the book. Will Lowry and I spent hundreds of hours during that period, and thousands more since, discussing punk rock and politics. He has had a great influence on my work and my thinking about San Francisco.

My primary companion at Candlestick Park in 1978 was my brother, Jonathan Mitchell. My brother died in 2014. He was with me every day in 1978 and is in my thoughts every day now. Christian Ettinger, Charles Karren and Michael Mason also were with me at the 'Stick in 1978 and still go to Giants games with me when I am in San Francisco. Charles A. Fracchia Jr. (who remains a great resource for any Giants-related information), Glenn Dickey, Hank Greenwald, Jon Leonadoukis, Marty Lurie, and particularly John Maschino also helped me think through the baseball sections of this book.

My wife, Marta Sanders, and sons Asher and Reuben Mitchell have patiently listened to countless anecdotes and memories from San Francisco in the 1970s. Isis the dog has for many years been my faithful writing companion.

In 1978 Susan Mitchell was a single mother in Cow Hollow trying to balance her career, two young sons, and a life of her own. During that year, she took care of my brother and me, made sure that we were fed and clothed, that we made it out to see the Giants a few dozen times, and that we did well in our Catholic school while remembering who we were and which side we were on. Four decades or so later, while I was writing this book, my mother continued to help in any way she could. This book, like everything else in my life, would not have been possible without my mother and is dedicated to her.

Notes

Preface

1 Kia Makarechi, "San Francisco's Inequality Rivals That of Developing Nations," *Vanity Fair*, May 20, 2014, https://www.vanityfair.com/news/business/2014/05/san-francisco-income-inequality-developing-nations.

Chapter 1   New Year's 1978

1 Advertisement, *San Francisco Chronicle,* December 31, 1977, 31.

2 Marshall Kilduff and Phil Tracy, "Inside Peoples Temple," *New West*, August 1, 1977, 30–34.

3 The use of the asterisk(s) in homophobic and racial slurs and in certain profanities is used by the author here and throughout this book.

4 Charles A. Fracchia Sr., interview with the author, June 7, 2017. Historian Charles A. Fracchia Sr. is the father of Charles A. Fracchia Jr., a longtime Giants fan. Both were valuable sources for this book.

5 *San Francisco Bay Guardian,* November 17, 1977.

6 Frances Fitzgerald, *Cities on a Hill: A Journey through Contemporary American Cultures* (New York: Simon & Schuster, 1981), 91.

7 City of San Francisco, *San Francisco Voter Information Handbook: Arguments and Statements* (San Francisco: Recorder Printing and Publishing Company, 1975), 20.

8 Harvey Milk, "Address to the Joint International Longshoremen & Warehousemen's Union of San Francisco and to the Lafayette Club September 30, 1973," in *An Archive of Hope: Harvey Milk's Speeches and Writings,* ed. Jason Edward Black and Charles E. Morris (Berkeley: University of California Press, 2013). ProQuest Ebook.

9 Harvey Milk, "Who Really Represents You?," in Black and Morris, *Archive of Hope*.

10 Art Agnos, interview with the author, March 6, 2018.

11 "US Presidential Elections: Jewish Voting Record," Jewish Virtual Library, http://www.jewishvirtuallibrary.org/jewish-voting-record-in-u-s-presidential -elections.

12 Les Ledbetter, "San Francisco Legislators Meet in Diversity," *New York Times,* January 12, 1978, A14; ibid., A14.

13 Herb Caen, "3-Dot Journalism Lives," *San Francisco Chronicle,* January 26, 1978, 31.

14 Jack Boulware and Silke Tudor, *Gimme Something Better: The Profound, Progressive, and Occasionally Pointless History of Bay Area Punk from Dead Kennedys to Green Day* (New York: Penguin, 2009), 37.

15 Alejandro Escovedo and Jeff Olener, "Decadent Jew," 1977.

16 Henry S. Rosenthal, interview with the author, July 25, 2017.

17 John Wasserman, "How I Got Punked On by the Sex Pistols," *San Francisco Chronicle,* January 16, 1978, 2.

18 Joel Selvin, "The Sex Pistols—Punks and Musicians," *San Francisco Chronicle,* January 16, 1978, 40.

19 Joseph Torchia, "Go Punk Yourself," *San Francisco Chronicle,* January 24, 1978, 12.

20 All the baseball data in this book including, but not limited to, individual statistics, game summaries, attendance records, team records and standings are from Baseball -Reference.com.

21 Marty Appel, *Casey Stengel: Baseball's Greatest Character* (New York: Doubleday, 2017), iBook edition.

22 OPS+ represents a player's on-base percentage plus slugging percentage normalized over era and ballpark. An OPS+ of 100 is the league average for any given year. Anything over 120 is very good. An OPS+ over 150 is considered great.

23 WAR stands for "wins above replacement" and attempts to measure the overall value of a player by looking at hitting, base running, and fielding indicators relative to the rest of the league that year. Five WAR a year is very good. Seven or so reflects All-Star status, and eight represents an MVP candidate. WAR is a composite measure that draws on other primary data such as plate appearances, home runs, and the like. In this book, I use the WAR formula and data from Baseball-Reference .com.

24 Bill James, *The New Bill James Historical Baseball Abstract* (New York: Free Press 2001), 436..

25 Ron Firmite, "The Cable Cars, the Fog—and Willie," *Sports Illustrated,* April 17, 1978.

26 Wells Twombly, "Toronto Convinced Giants Are on the Way," *San Francisco Examiner* January 21, 1976.

27 Fitzgerald, *Cities on a Hill,* 44–45.

28 David Talbot, *Season of the Witch: Enchantment, Terror, and Deliverance in the City of Love* (New York: Free Press, 2012), xvii.

29 Charles A. Fracchia Sr., interview with the author, June 7, 2017.

30 Rich Schlackman, interview with the author, July 28, 2017.

31 Joel Selvin, interview with the author, June 6, 2017.

Chapter 2   San Francisco in 1978

1 Wallace Turner, "Magical 'Happy' San Francisco Also Has Problems, and Tears," *New York Times,* December 11, 1975, 47.

2 Ibid., 47.

3 Russ Cone, "New Mayor: 28 Days to Saddle a Tiger," *San Francisco Examiner*, December 12, 1975.

4 Stephen C. Brooks, "Politics of Crime in the 1970s: A Two City Comparison," Reactions to Crime Project (1980), http://www.skogan.org/files/Brooks.Politics _of_Crime_in_the_1970s_A_Two_City_Comparison.1980.pdf; and Nuala Sawyer, "2016 Closes with 59 Homicides in S.F.," *SF Weekly*, January 2, 2017, http://www.sfweekly.com/topstories/2016-closes-59-homicides-s-f/.

5 Chris Mitchell, "The Killing of Murder," *New York Magazine*, January 7, 2008, http://nymag.com/news/features/crime/2008/42603/.

6 *San Francisco Police Department Year-End Crime Statistics, 2017*, San Francisco Police Department, Crime Analysis Unit, February 15, 2018, https:// sanfranciscopolice.org/sites/default/files/Documents/PoliceDocuments /CompStat/SFPD-YearEnd-Stats-2017-Amended.pdf; Megan Cassidy, "Homicides Fall across Bay Area in 2018, Posting a 26 Percent Decline in Two Years," *San Francisco Chronicle*, January 5, 2019, https://www.sfchronicle.com/crime/article /Homicides-fall-across-Bay-Area-in-2018-posting-a-13510327.php.

7 Christine Lamberson, "The Zebra Murders: Race, Civil Liberties and Radical Politics in San Francisco," *Journal of Urban History* 42, no. 1 (2016): 201–225.

8 "Industrial Land in San Francisco: Understanding Production, Distribution, and Repair," San Francisco Planning Department, July 2002, 16, http://sf-planning.org /sites/default/files/FileCenter/Documents/4893-CW_DPR_chapter5_2.pdf.

9 Ibid., 8.

10 Helene Whitson, "STRIKE! . . . Concerning the 1968–69 Strike at San Francisco State College," FoundSF.org, http://www.foundsf.org/index.php?title=STRIKE! . . . _Concerning_the_1968-69_Strike_at_San_Francisco_State_College.

11 Charles A. Fracchia Sr., interview with the author, June 7, 2017.

12 Quentin Kopp, interview with the author, March 6, 2018.

13 Rich Schlackman, interview with the author, July 26, 2017.

14 Robert W. Bailey, *Gay Politics, Urban Politics: Identity and Economics in the Urban Setting* (New York: Columbia University Press, 1999), 283.

15 Richard DeLeon, *Left Coast City: Progressive Politics in San Francisco 1975–1991* (Lawrence: University of Kansas Press, 1992), 51.

16 Ibid., 48.

17 Corey Busch, interview with the author, July 27, 2017.

18 Quentin Kopp, interview with the author, March 6, 2018. Jack Ertola was a Superior Court judge who finished fourth in the first round of that election. Milton Marks, a state senator, finished fifth.

19 Ibid.

20 Art Agnos, interview with the author, March 6, 2018.

21 "Can You Afford Moscone?," John Barbagelata campaign flyer, 1975.

22 Ibid., ellipses in original.

23 Moscone's use of the uppercase "C" in "city" to refer to San Francisco reflected the generally accepted practice San Franciscans used well into the twenty-first century.

24 Michael Harris, "The Neighborhood Vote-Election Split the City," *San Francisco Chronicle* December 12, 1975, 1.

25 "How They Voted in Precincts," *San Francisco Examiner,* December 12, 1975.

26 John M. Crewdson, "Followers Say Jim Jones Directed Voting Frauds," *New York Times*, December 17, 1978, 42.

27 Corey Busch, interview with the author, July 27, 2017.

28 Rudy Nothenberg, interview with the author, June 29, 2018.

29 Corey Busch, interview with the author, July 27, 2017.

30 Ibid.

31 "Table 33. New York—Race and Hispanic Origin for Selected Large Cities and Other Places: Earliest Census to 1990," US Census, accessed July 4, 2018, https://www.census.gov/population/www/documentation/twps0076/NYtab.pdf.

32 Herb Caen, "Pull Cord to Stop Press," *San Francisco Chronicle,* February 22, 1978, 31.

Chapter 3   Spring Training

1 These three numbers represent Whitfield's batting average, on-base percentage, and slugging percentage. They are presented to give a fuller picture of a player's offensive contribution and are referred to as a player's slash line.

2 Zander Hollander, *The Complete Handbook of Baseball 1978 Edition* (New York: Signet, 1978), 172.

3 Ibid., 205.

4 Glenn Dickey, "Survey Offers Solution to Bay Area Problem," *Sporting News,* March 4, 1978, 25.

5 "Moscone Was the Key to Giant Deal," *Daily Independent,* February 27, 1978. A few days after this article, Bud Herseth replaced Bob Short as partner to Bob Lurie.

6 Remarks at March 13, 1978, press conference, reported in "S. F. Label Pivotal to Moscone," *Contra Costa Independent,* March 14, 1978, Moscone Archives, University of Pacific Library.

7 Tom Weir, "Davis' Deadline Passes; A's Are Left in Limbo," *Sporting News,* February 2, 1978, 44.

8 Rudy Nothenberg, interview with the author, June 29, 2018.

9 Memo from San Francisco Commission of Recreation and Parks, March 1978.

10 Letter from George Moscone to Quentin Kopp, February 21, 1978, Moscone Archives, University of Pacific Library.

11 Letter from George Moscone to Charles Feeney, March 3, 1976, Moscone Archives, University of Pacific Library.

12 Ron Firmite, "A Specialist in Flying Objects," *Sports Illustrated,* June 2, 1986, https://www.si.com/vault/1986/06/02/638351/a-specialist-in-flying-objects.

13 This was probably May 8, July 22 (game 1), or July 23, 1979.

14 Charles A. Fracchia Jr., interview with the author, August 28, 2017.

15 John Maschino, interview with the author, July 8, 2018.

16 W. A. Van Winkle, "Look Who's in First," *San Francisco Bay Guardian,* June 15, 1978.

17 "Thomas Won't Be Second at Second," *San Francisco Chronicle,* April 5, 1977, 41.

18 Bob Stevens, "Vida: New Team, New Attitude," *San Francisco Chronicle,* March 20, 1978, 53.

19 Glenn Dickey, "The Trade's Many Facets," *San Francisco Chronicle,* March 17, 1978, 82.

20 Ron Firmite, "The West," *Sports Illustrated,* April 10, 1978, https://www.si.com /vault/1978/04/10/106772675/the-west.

21 Van Winkle, "Look Who's in First."

22 Hank Greenwald, interview with the author, June 6, 2017.

23 John Maschino, interview with the author, July 8, 2018. "Deals" is a baseball term referring to good pitching.

24 Glenn Dickey, interview with the author, June 6, 2017.

25 Firmite, "The West."

26 Jerry Roberts, *Dianne Feinstein: Never Let Them See You Cry* (New York: Harper-CollinsWest, 1994), 98–99.

27 John Geluardi, "Dan White's Motive More about Betrayal than Homophobia," *SF Weekly,* January 30, 2008, http://www.sfweekly.com/news/dan-whites-motive -more-about-betrayal-than-homophobia/.

28 Les Ledbetter, "Bill on Homosexual Rights Advances in San Francisco," *New York Times,* March 22, 1978, 21.

29 Ibid, 21.

30 Ibid, 21.

31 Golden Gate Business Association, 1978 Annual Dinner Program.

32 "78 CSL Season Opened by Mayor Moscone," *San Francisco Gazette,* April 24, 1978.

Chapter 4 Heading to the 'Stick

1 Raymond Pepperell, interview with the author, July 27, 2017.

2 Art Agnos, interview with the author, March 6, 2018.

3 Joe Dirt, interview with the author, June 29, 2018.

4 Charles A. Fracchia Sr., interview with the author, June 6, 2017.

5 Herb Caen, "This Old Town," *San Francisco Chronicle,* February 26, 1978, 117.

6 Hank Greenwald, interview with the author, June 6, 2017.

7 Charles A. Fracchia Jr., interview with the author August 28, 2018.

8 Glenn Dickey, interview with the author, June 27, 2017.

9 Zander Hollander, *The Complete Handbook of Baseball 1978 Edition* (New York: Signet, 1978), 173.

10 Concerned Relatives and Citizens flyer, April 14, 1978.

11 "Peoples Temple Plea," *San Francisco Chronicle,* April 12, 1978, 14.

12 Concerned Relatives and Citizens flyer.

13 Corey Busch, interview with the author, July 27, 2017.

14 Rich Schlackman, interview with the author, July 28, 2017.

15 Carol Ruth Silver, interview with the author, June 26, 2018.

16 Busch, interview with the author.

17 Tim Reiterman and John Jacobs, *Raven: The Untold Story of the Rev. Jim Jones and His People* (New York: Penguin Press, 1982), 306.

18 Quoted in Reiterman and Jacobs, *Raven,* 308.

19 Schlackman, interview with the author.

20 Busch, interview with the author.

Chapter 5   Harvey Milk

1 Allen Bennett, interview with the author, August 3, 2017.
2 Charles A. Fracchia Sr., interview with the author, June 7, 2017.
3 Glenn Dickey, interview with the author, June 6, 2017.
4 Hank Greenwald, interview with the author, June 6, 2017.
5 The Shot Heard 'Round the World is considered by many to be the most dramatic home run in baseball history. It occurred in the bottom of the ninth inning of the third game of a best-of-three playoff between the Dodgers and Giants after the two teams ended the 1951 regular season tied for first place in the National League.
6 John D'Acquisto and Dave Jordan, *Fastball John* (New York: Instream Books, 2015), 168–169 (ellipsis in original).
7 Bodie was born Francesco Stephano Pezzolo.
8 Charles A. Fracchia Jr., interview with the author, August 28, 2017.
9 Herb Caen, "Bay Area Rapid Typewriter," *San Francisco Chronicle*, May 31, 1978, 29.
10 Art Spander, "Giants Race up the Hill with Blue Streak," *Sporting News*, June 3, 1978, 10.
11 "Affidavit of Deborah Layton Blakey Re: The Threat and Possibility of Mass Suicide by Members of the Peoples Temple," June 14, 1978, https://jonestown.sdsu.edu/?page_id=18599.
12 Marshall Kilduff, "Grim Report from Jungle," *San Francisco Chronicle*, June 15, 1978, 2.
13 Ron Javers, "240,000 at Gay Parade: Harsh Words against Briggs Initiative," *San Francisco Chronicle*, June 26, 1978, 1.
14 Matt Johanson and Wylie Wong, *Where Have You Gone? Catching Up with Will Clark, Bob Brenly, Willie McCovey, and Other Giant Favorites* (Champaign, IL: Sports Publishing, 2005), 79.
15 Quoted in Nick Peters, "Willie's 500th HR More Relief Than Thrill," *Sporting News,* July 22, 1978, 9.
16 John Maschino, interview with the author, July 8, 2018.
17 Ibid. McCovey only hit four home runs at home in 1978.
18 Nick Peters, "Better Attitude Boosts Clark Play as a Giant," *Sporting News*, June 10, 1978, 10.
19 John Maschino, interview with the author, July 8, 2018.
20 Hank Greenwald, interview with the author, June 6, 2017.
21 Glenn Dickey, interview with the author, June 6, 2017.
22 Nick Peters, "Better Attitude Boosts Clark Play as a Giant," 10.

Chapter 6   The Band Is Called What?

1 Although the examples above, other than "Whoopie Guns" are my own, this point, and that example, arose from a discussion I had circa 1983 with San Francisco drummer and punk rock raconteur Will Lowry.
2 Joel Selvin, interview with the author, June 6, 2017.
3 Dead Kennedys were not the only band whose name drew on the famous Democratic family. Another much lesser known Bay Area band in the early 1980s was known as the Ted Kennedys. Their one reasonably memorable song was a takeoff on the Dead Kennedys song "Too Drunk to F**k." The Ted Kennedys, in tribute to

events a decade earlier in Chappaquiddick, wrote a song called "Too Drunk to Swim."

4 Raymond Pepperell, interview with the author, July 27, 2017.
5 Herb Caen, "Here Today," *San Francisco Chronicle,* November 17, 1978, 41.
6 Penelope Houston, interview with the author, June 8, 2017.
7 Jello Biafra, interview with the author, August 16, 2018.
8 Joseph Torchia, "Go Punk Yourself," *San Francisco Chronicle,* January 24, 1978, 12.
9 Ibid.
10 Michael Fox, interview with the author, July 3, 2018.
11 Ginger Coyote, interview with the author, July 5, 2018.
12 Jennifer Blowdryer, *White Trash Debutante* (New York: Galhattan Press, 1997), 26–27.
13 Jennifer Blowdryer, interview with the author, July 12, 2018.
14 Biafra, interview with the author.
15 Ibid.
16 Houston, interview with the author.
17 John Gullak, interview with the author, March 8, 2018.
18 Howie Klein, interview with the author, July 8, 2018.
19 Henry S. Rosenthal, interview with the author, July 25, 2017.
20 Rosenthal, interview with the author.
21 Michael Goldberg, "What Do Punk Rock and Striking Coal Miners Have in Common? Well . . . ," *San Francisco Bay Guardian,* April 1978.
22 Michael Stewart Foley, *Dead Kennedys' Fresh Fruit for Rotting Vegetables* (New York: Bloomsbury, 2015), 70.
23 Scott Stalcup, "Noise, Noise, Noise: Punk Rock's History since 1965," *Studies in Popular Culture* 23, no. 3, (2001): 52.
24 Howie Klein, interview with the author, July 8, 2018.
25 Alex Ogg, *Fresh Fruit for Rotting Vegetables: The Early Years* (Oakland: PM Press, 2014), 108.
26 Howie Klein, "The Dils: Political Punk and the Big Threat," *BAM (Bay Area Music),* February 1978, 66.
27 Fox, interview with the author.
28 Jello Biafra, interview with the author, August 16, 2018.
29 Chris Carlsson, "When Punk Mattered: At the Birth of the Neoliberal City," *Boom California,* September 10, 2015, https://boomcalifornia.com/2015/09/08/when-punk-mattered-at-the-birth-of-the-neoliberal-city/.
30 "Dead Kennedys!" *Search and Destroy,* September 1978. The interview was with the entire band, but Biafra did almost all the talking.
31 Ibid.
32 Ibid.
33 Penelope Houston, "The American in Me," 1978.
34 Ibid.
35 Joe Dirt, interview with the author, June 29, 2018.
36 Ogg, *Dead Kennedys,* 9.
37 Jeff Goldthorpe, "Punk Rock," FoundSF.org, accessed July 4, 2018, http://www.foundsf.org/index.php?title=PUNK_ROCK.
38 Rosenthal, interview with the author.
39 Biafra, interview with the author, August 16, 2018.

40 Gullak, interview with the author.

41 Jack Boulware, interview with the author, July 28, 2017.

42 Blowdryer, interview with the author. Alvin refers to Jennifer and the Blowdryers' lyricist Alvin Orloff.

43 Dead Kennedys, "California Über Alles," 1978.

44 Ogg, *Dead Kennedys*, 46–47.

45 Biafra, interview with the author, August 16, 2018.

46 Ibid.

47 Dead Kennedys, "We've Got a Bigger Problem Now," 1984.

48 Maggie Serota, "For Jello Biafra, It's 'California Über Alles' All Over Again—and Again, and Again," *AV Club*, March 28, 2010, https://music.avclub.com/for-jello -biafra-its-california-uber-alles-all-over-1798219494.

49 Pepperell, interview with the author.

50 Selvin, interview with the author.

51 Rosenthal, interview with the author.

52 Michael Lucas, interview with the author, July 26, 2017.

53 Biafra, interview with the author, August 17, 2018.

54 Quoted in James Stark, *Punk '77: An Inside Look at the San Francisco Rock n' Roll Scene, 1977* (San Francisco: Research, 1999), 6.

55 Jack Boulware and Jack Silke Tudor, *Gimme Something Better: The Profound, Progressive, and Occasionally Pointless History of Bay Area Punk from Dead Kennedys to Green Day* (New York: Penguin Press, 2009), xv. Klein was the founder of 415 Records. Biafra was the lead singer of Dead Kennedys. Dictor was the lead singer for MDC. Volume played guitar in many bands, most notably the Naked Lady Wrestlers. Stark was a punk photographer and graphic artist. Rezabek was the lead singer in Negative Trend. Miro was the lead singer for the Nuns.

56 Houston, interview with the author.

57 Gullak, interview with the author.

58 Dirt, interview with the author.

59 Fox, interview with the author.

60 Klein, interview with the author, July 8, 2018.

61 Houston, interview with the author.

62 Joel Selvin, interview with the author, June 5, 2017.

63 Rosenthal, interview with the author.

64 Dirt, interview with the author.

65 Michael Lucas, interview with the author, July 26, 2017.

66 Howie Klein, "The Avengers Leave 'Summer of Hate' Behind," *BAM (Bay Area Music)*, December 1977.

67 Houston, interview with the author.

68 Stephen Duncombe and Maxwell Tremblay, "White Riot?" in *White Riot: Punk Rock and the Politics of Race,* ed. Stephen Duncombe and Maxwell Tremblay (New York: Verso, 2011), 5–6.

69 Biafra, Jello, "Nazi Punks F**k Off," 1981.

70 Coyote, interview with the author.

71 Quoted in Jim Bessman, *Ramones: An American Band* (New York: St. Martin's Press, 1993), 131.

72 American Jewish Congress, *American Jewish Year Book*, vol. 79, (New York: American Jewish Committee, 1979).

73 Steven Lee Beeber, *The Heebie Jeebies at CBGB's: A Secret History of Jewish Punk* (Chicago: Chicago Review Press, 2006), 8.

74 Ibid., 2.

75 Ibid., 225.

76 Klein, interview with the author.

77 Ibid.

78 Houston, interview with the author.

79 Selvin, interview with the author, June 6, 2017.

80 Coyote, interview with the author.

81 Code of Honor, "What Are We Gonna Do?" 1982.

82 Joel Selvin, interview with the author, June 7, 2017.

83 Boulware, interview with the author.

84 W. A. Van Winkle, "Look Who's in First," *San Francisco Bay Guardian,* June 15, 1978, 10.

85 "Moscone: McCovey Should Be All-Star," *San Francisco Progress,* June 7, 1978.

86 Larry Keith, "These Giants Are Jolly Blue," *Sports Illustrated,* May 29, 1978, https://www.si.com/vault/1978/05/29/822679/these-giants-are-jolly-blue-it-has -been-veni-vidi-vici-for-vida-in-san-franciscos-stunning-ascent-in-the-national -west. "Blue blazer" refers to Blue's famous fastball.

87 Tom Clark, *Baseball* (Berkeley, CA: Serendipity Books, 1976), 17.

88 FIP is an acronym for "fielding independent pitching." It is an advanced metric that seeks to evaluate a pitcher based on what he, rather than the team around him, does. Like ERA, a lower FIP is better. ERA+ is a statistic that seeks to normalize ERA over time and ballpark. An ERA of 100 is the league average. Better pitching is reflected by a higher ERA+.

89 Leonard Koppett, "Giants Benefit from Sharp Promotion," *Sporting News,* July 8, 1978, 4.

90 Roger Kemp, "California's Proposition 13: A One-Year Assessment," *State and Local Government Review* 14, no. 1 (1982): 44.

91 Ibid., 46.

Chapter 7 The Pennant Race

1 Ron Firmite, "The Battle Is Rejoined," *Sports Illustrated,* August 7, 1978, https://www.si.com/vault/1978/08/07/822865/the-battle-is-rejoined-with-the-giants -contending-again-the-old-san-francisco-los-angeles-rivalry-has-been-rekindled-as -have-memories-of-dodger-giant-feuds-past.

2 William Endicott, "Gloom to Glow: Giants Mania: New Spirit in Old Ball Town," *Los Angeles Times,* August 1, 1978.

3 Nick Peters, "Fundamental Problems Surface as Giants Sink," *Sporting News,* September 30, 1978, 18.

4 Channel Five Eyewitness News, https://www.youtube.com/watch?v =7Lq6HZiSbds, accessed July 17, 2018.

5 Terry Pluto, *The Greatest Summer: The Remarkable Story of Jim Bouton's Comeback to Major League Baseball* (Englewood Cliffs, NJ: Prentice Hall, 1979), 159.

6 Peters, "Fundamental Problems Surface," 18.

7 Sharyn Saslafsky, interview with the author, March 5, 2018.

8 Ibid.

9 Hillary Cassell, "Stuart Milk Inspires Jewish LGBT Leaders," *Bay Area Reporter*, July 8, 2010, https://sanfrancisco.edgemedianetwork.com/index.php?ch=news&sc =&sc2=news&sc3=&id=107748.

10 Allen Bennett, interview with the author, August 31, 2017.

11 Saslafsky, interview with the author.

12 Randy Shilts, *The Mayor of Castro Street* (New York: St. Martin's Press, 1982), 23.

13 Ibid., 364.

14 "Interview with Harvey Milk," in *Archive of Hope: Harvey Milk's Speeches and Writings*, ed. Jason Edward Black and Charles E. Morris (Berkeley: University of California Press, 2013).

15 Ibid., 371.

16 David Johnston, "Dan White's 'Hot Potato' Lobbying for Warren Simmons," *San Francisco Bay Guardian*, September 28, 1978, 4.

17 Ibid.

18 Shilts, *Mayor of Castro Street*, 200. The potatoes, however, were baked as well as fried.

19 Quoted in Herb Caen, "The Last Dinosaur," *San Francisco Chronicle*, October 19, 1978, 33.

Chapter 8   A Month Like No Other

1 Telegram from Congressman Leo Ryan to Reverend Jim Jones, November 1, 1978, https://jonestown.sdsu.edu/?page_id=13922.

2 Letter from Mark Lane to Congressman Leo Ryan, November 6, 1978, https:// jonestown.sdsu.edu/?page_id=13921. The two countries in question were the USSR and Cuba.

3 Mervin D. Field, "Public Opinion Trending Strongly against Prop. 6, Homosexual Teacher Initiative," October 5, 1978, http://ucdata.berkeley.edu/pubs/CalPolls/990 .pdf, 2.

4 "Anti-Prop. 6 Fund-Raiser," *San Francisco Chronicle*, September 29, 1978, 2.

5 Statement by Mayor George Moscone, May 9, 1978, Moscone Archives, University of the Pacific Library.

6 Howie Klein, interview with the author, July 5, 2018.

7 Ginger Coyote, interview with the author, July 5, 2018.

8 Daniel Nicoletta, interview with the author, July 9, 2018.

9 Ibid.

10 Frances Fitzgerald, *Cities on a Hill: A Journey through Contemporary American Cultures* (New York: Simon & Schuster, 1981), 68.

11 Herb Caen, "The Way We Are," *San Francisco Chronicle*, September 10, 1978, 149.

12 Quoted in Marshall Kilduff, "Supervisor Dan White Resigns from Board," *San Francisco Chronicle,* November 11, 1978, 1.

13 Linda Ronstadt has an odd connection to baseball through what was perhaps her most famous song, "Blue Bayou." This song gave rise to a great piece of baseball slang, sometimes attributed to Mets and Phillies reliever Tug McGraw. The so-called Linda Ronstadt fastball is a pitch that is so fast that the batter never has a chance to hit it—that is, the pitch "blew by you."

14 Marshall Kilduff, "White Wants Supervisor's Job Back," *San Francisco Chronicle*, November 15, 1978, 1.

15 Letter from Dan White to George Agnost, November 22, 1978, Moscone Archives, University of the Pacific Library.

16 Letter from Gilbert Boreman to George Agnost, November 22, 1978, Moscone Archives, University of the Pacific Library.

17 Randy Shilts, *The Mayor of Castro Street* (New York: St. Martin's Press, 1982), 254–255 (italics in original).

18 Rudy Nothenberg, interview with the author, June 29, 2018.

19 Carol Ruth Silver, interview with the author, June 26, 2018.

20 Shilts, *Mayor of Castro Street*, 255.

21 Silver, interview with the author.

22 Corey Busch, interview with the author, July 27, 2017.

23 Art Agnos, interview with the author, March 6, 2018.

24 Rudy Nothenberg, interview with the author, June 29, 2018.

25 Quentin Kopp, interview with the author, March 6, 2018.

26 Ron Jarers, "Peoples Temple Shuts Door on U.S. Visitors," *San Francisco Chronicle*, November 16, 1978, 1.

27 Tim Reiterman and John Jacobs, *Raven: The Untold Story of the Rev. Jim Jones and His People* (New York: Penguin, 1982), 494.

28 Ibid., 512.

29 John Jacobs, *A Rage for Justice: The Passion and Politics of Phillip Burton* (Berkeley: University of California Press, 1995), 404–405.

30 Mayor George Moscone, press statement (never issued), November 27, 1978, Moscone Archives, University of the Pacific Library.

31 Corey Busch, interview with the author, July 26, 2017.

32 Nothenberg, interview with the author, July 29, 2018.

33 Rachel Gordon, "Feinstein Recalls S.F.'s 'Day of Infamy,'" *San Francisco Chronicle*, November 26, 2008, https://www.sfgate.com/bayarea/article/Feinstein-recalls-S-F-s-day-of-infamy-3260395.php.

34 Kopp, interview with the author.

35 Dianne Feinstein Press Conference, November 27, 1978, https://www.youtube.com/watch?v=5NikqzmwbgU, accessed July 17, 2018.

36 Quoted in Jerry Roberts, Dave Farrell, et al., "'I Do Best during the Most Difficult Times,'" *San Francisco Chronicle*, August 31, 1987, 4.

37 Nothenberg, interview with the author, June 29, 2018.

38 On June 7, 1984, the UPI wrote of Feinstein that "she is on the former vice president's 'short list' of women being considered."

39 David Johnston, "The Guardian Intelligencer," *San Francisco Bay Guardian*, October 12, 1978.

40 Jerry Burns, "No One Yet Taking On Moscone," *San Francisco Chronicle*, September 1, 1978, 6.

41 Jerry Roberts, *Dianne Feinstein: Never Let Them See You Cry* (New York: HarperCollinsWest, 1994), 12.

42 Ibid., 23.

43 Helene Myers, "Got Jewish Milk? Screening Epstein and Van Sant for Intersectional Film History," *Jewish Film and New Media* 5, no. 1 (2017): 8.

44 Nicoletta, interview with the author.

45 Busch, interview with the author, July 27, 2017.

46 Charles A. Fracchia Sr., interview with the author, June 7, 2017.

47 Silver, interview with the author.

48 Allen Bennett, interview with the author, August 31, 2017. The "White Nights" to which Bennett referred are the demonstrations following the sentencing of Dan White in 1979.

49 Channel Two nightly news, November 27, 1978, http://www.ktvu.com/news/ktvu -archives-assassination-of-mayor-george-moscone-supervisor-harvey-milk.

50 Herb Caen, "Gray Day," *San Francisco Chronicle*, November 28, 1978, 31.

51 Lawrence Ferlinghetti, "An Elegy to Dispel Gloom," in *These Are My Rivers: Selected and New Poems: 1955–1933* (New York: New Directions Press, 1978), 235.

52 Fracchia Sr., interview with the author.

53 David Talbot, *Season of the Witch: Enchantment, Terror, and Deliverance in the City of Love* (New York: Free Press, 2012), 333.

54 Joel Kotkin, Paul Grabowicz, and Francis Moriarty, "San Francisco: A City of Violence," *Washington Post*, November 29, 1978, https://www.washingtonpost.com /archive/politics/1978/11/29/san-francisco-a-city-of-violence/3959fded-f13d-4c98 -9060-ffb7fd5abc85/.

55 "Guyana Holocaust," *National Review*, December 8, 1978, 1524.

56 Mervyn Dymally Jonestown Letter, June 7, 1977, https://scholarlycommons.pacific .edu/cgi/viewcontent.cgi?article=1026&context=mayor-moscone.

57 Marshall Kilduff and Phil Tracy, "Inside Peoples Temple," *New West*, August 1, 1977, 30–34. This article described Dymally as being "impressed" by what he saw in Jonestown.

58 A. J. Delgado, "The Unburied Truth about Jim Jones," *National Review*, May 6, 2014, https://www.nationalreview.com/2014/05/unburied-truth-about-jim-jones-j -delgado/.

59 George Russell, "The Left's Great Crime: Jim Jones, Marxist Mass Murderer," *Commentary*, January 1, 2012, 38.

60 1976 California State Resolution, RYMUR 89-4286-A-39-b-10.

61 Peoples Temple, "Statements about Rev. Jim Jones and the Peoples Temple," https://jonestown.sdsu.edu/?page_id=18355.

62 Ibid.

63 George Cothran, "Barbagelata's Return?" *SF Weekly*, November 18, 1998, https:// archives.sfweekly.com/sanfrancisco/cothran/Content?oid=2135846.

64 Michael Harris, "The Neighborhood Vote-Election Split the City," *San Francisco Chronicle*, December 12, 1975, 1.

65 Art Agnos, interview with the author, March 6, 2018.

66 Ibid.

67 Silver, interview with the author.

68 Nothenberg, interview with the author, June 29, 2018.

69 Letter from Jim Jones to George Moscone, May 1978, Moscone Archives, University of the Pacific Library. Talley was listed in the letter as "Noreen," but her real · first name was Maureen.

70 Letter from Jim Jones to George Moscone, June 3, 1978, Moscone Archives, University of the Pacific Library.

71 Letter from Jim Jones to George Moscone, July 12, 1978, Moscone Archives, University of the Pacific Library.

72 Agnos, interview with the author, March 6, 2018. The event occurred in 1978, not 1977.

73 Daniel J. Flynn, "Drinking Harvey Milk's Kool-Aid," *City Journal* May 21, 2009, https://www.city-journal.org/html/drinking-harvey-milk's-kool-aid-10574.html.

74 Talbot, *Season of the Witch*, 31.

75 Josh Sides, *Erotic City: Sexual Revolutions and the Making of Modern San Francisco* (Oxford: Oxford University Press, 2009), 141.

76 Talbot, *Season of the Witch*, 329.

77 Busch, interview with the author.

78 Al Casciato, "Policemen Quitting Blindly," *San Francisco Policemen,* April 1976, https://sfpoa.org/journal_archives/Vol_7_No_4_April_1976.pdf.

79 "Daniel White Was Always Serving People-In Various Capacities," *Palo Alto Times*, November 28, 1978. The reference to French fries was an allusion to White's potato stand at Pier 39, a franchise that he received after agreeing to support the development.

80 Maura Dolan, "Dan White in Jail: It's a Family Affair," *San Francisco Examiner*, December 17, 1978.

81 Kopp, interview with the author.

82 Silver, interview with the author.

83 Campaign flyer, George Moscone for Mayor 1975.

84 George Moscone, submission to *San Francisco* magazine, October 23, 1978.

85 Ibid.

86 Herb Caen, "The Moving Finger," *San Francisco Chronicle*, December 19, 1978, 19.

Chapter 9   The Long Shadow of 1978

1 Grateful Dead Online Archive, https://archive.org/details/gd1978-12-31.fob .akgd224e.holwein.motb-0130.106102.flac16.

2 Chester Hartman and Sarah Carnochan, *City for Sale: The Transformation of San Francisco* (Berkeley: University of California Press, 2002), 252.

3 Dave Farrell, Jerry Roberts, et al., "Poll Finds Mayor 'Amazingly' Popular," *San Francisco Chronicle*, September 1, 1987, 1.

4 Dave Farrell, Jerry Roberts et al. "I Do Best During the Most Difficult Times,'" *San Francisco Chronicle*, August 31, 1987, 4.

5 Carol Ruth Silver, interview with the author, June 26, 2018.

6 Rudy Nothenberg, interview with the author, June 29, 2018.

7 Judy Stone, "Dianne Feinstein: A Brave New Mayor," *Ladies' Home Journal*, May 1979, 162.

8 Nothenberg, interview with the author.

9 Richard DeLeon, *Left Coast City: Progressive Politics in San Francisco 1975–1991* (Lawrence: University of Kansas Press, 1992), 52.

10 Katy Butler, "Anatomy of a Gay Riot," *San Francisco Chronicle*, May 23, 1979, 11.

11 Michael Fox, interview with the author, July 3, 2018.

12 Henry Schulman, "CANDLESTICK CLASSICS / #3 / Day of Sweet Revenge / Joe Morgan's Clutch Homer Knocked the Dodgers Out of the Pennant Race on the Final Day of the 1982 Season and Made the Braves Champions," *San Francisco Chronicle*, September 7, 1999, https://www.sfgate.com/sports/article /CANDLESTICK-CLASSICS-3-Day-of-Sweet-Revenge-2909897.php.

13 Corey Busch, interview with the author, July 27, 2017.

14 Penelope Houston, interview with the author, June 8, 2017.

15 Joel Selvin, interview with the author, June 6, 2017.
16 Ibid.
17 Ibid.
18 Henry S. Rosenthal, interview with the author, July 25, 2017.
19 Joe Dirt, interview with the author, June 29, 2018.

Chapter 10   Neighborhoods, Natives, and Those Hills

1 Penelope Houston, interview with the author, June 8, 2017.
2 Rebecca Moore, "Demographics and the Black Religious Culture of Peoples Temple," in *Peoples Temple and Black Religion in America,* ed. Rebecca Moore, Anthony Pinn, and Mary Sawyer (Bloomington: Indiana University Press, 2004) 57.
3 Michael Stewart Foley, *Fresh Fruit for Rotting Vegetables* (New York: Bloomsbury, 2015), 74.
4 Henry S. Rosenthal, interview with the author, June 25, 2017.
5 John Gullak, interview with the author, March 8, 2018.
6 Michael Fox, interview with the author, July 3, 2018.
7 Jello Biafra, interview with the author, August 16, 2018.
8 Foley, *Fresh Fruit for Rotting Vegetables*, 96.
9 Biafra, interview with the author.
10 Joel Selvin, interview with the author, June 6, 2017.
11 Carol Ruth Silver, interview with the author, June 26, 2018.
12 Milk made a recording that was to be played in the case of his death where he mentioned Britt as the person he wanted to succeed him if he died.
13 Allen Bennett, interview with the author, August 31, 2017.
14 John Geluardi, "Dan White's Motive More about Betrayal than Homophobia," *SF Weekly,* January 30, 2008, http://www.sfweekly.com/news/dan-whites-motive-more-about-betrayal-than-homophobia/.
15 Silver, interview with the author.
16 Charles A. Fracchia Jr., interview with the author, August 28, 2017.

Index

About the Author

LINCOLN A. MITCHELL is an adjunct associate professor of political science at Columbia University, where he also serves as an associate scholar in the Arnold A. Saltzman Institute of War and Peace Studies. He has authored many books on the former Soviet states, democracy, and baseball, including *Baseball Goes West: How the Giants and Dodgers Shaped the Major Leagues* (2018). Lincoln grew up in San Francisco in the 1970s and 1980s and currently lives in New York City.